BATANG KALI

*Six decades of relentless British concealment undertaken by
senior politicians, high ranking military officers and top civil
servants to protect national prestige and the mystique
of an elite fighting force.
An official cover-up that remains in place to this day.
For the first time in 60 years, a comprehensive examination
of a brutal colonial episode with telling lessons for
our contemporary world.*

MEDIA MASTERS
SINGAPORE

BATANG KALI

Copyright © 2008 by Media Masters Pte Ltd

Published by:

Media Masters Pte Ltd
Newton Road PO Box 272
Singapore 912210

Email: mediamasters@pacific.net.sg
            mediam@bigpond.com
Website: www.mediamasters.com.sg

First published June 2009

Design: O'Art Creative Pte Ltd, Singapore
Printed by: Konway Printhouse Sdn Bhd

ISBN: 978-981-08-1303-1

Foreword

No one has ever denied that a mass killing of Chinese plantation workers resulted when a patrol of Scots Guards raided a Malayan rubber estate near the township of Batang Kali in early December, 1948. This fact could never be fully concealed, not even in the slaughter's immediate aftermath.

Our book has been written because there is infinitely more to the Batang Kali saga. The sinister efforts to deny accountability and withhold justice must be recorded in a comprehensive manner.

An elaborate programme of concealment was instigated by senior officers within Britain's anti-insurgency High Command in Kuala Lumpur. They worked in close collaboration with top colonial police and civil administrators.

It was a time when the Malayan Emergency was barely six months old and the insurgents appeared to be gaining ground.

London then had her own preoccupations. There were the repercussions associated with the evolving Cold War.

Britain was also saddled with huge post-war debts. She required reassurance that the much needed dollar earnings from the little understood colony called Malaya – her richest source of foreign exchange – would not be disrupted by a ragtag bunch of 'unlettered bandits'.

There were other compelling considerations requiring an official cover-up.

National pride and prestige were at stake. And there was the cherished image of an elite fighting unit to protect.

The overall effect of the cover-up's imposition and the immediate political support it achieved in Westminster ensured that the full Batang Kali story remained undisclosed.

Over the years, several attempts to get to the bottom of Batang Kali have been launched. Fleet Street did its share in 1970; Scotland Yard initiated an investigation shortly thereafter. The British Broadcasting Corporation (BBC) produced a documentary in 1992. The Malaysians formed their own probe team.

But every effort was firmly thwarted. Whenever the issue was raised, politicians of the day were a step ahead, displaying a spirited will to sustain the fudging begun in 1948.

This book stands as the first attempt to present a cohesive study of the Batang Kali episode in its entirety.

A number of official doors, not unexpectedly, remained locked to us in the four years we spent researching the subject. But we also gained access to never-before revealed investigative reports, photographs and signed statements of eyewitnesses.

In the light of evidence presented here, we are compelled to ask how much longer can Britain's cover-up be sustained, the historical record be ignored and justice be denied the surviving kin of the Batang Kali dead.

Ian Ward
Norma Miraflor
Singapore, March, 2009

CONTENTS

Maps of the era

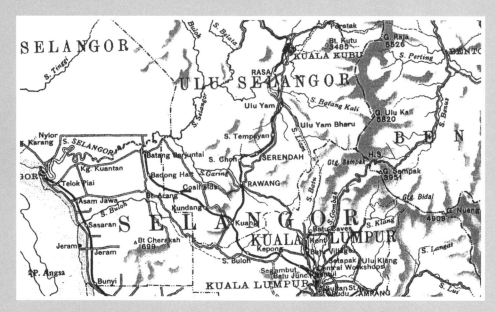

A segment of a 1940s Peninsular Malaya map showing the old north-south main highway linking the colonial administrative capital of Kuala Lumpur with Ulu Selangor. The highway threaded, as it still does today, from Kuala Lumpur through Rawang, Serendah, Ulu Yam and Kuala Kubu Bahru.

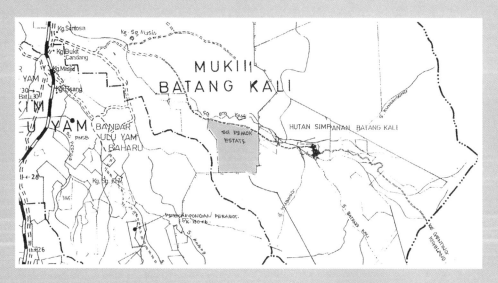

A Batang Kali district map of the time illustrating the position of Sungei Remok Estate – scene of the 1948 mass killing of rubber estate workers by a patrol of Scots Guardmen – along the Genting Highlands road.

Chapter 1

Sungei Remok Estate:
December 11 – 12, 1948

Humidity choked the late afternoon as the sweat-drenched patrol of British soldiers, weapons at the ready, advanced cautiously across the wooden bridge spanning a boulder-littered stream of tumbling water. Ahead, a dirt road ran parallel to the stream for a muddy stretch before snaking its way off to the right down a row of mature rubber trees, their chiseled trunks supporting familiar latex-gathering cups. A sign from the head of the single-file line of figures brought the advance to a halt.

To a man, the patrol dropped to their haunches. All were exhausted. They had been trudging without break through the stifling Malayan heat for just on two hours. Shade beneath the canopy of rubber tree foliage provided welcome, albeit minor, relief. In the distance, a dog yelped. Focusing through the patchwork of tree trunks ahead, forward members of the patrol could just discern the outline of vague wooden structures. A quick review of map coordinates by the youthful patrol leader confirmed they had finally reached the target of the day's mission.

The map showed the Genting Highlands road marking the northern boundary of Sungei Remok Estate. Neat rows of rubber trees began a few yards in from the roadway. These ran down a steep incline to the stream and continued away from the opposite bank. From there tree rows spread across a hundred yards or so of river-flat terrain before running uphill to the estate's southern border that lay beyond the undulating crest.

Resuming their wary approach, the 14 British troops, along with their three local guides – a Chinese, a Malay and a Tamil – moved to within yards of a clearing situated roughly in the centre of the plantation's river-flat area. Although anti-insurgency novices, the soldiers' manoeuvre thus far had been faultless. To the left, discernible through the trees, lay the banks of the stream they had just crossed. Their approach had been undetected. From where they had positioned themselves the patrol could observe Sungei Remok's entire production hub. What had initially been indistinct images now presented as living quarters, storage facilities, a smokehouse, an office and odd pieces of plantation equipment. The human factor was now vividly apparent. Men, women and children were going about their late afternoon routines.

The scene confronting the patrol portrayed a seemingly mundane picture of plantation life, far from the threatening outpost of subterfuge they had been briefed to expect. A shirtless youth, in shorts and sandals, toweled his dripping hair as he strolled back along one of two narrow tracks leading directly from the stream. Plantation children had transformed stretches of open ground between the clearing's three communal living quarters into a varied playground. In one section a game of tag was in progress. Boys and girls, no more than five or six years old, chased each other, their excited cries punctuating the muggy afternoon.

Unbeknown to the poised British patrol, torrential monsoon rains which had begun their deluge shortly after midnight, had cancelled any hope of production work on the estate that day. Chinese labourers, living with their families in spartan compartments along the communal lines, were forced to remain indoors. By the time the rain eased it had been too late to venture into the plantation proper to gather the valuable latex and further shave off slithers of bark ensuring the continued slow oozing of the pungent white sap. The overnight drenching had also affected a scheduled arrival of extra contract labour. Additional tappers, grass-cutters and workers were normally trucked-in around 6 am daily from nearby Ulu Yam Bahru village. Generally the same transport carried daily food supplies for the resident community. That morning, however, the supply lorry had failed to appear. With no prospect of work in the offing, one or two of the estate staff had left to visit friends or relatives nearby. By late afternoon a few of the tappers could be seen, dotted around the clearing, idly honing stone on steel as they sharpened their knives and chisels in preparation for the next day's work. The infantrymen had arrived at their target on a decidedly slow day.

Erected on stilts, the wooden living quarters, referred to locally as *kongsis*, had flights of steps at each end leading to planked balconies. Evenly spaced down the length of each balcony were ten individual doorways marking the separate living spaces allotted to resident plantation staff. Some were lone occupiers. Others were accompanied by their families.

Still toweling his hair, the youth slowly climbed the stairs to one of the three *kongsis*. He looked back briefly on the children at play, took a few steps down the balcony, then disappeared through one of the doorways.

He had barely shut the door when the pre-dusk calm was shattered by an order screeched in Chinese Hakka dialect. Startled children stopped in their tracks.

A Chinese man stood on the estate road in front of the first *kongsi*. Flanked by two white men in jungle green, he repeatedly shouted his order for everyone to come down from the living quarters and assemble on the open ground.

Agitated men and women emerged from their doorways and stood tentatively along the balconies. Among the last to appear was a young woman breast-feeding her baby. By this time all 14 patrol members had cordoned-off the clearing, blocking any possible escape route to the surrounding rows of rubber trees and beyond. The impact of barked orders intensified as the troops swept their raised weapons menacingly along the lines of frightened faces – men, women and children. Ignorant of any local language, the soldiers added to the moment's confusion with a cacophony of bellowed demands in variously accented English.

Cowed as much by the wild gesticulations of the uniformed intruders as by the frenetic commands of their Chinese guide, the estate's residents rushed to comply. They soon found themselves herded in an open space between the first *kongsi* and the estate road traversing the front section of the clearing. The smell of boiling rice from abandoned kitchens filled the air. Its normally calming effect was lost on the workers. On any other day the aroma would have signalled a hearty, if simple, meal.

Detailing three or four troops to guard their suspects, the patrol leader ordered the remainder of his men conduct an extensive search of all living quarters. As the soldiers moved off, the Chinese guide informed the dumbfounded gathering he was a police detective working with the troops. They had arrived to track down communist guerrillas and their sympathisers operating in the area. The authorities, he said, were aware people working on the estate had been aiding the enemy. Some, he added, might even be communist party members.

Without pausing, the detective singled out a male tapper for interrogation. As other residents stood watching and listening, the officer demanded the names of all those supplying food to the guerrillas. The tapper insisted armed communists had never once ventured onto the estate. The remark drew a roar of protest from the detective and a barrage of further questions. Despite the policeman's increasing impatience, the tapper stood his ground.

Exasperated, the detective swung his attention to the women and children. The first woman questioned staunchly denied having any connection with the communist movement or its army. A terrified boy tearfully asked: what were communists? What did they look like? A woman with two toddlers clinging to her loose black trousers pleaded to be allowed back to her quarters. It was well past time for her children's evening meal and they were crying with hunger. Another woman began weeping as the detective pursued his interrogation.

Through the interpreter a British soldier ordered this woman to stop crying. How could she stop, the woman retorted. Every time she denied knowing any communists she was told she was lying. She felt helpless. Ignoring her, the detective switched his attention back to the men. This time he ordered them to empty their pockets. Moving from one set of outstretched palms to another, he scrutinised an innocuous array of objects. He inspected pencils, odd cigarettes, rolling tobacco and papers, matches, receipt slips, handkerchiefs, small medicinal bottles, some crumpled Straits dollar currency notes and a handful of coins.

During the questioning process, the Chinese detective, along with a soldier, took a number of workers, one at a time, out of sight behind a *kongsi* and there subjected them to heavy interrogation. Threats that they would be shot unless they cooperated were followed by rounds fired off close behind their heads – but into the air.

One of the workers became so traumatised by these tactics that he collapsed, turned deathly pale and unable to move. The interrogators surmised he had suffered a heart attack. To them it seemed unlikely he would survive the night. Identified as Chan Loi, a rubber tapper and the father of several children, he was carried to a nearby *kongsi* verandah and left to die. His wife was summoned to look after him.

Meanwhile, the search through the *kongsis*, in progress now for well over an hour, was wrapping up. One by one, patrol members were rejoining the guard assigned to the estate residents. The living quarters, it seemed, had revealed nothing out of the ordinary. The soldiers appeared to be returning empty-handed. At least nothing recovered from personal possessions was presented to those assembled as evidence of their alleged guilt.

A heated exchange between the detective and a young male caught the attention of the British patrol leader. The soldier shoved his way through family groupings to demand what the shouting was all about. A 19 year-old rubber tapper was insisting that a piece of paper he had been carrying was nothing more than confirmation allowing him to gather durian fruit. It had been provided, he said, by a nearby community of Orang Asli (local aborigines) with whom he conducted intermittent business.

Translated, the explanation infuriated the patrol leader. Another burst of questioning followed. The paper was an obvious order for supplies from the communists, insisted the detective. 'Admit it!' he bellowed. When the youth appeared unmoved the vexed detective demanded his name.

'Loh Kit Lin,' came the reply. The Chinese police officer then leant close to the young tapper's flushed face. To the horror of the other plantation staff he yelled in Hakka: 'You're dead.' The policeman and patrol leader seized the youth and separated him from the rest.

Another set of orders, promptly translated, sent the soldiers separating the flustered Sungei Remok folk into two batches – men in one, women and children in the other. As this was being done, the patrol leader and detective turned back towards the young rubber tapper standing apart. Loh looked apprehensive but did not struggle when the two men dragged him aside and out onto the estate road.

Another soldier who had been standing guard followed.

As Loh was led off down the estate road, other soldiers began herding the women and children towards a room in the first *kongsi*. The men were marched off to a second room in the same living quarters.

All the ominous threats of the past hours consolidated instantly at the unmistakeable crack of a single shot. It rang out across the clearing from the direction taken by the tapper and his escorts. Instinctively, the braver among the women climbing the steps looked back. Less than 100 yards away, Loh Kit Lin lay face up on the centre of the estate road. The patrol leader and Chinese detective were close by. The third escorting officer stood a few paces away.

The shooting accelerated the herding of captives into their separate holding areas. Shortly after doors slammed shut, the sound of a second shot was heard. It rendered both rooms silent, rooted in fear.

Inside their crowded confinement, the male detainees, once recovered from the shock of gunfire, conversed in hushed tones. It was oppressively hot and dark. The inmates could discern only outlines of those sharing the room. Teenagers formed clusters as if seeking strength in one another's company. The youth who had bathed in the stream just prior to the arrival of the troops, withdrew to a corner. There he refused to speak to anyone, not even to his brother who sat nearby.

In the other holding room, women attempted to comfort the children. By now, what had been pitiful whimpering had degenerated into loud, anguished wailing. The young were hungry. They were thirsty.

Older children kept asking why they were being locked up at mealtime without food or water. Where were their fathers? They also wanted to know why the white men were so upset. What did the strangers want?

All efforts at pacifying failed. At one point the door swung open and the Chinese detective poked his head into the room. He had grown more agitated. 'The tapper is dead,' he announced, loud enough to be heard above the plaintive noise that filled the room. He demanded silence. Before leaving, he told the women they must consider his earlier questions. He warned that should they remain uncooperative they would be in very serious trouble indeed. Then he was gone and the door was locked once more.

An hour or two later the door opened again and two soldiers entered, carrying milk for the children. Without a word they set the small supply on the *kongsi* floor and left, again locking the door behind them. The mothers felt slightly relieved but could hardly be grateful. The same soldiers who had arrived with milk had earlier been shouting at them, pushing them and pointing guns at them.

As much a centre of Kuala Lumpur social life today as in colonial times, the Selangor Club still functions from its location overlooking the padang. The club was originally established in 1884 as a gathering point for British colonial planters, businessmen and government officials. Curiously, it still retains its colonial era nickname, 'The Spotted Dog'– sometimes shortened to 'The Dog'. Tom Menzies, Chairman of the Estate Owners' Association, regularly used the club premises for planter meetings.

Thomas Hutchison Menzies, owner of the 646-acre Sungei Remok rubber estate fronting the Batang Kali Forest Reserve, was the quintessential planter's planter. He'd been in the area for years. Long before the Japanese invasion of Malaya in December, 1941, he had established his credentials as one of the colonial territory's most knowledgeable rubber experts. He knew all there was to know about the planting and nurture of trees. He understood management of plantation labour and the various critical aspects of preparing raw latex for the processing plant.

It was therefore no surprise among the planting fraternity, returning to their properties after the Allied defeat of Japan in August, 1945, that the popular Tom Menzies became quickly re-instated as chairman of the territory's Estate Owners' Association. As such he was well recognised as a local authority and a figure to whom fellow planters could readily turn for advice and reassurance.

Association gatherings at the Selangor Club – the legendary 'Spotted Dog' – focal point for expatriate social life in Kuala Lumpur, were popular and frequent. Invariably, they were politically-charged events at which the chairman's thick Scottish brogue was much anticipated. Menzies' opinions mattered. An anti-communist Emergency had been proclaimed throughout Malaya by British colonial authorities on June 16, 1948. What was Tom's take on colonial Britain's latest moves against the insurgents? The first six months of warfare against the godless communists had been nothing short of disastrous. What advice did he have for intensifying the lobbying of both high-level civil administrators and military top brass?

As far as the planters were concerned, and this went for the mining community as well, the government's decision to take military action against the Communist Party of Malaya (CPM) had been long overdue. Indeed, when the Emergency was finally imposed, so many of its measures appeared to fall lamentably short of the sort of 'anti-bandit' action planters and miners had been urging throughout 1947 and the first half of 1948.

The widely portrayed image of colonial plantation owners in Malaya doggedly inhabiting their holdings in order to battle it out personally with marauding communist guerrillas is more a reflection of film script writers and novelists of the day than reality. Some did, of course. But a significant number didn't. Those who didn't placed control of plantation activities with local Chinese contractors. These on-the-spot specialists handled the full range of logistics associated with labour supply, labour provisioning, production and transportation.

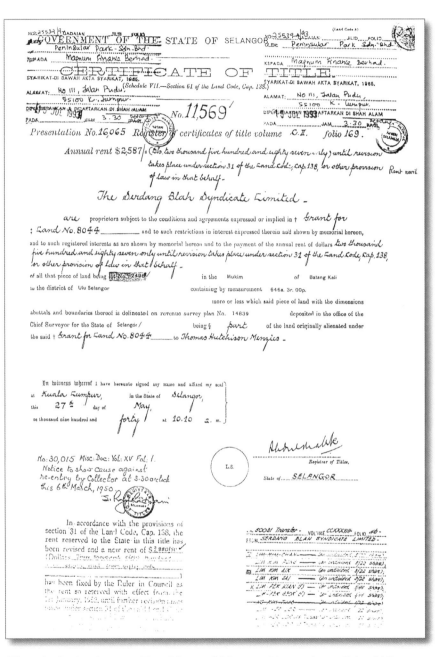

The title deed indicating Tom Menzies' May, 1940, purchase of the 646-acre tract of land he would later rename Sungei Remok Estate.

Tom Menzies was in this second category – an absentee plantation owner. He lived in Kuala Lumpur where Association duties took up much of his time. His visits to Sungei Remok were infrequent. Indeed, so infrequently had he been spotted anywhere on the estate's steep hilly terrain, which formed such a dramatic backdrop to the mountain stream marking its frontage, the popular assumption among plantation workers and their families was that the *tuan* lived in England and only visited Malaya once a year.

For all Tom Menzies' much vaunted rubber-growing expertise, the truth was his relationship to the Sungei Remok land tract had been anything but the glowing success story his Association colleagues might otherwise have expected. He was clearly reading the international situation wrongly when, in late May, 1940, he saw value in expanding his holdings in Malaya. He purchased Serdang Blah Syndicate Ltd, a company owning the rights to operate the 646-acre estate, by virtue of original government land grant No 8044. The Scottish planter took possession of the property on May 27 that year and transferred one or two trusted staff from his other interests. He was barely 18 months into operating the newly acquired estate, paying an annual rental of $2,587.00 (Straits dollars) to the government, when the Pacific War erupted on December 7, 1941.

Japan's rapid 25th Army invasion down the Malayan peninsula determined that Tom's newest estate was, six weeks later, well within Japanese-held territory. By this time, however, the Scotsman, along with a large majority of his expatriate colleagues, had made good their evacuation south to Singapore.

As the crow flies, Sungei Remok Estate lay just 45 miles north-west of Kuala Lumpur. Yet the very topography of its location, slashed from a vast tract of undulating, triple-canopied jungle, deep in the hinterland area known as Ulu Selangor, had its advantages. It would provide a curious form of protection for those who remained there throughout the three-and-a-half years of Japanese occupation. Tappers and other plantation workers would later report that their normal lives had remained largely undisturbed during this period. Neither the Japanese military, nor guerrilla fighters of the then British-backed, communist-led Malayan People's Anti-Japanese Army (MPAJA) had seen reason to intrude into the estate's isolation. But if the invading Japanese were prepared to ignore those living on fringe jungle areas of Ulu Selangor in wartime, the returning British viewed things very differently. To them, there was every reason to regard the same people with deepest suspicion.

By late 1948, intelligence reports were suggesting that, Malaya-wide, Chinese civilian sympathisers of the 5,000-strong CPM guerrilla army numbered a staggering 500,000. In the main, these supporters, termed the *Min Yuen*, shunned direct Party membership. But they were more than happy to help the anti-colonial cause by providing food and finance within their means, along with moral support, for those willing to put their lives on the line via armed revolt. The overwhelming majority of *Min Yuen*, according to these estimates, lived along jungle fringe areas where their livelihood stemmed from some form of agricultural labour. The increasingly intense guerrilla activity across Ulu Selangor led the authorities to assume that all isolated communities of Chinese throughout this region were now in league with the enemy.

The early north-east monsoon rains in 1948 began their onslaught in the first week of December. By this stage, field statistics had firmly established Ulu Selangor as one of the most critical focal points for what colonial officialdom then preferred to categorise as 'bandit activity'. On Tuesday, December 7, three communists brazenly walked the streets of nearby Rawang township distributing leaflets declaring the 8th Regiment of the Malayan People's Anti-British Army (MPABA) would be imposing a dusk-to-dawn road curfew along an approximately 40-mile segment of Malaya's main north-south trunk route. This would run, the leaflets stipulated, between 1900 hours and 0530 hours daily from December 12 to December 18. The affected section would stretch from the recognised CPM stronghold of Kanching village, near Batu Caves just north of Kuala Lumpur, through the main Selangor state townships of Rawang, Serendah and Batang Kali, past the turn-off to Kuala Kubu Bahru and on to Tanjong Malim.

Quite aside from the threatened disruption to plantation, mining and general commerce posed by the communist announcement, both military and police regarded the 8th Regiment's leaflet as a major provocation. They interpreted it as a demonstration of both the enemy's escalating numerical strength and political arrogance. Whether the curfew would be successfully sustained or not, the threat alone would, the authorities feared, result in a substantial propaganda coup for the CPM.

Colonial intelligence-gathering activity since the beginning of the Emergency had shown itself to be severely wanting. Even so, the police Special Branch had managed to detect very obvious and disturbing indications for Ulu Selangor. Since late September the CPM's 8th Regiment had been making no secret of its intentions to transform the region into an important theatre for substantial and expanding guerrilla attacks. In order to counter this, the 2nd Battalion Scots Guards, part of a Guards Brigade reinforcement of three infantry battalions that had arrived in Malaya by sea from Britain in October, was quickly committed to Ulu Selangor.

These soldiers came backed by a proud history spanning more than three centuries and with professional officers quietly schooled to understand that among all Guards regiments theirs was clearly the elite force. They were, from the regimental viewpoint, the elite of the elite.

Originally assembled on March 16, 1642, the unit formally became an integral part of the English Army 44 years later, winning its first major battle honour at the Siege of Namur in 1695. On establishment within the English Army, the same unit became designated the 3rd Regiment of Foot Guards. Between the years 1831 and 1877 it was known as the Scots Fusilier Guards. The designation Scots Guards came in 1877.

Regimental records establish that, since inception, the Scots Guards have fought in practically all campaigns waged by the British Army. They served in the English Civil War, the Marlborough Wars, the War of the Austrian Succession, the Seven Years War, the French Revolutionary Wars, Waterloo, the Crimean War, the Egyptian Campaign, the South Africa War of 1899-02, as well as World Wars I and II.

This time the regiment was participating in a very different type of conflict – one defined by the colonial leaders as an Emergency, not a war. The Scots Guards headquarters and main base in Malaya were quickly established in the township of Kuala Kubu Bahru itself, on an open field adjacent to the local Chinese school and police billets.

For Tom Menzies, word of the elite Scottish unit's injection so close to his holding came as a major morale booster. His schedule in Kuala Lumpur was such that he would have no direct association with the newly installed guardsmen. But he acknowledged their presence would be a reassuring contact point for his Chinese plantation contractor, even if formal links had to be pursued via the local police.

Early deployment of the young Scots Guards on patrols only underlined their appalling inexperience in confronting the harsh realities of an anti-insurgency campaign largely confined to jungle terrain. The novice soldiers proved inadequate, even in basic elements of jungle warfare techniques. The speed of their dispatch from the United Kingdom in answer to urgent demands for troop reinforcements from Military High Command, Malaya, had been a factor. This, coupled with the unit's then hasty introduction in the hopes of stemming the security rot in Ulu Selangor, had determined that all chances of adequate training sessions in preparation for the rigours of combat in the tropics had been abandoned.

Scots Guards officers experimented with all manner of tactics as they sought to initiate their men, fresh from the ceremonial world of guarding Britain's royal palaces, into direct hinterland contact with communist insurgents. Overall advice handed down from Malaya High Command did little to assist the preparatory programmes for jungle warfare. Despite their earlier shrill demands for reinforcements, top generals persisted in categorising the so-called 'bandits' of Malaya as decidedly inferior to anything similar encountered by British forces post-World War 11.

General Officer Commanding Malaya, Major General Sir Charles Hamilton Boucher, comes to his colonial posting in Kuala Lumpur with an impressive World War 11 military record. Never shy about providing public statements and observations, General Boucher, within days of his arrival, tells local journalists the Emergency is 'the easiest problem' he has ever tackled.

No less a figure than Britain's General Officer Commanding (GOC) Malaya, Major General Sir Charles Hamilton Boucher, was happy to confirm this publicly. He had confidently gone on record in the local press saying: 'I can tell you this is by far the easiest problem I have ever tackled. In spite of the appalling country, the enemy is far weaker in technique and courage than even the Greek or Indian Reds.'

Still, teenage guardsmen, thrust into the bitter Malayan Emergency war zone while meeting national service obligations, quickly discovered the shattering difference between lying in ambush on a sodden, leech-infested jungle floor and parading ceremoniously before Buckingham Palace, Windsor Castle or the Tower of London.

Setting up ambush positions, as it happened, quickly developed as a primary aspect of the Scots Guards counter-insurgency programme. They attempted them in rubber estates, along deep jungle tracks and particularly on approaches to outlying communities of Chinese squatters and plantation workers. These isolated pockets of humanity had become, according to police briefings, hotbeds of the *Min Yuen*.

With Special Branch impregnation of CPM ranks still in its infancy, and reliable information on guerrilla movements sparse to the point of being non-existent, such villages and *kongsis* emerged as vital areas of counter-insurgency interest for the freshly arrived troops. Ambushes associated with them were laid with the aim of intercepting and killing guerrillas moving to receive *Min Yuen* supplies. But for all the effort expended, results from these tactics throughout November and the early days of December, 1948, proved dismal. Whether 'weaker in technique and courage' or not, the communists in Ulu Selangor displayed a remarkable propensity for skilful avoidance of all Scots Guards traps.

Communist guerrillas, throughout the same general time-frame – and in precisely the same operational area – were able to employ a series of their own ambushes with deadly effect. A 13-man Police Jungle Squad from Rawang was wiped out by a bandit ambush on the region's prominent Bukit Manchong rubber estate. On the Ulu Caledonian property nearby, another police squad, comprising special constables, drove into a road ambush, suffering heavy casualties. The police vehicle and all bodies aboard were torched.

Some days later, in a follow-up action on the same estate, a British infantry patrol was caught in a furious gunfight after stumbling into yet another enemy trap. This time the communists had positioned themselves on an S-shaped bend along high ground at the main entrance road to the estate. The guerrillas allowed the troops to pass onto the property and carry out their patrolling duties. Then, as the British unit began its withdrawal aboard a three-ton military truck, accompanied by an armoured Lynx car sporting two Bren-guns, the communists sprang their ambush.

Police reinforcements sent to the scene found two dead guerrillas on the high ground and claimed to have shot a further two unarmed communists shortly thereafter. But in the ambush 'killing zone' they discovered bodies of British patrol members and their Iban tracker guides still in the truck, underneath the vehicle and scattered along the roadside.

Fearful of the demoralising impact that might result, the authorities made certain no information on these events would be released publicly. No mention of them appeared in the local or UK press. Furthermore, in an obvious propaganda counter-measure, the High Command went ahead to issue a special release on December 10 geared to reassuring the general public that the Scots Guards and other recently introduced British units were indeed being effective.

The release claimed security forces were making broader use of mortar fire to 'flush' areas into which armed communists were escaping from pursuing troops. Carried prominently in the following day's Malaya and Singapore newspapers, it went on to reveal that normal equipment of all infantry units now included both two-inch and three-inch mortars. A Scots Guards patrol was said to have fired a number of two-inch mortar rounds into an area where Chinese terrorists had fled from advancing columns. An infantry officer engaged on operations was quoted as saying: 'When bandits escape into light copses and undergrowth it is quite likely that several well-directed mortar bombs will prove successful, whereas rifle fire is not likely to achieve results.'

In stark contrast to the High Command's calculated statements, there was no stopping news of the alarming security deterioration spreading by word of mouth throughout Ulu Selangor, particularly so among police and military troops assigned locally.

By the onset of the weekend of December 11-12, tension across the region's main population centres had peaked. On the evening of Saturday, December 11, the communists' 8th Regiment, in a blatant display of audacity, took over literally – though briefly – Rawang township, then an important mining and rural centre just 16 miles north of the Federal capital, Kuala Lumpur.

As dusk fell, approximately 50 guerrillas in civilian clothes infiltrated the town. They came in groups of four to six. Some moved along side-roads. Others boldly swaggered, Sten-guns under loose fitting shirts, down the centre of the town's main thoroughfare. Once positioned, they began firing simultaneously from ten pre-determined locations. The police and railway stations became main targets. Indiscriminate fire was also directed into houses and shops. Widespread panic followed as inhabitants rushed to the safety of their homes or sought refuge in any available shelter.

Still existing where they stood six decades ago, the old Rawang Police Station buildings (top photo) serve as back-up quarters to a newer administrative wing. But a lone police pillbox position (lower photo) remains looking north along old Rawang township's main street. From here, armed police on the evening of December 11, 1948, defend their station against guerrillas from the CPM's 8th regiment advancing from the north down Rawang's popular shopping thoroughfare. Just 50 yards away to the west of the police compound, down a sharp incline, lies another target for the communists that day – the Rawang Railway Station.

The Penang day train, en route to Kuala Lumpur, had arrived and was taking on passengers at Rawang's railway station as the first shots rang out. The stationmaster had the presence of mind to speed up the train's departure. It left, packed with startled passengers and considerably ahead of schedule.

John McCormick, a visiting British engineer working for the large Anglo-Oriental mining concern, Rawang Tin Fields, farewelled his wife, a passenger on the train, then rushed to where he had parked his armour-plated pick-up van. McCormick's company vehicle came complete with a steel-encased pillbox firing station. The engineer drove quickly into Rawang's main street in an effort to assist the police who were leading the counter-attack. But as suddenly as the chaos had begun, it ceased. McCormick spent the next three hours patrolling the deserted streets.

The action had lasted barely 30 minutes but in that time it was estimated the intruding guerrillas and security forces exchanged more than two thousand rounds of ammunition. Extraordinarily, only two people died during the raid. Both were males – a Chinese and a Tamil. They were bystanders caught in crossfire, an indication that the communists had planned this unprecedented strike as a stunning demonstration of their increasing strength and influence rather than as a killing spree. Reportedly, the intruders suffered no casualties. Certainly no communist dead or wounded were left at the scene.

So spectacular was the CPM's incursion into Rawang that evening that this time the authorities had no hope of keeping details under wraps. Days later, when the High Command was putting the best possible gloss on events, Boucher publicly attributed the increase in Ulu Selangor enemy activity to stimulation generated within communist ranks by 'the arrival of a new bandit leader'. At the same time, the authorities were emphasising the CPM's inability to stay and fight it out on the streets of Rawang. In fact, there had been no switch in the 8th Regiment leadership and it would remain unchanged for months to come. At Rawang, the guerrillas were merely employing their tried and tested 'strike and withdraw' tactics.

— ✺ —

Within hours of the previous Tuesday's dispersal of communist leaflets announcing the CPM's Kanching to Tanjong Malim road curfew, counter-insurgency experts had begun instituting a major drive against bandit operations throughout Ulu Selangor. A battalion-sized combined force of Scots and Grenadier Guards, together with police, had been rapidly detailed for the campaign. In addition, units of Britain's 4th Hussars, along with armoured vehicles, had been introduced on round-the-clock patrols along the Kuala Lumpur to Tanjong Malim link. From the psychological viewpoint, no communist threat could ever be allowed to disrupt such a vital road.

Part of this intensified security effort called for a number of British military patrols to be dispatched to outlying rubber plantations and tin mines in an effort to stem *Min Yuen* activities. Special Branch officers were called in to identify, for participating forces, those fringe jungle communities and *kongsis* considered hottest targets most likely to be aiding the enemy. Among the patrols selected for these specific duties was a 14-man section of 7 platoon, G Company, 2nd Battalion Scots Guards, whose home base was with the Guards headquarters in tents on the Kuala Kubu Bahru field beside the Chinese school.

Senior Scots Guards officers, charged with assembling patrols and organising lines of command for substantially expanded operations, quickly discovered that the battalion line-up seriously lacked men with solid combat experience. When it came to deciding the make-up of the unit to be dispatched to the Mukim of Batang Kali, along the hazardous road to Genting Highlands, they settled on a 22 year-old career army sergeant as patrol leader. A lance-sergeant, also a professional soldier, was chosen to be second-in-command. Those responsible for the selection ignored the fact that the second-in-command, an older man, had seen active duty in Greece during World War 11, whereas the chosen patrol leader had yet to experience any real combat conditions. The remaining 12 members picked for this patrol were national servicemen in their late teens. All had yet to see shots fired in anger.

Before departing their base camp, the national servicemen and their leaders attended an early morning briefing session. There, a senior Scots Guards officer outlined all objectives of the mission ahead. The patrol leader received military maps of the intended operational area together with precise co-ordinates defining the terrain within which his men should concentrate their activities.

One of the maps showed the Genting Highlands road, an important passage for the transportation of plantation produce, as it wound its way past the Sungei Remok Estate and on through foothills of the central mountain range up to the developing Genting Highlands station. Underlying the information being passed to the 14 young soldiers was the clear indication that the Sungei Remok property was to be regarded as a priority target for scrutiny and possible military action. Police intelligence pointed to the high probability of the estate being a source of support for the communists.

At the same briefing session, patrol members met a fresh-faced Chinese policeman, a member of the elite Special Branch. Speaking English, Cantonese and Hakka, he had been assigned as the key guide and interpreter for the intended foray

Makeshift former military huts are today scattered across the Kuala Kubu Bahru field that in 1948-49 served as advanced headquarters for G Company, 2nd Battalion, Scots Guards. From this location a section of the Company's 7 platoon set out on its December 11, 1948, raid on Sungei Remok Estate.

into the almost exclusively – though sparsely – Chinese inhabited operational area. None of the British patrol members spoke any of the local languages or dialects. Thus, two more police – a Malay and a Tamil – would, in the hours ahead, be required to join the grouping.

—⁓—

On Sungei Remok Estate that night the milk brought in by the soldiers temporarily calmed the children. The adults, though, got no consolation. It would take hours before sheer exhaustion overtook their fear, apprehension, hunger and thirst. Any relief brought on by sleep came all too briefly. The established plantation regimen of pre-dawn rubber tapping ensured that the incarcerated, held in the guarded *kongsi* rooms, were well-awake long before the Scots Guards made their first early morning moves.

The familiar rumble of the approaching supply lorry from nearby Ulu Yam Bahru, resuming its regular delivery schedule, could be heard as the vehicle entered the estate clearing. By the time the escorted women and children were brought blinking into the subdued light, the lorry had come to rest just beyond the sprawled body of the tapper shot the previous evening. Visible to the new arrivals was his corpse lying on the road centre. Intestines spewed from a massive stomach wound. Coagulated blood led to another huge wound, this time to the head.

Seven or eight guardsmen surrounded the lorry. With the Chinese detective again acting as interpreter, the driver and all passengers were commanded to alight and stand at the road edge. This they did, a short distance from the first *kongsi* house outside which stood the women and children held overnight. More interrogations followed, culminating in the driver and two men – a head grass cutter and the plantation's *kepala* (headman) – being separated and taken away under guard.

The detective and Scots Guards patrol leader could be seen in intense conversation beside the lorry. Thereafter, a group of casual workers who had alighted from the vehicle were led off to a nearby storeroom and there detained by two guardsmen. Some half-an-hour elapsed before the lorry driver returned. The grass cutter and the clerk who had been taken away with him were nowhere to be seen. The women and children from the lorry, standing as instructed at the roadside, were subsequently directed to re-board the vehicle. The still slumped body of Chan Loi, the man who had broken down during interrogation, was lifted by two soldiers and dumped in the rear of the truck.

Shortly thereafter the Chinese detective returned to the women and children detained overnight. The women were given a last chance to go back to their respective living quarters for personal belongings. They were informed their homes were to be torched. In their rush they retrieved very little. One returned with a blanket. Another came back with cooking utensils. One or two mothers collected clothing and tins of food. Any woman found lingering in the confines of her home was brusquely hustled along by guardsmen. Finally, the women and children were ordered aboard the lorry.

A precise timetable for the ghastly episode that followed is impossible to compile. Those present on the plantation who escaped the fury had no watches or clocks in their possession as events unfolded. Quite inexplicable has been the total absence of Scots Guards operational reports that should have revealed a complete schedule of all activities – and their time-frames – throughout the operation.

But while exact time-frames may be blurred, the reality of what transpired is patently clear.

It was now about 9 am. The women, whose attentions were not dominated by the requirements of child-care, could look back down the estate road from their position on the lorry towards the *kongsis*. They could see the male prisoners being brought from their overnight holding area to the open ground beside the estate road. The women had no way of knowing exactly how many men were gathered there. But in the group stood the two men detained with the lorry driver earlier that morning. One woman recognised the head grass cutter. Another spotted her spouse, the *kepala*. A third saw the husband she realised had been detained all night with the other workers. A teenage girl identified her fiancé. Another caught a glimpse of her brother-in-law.

The women watched as the soldiers divided the detained men into three or four groups and began taking them at gunpoint in different directions. Two groups seemed headed towards the stream via the separate walking tracks that led away from the estate road. The rest disappeared behind the *kongsis* and looked as if they were being directed towards the plantation hill beyond the clearing.

When the Chinese detective gave the order for the lorry to leave, it required some deft manoeuvring on the part of the driver to swing round and face the opposite direction. The road was narrow and the corpse lay on its centre. With the turning completed, the driver came to a halt. The vehicle was barely 100 yards away from the closest *kongsi* house. Those standing at the back of its open passenger section had an unrestricted view of the scene they were about to leave.

A wife spotted her husband walking in front of those moving along the estate road, past the smokehouse. The men came directly towards the parked lorry. She kept watching as the soldiers shepherded her husband and his companions through a right hand turn into the first track leading down to the stream. The spacing of the rubber tree rows and intermittent ponds allowed the monitoring of her husband's progress right down to the stream's nearest bank. Simultaneously, the second group went out of sight as it turned into the other pathway to the stream further back down the road. Those taken behind the *kongsis* were, by then, well out of the fields of view of anyone aboard the lorry.

As the scene unfolded before them, the women began howling. A crescendo of wailing erupted as the children joined in. Frantic struggles broke out. Several women attempted to jump down and run to their men. Fellow occupants in the lorry lunged forward in desperate bids to restrain them. At road level, two soldiers, detailed to guard all those aboard and oversee their departure, ran back and forth blocking the descent of women on the verge of tumbling to the ground.

In the middle of the melee came the blast of automatic weapons' fire. It sounded from the direction of the estate workers by the stream, the group nearest the lorry. As if on cue, another spate of firing erupted further upstream, close to where the second group of detained men had been seen walking in front of their captors. Then came a third, then a fourth burst of rapid-fire – these from the general area behind the *kongsis*. For the horror-struck spectators, the staccato volleys that followed felt like an eternity. In truth, they probably lasted less than two minutes.

By the time the supply lorry had moved off down the estate road, negotiated the wooden bridge and was heading for the dingy streets of Ulu Yam Bahru, the soldiers' threats to torch the *kongsis* had been fulfilled. All structures in the clearing were well alight.

Pomp and pageantry play a vital role in the mindset of British colonialists when it comes to imposing authority in far flung territories. Malaya is no exception.
Sir Henry Gurney chooses a matter-of-fact business suit for his initial arrival to become High Commissioner in Kuala Lumpur (left). But he is soon donning the required paraphernalia of high office (below) when attending formal occasions.

Chapter 2

'Best news in weeks'

As far as the colonial territories of Malaya and Singapore were concerned, there was very little good news about – local or international – as the December, 1948, run-up to Christmas began.

Colonial rubber planters and tin miners, who together amounted to the territory's most powerful political lobby, were as one in their vehement criticism of the way the authorities were handling Emergency measures. The government, they insisted, was complacent and Britain's Kuala Lumpur-based High Commissioner, Sir Henry Gurney, was ineffective. Unless far stronger measures were taken against the CPM and its guerrilla army, London stood to lose the one colonial territory with financial muscle enough to extract the mother country from its huge post-war debt. Latest reports from Westminster indicating Malayan police would soon be getting more armoured cars didn't impress the critics. They regarded such promises as far too little, far too late. In their view, the whole anti-insurgency effort was being mishandled and the colonial administration needed revamping from top to bottom.

And if the local scene was alarming, the international one was more so. Communiqués from China described the inexorable advances being made by communist troops in virtually all strategically important areas of that country. Mao Tse Tung's units had moved to within a few miles of Peking and were directly threatening to capture the city. They had cut the government's railway lifeline to the Huai River defences at a point only 50 miles from the administrative capital of Nanking. They had also encircled two major government forces, 145 miles and 185 miles north-west of Nanking.

On December 10, Winston Churchill, leader of the Conservative opposition, expressed the obvious in the House of Commons when he remarked that the advance of communism in China 'seems to be gaining momentum every day'. He quickly went on to reassure the House that, come what may, 'British forces will be defending the colony of Hong Kong from any assault'. Morale boosting stuff, perhaps. But if the same British forces were unable to handle a bunch of Chinese communist bandits in the jungles of Malaya – and they had certainly failed to notch up much success during the first six months of the Emergency – what chance would they have in Hong Kong against Mao Tse Tung's mainland marauders?

The Straits Times

MALAYA'S LEADING NEWSPAPER ESTABLISHED 1845

EIGHT PAGES.　　　　SINGAPORE, MONDAY, DECEMBER 13, 1948.　　★　PRICE TEN CENTS.

POLICE, GUARDS KILL 28 BANDITS IN DAY

Biggest Success For Forces Since Emergency Started

From Our Own Correspondent
KUALA LUMPUR, Sunday.

TWENTY eight bandits were killed by police and Scots Guards operating in the Batang Kali and Rawang areas of north Selangor in the past 24 hours.

In one operation a patrol shot dead 26 Chinese. This constitutes the biggest success in any one day's operation in one area since the emergency began.

In addition, one armed Chinese, declared by the police to be a well-known bandit leader, was seriously wounded and five others were captured.

A tin miner in the Rawang area said tonight when told about the news: "It's wonderful. It is the best news I have heard for many weeks."

It was one of the last few days has been the focal point of terrorist and anti-terrorist operations and a large scale fire was opened by the security forces of the week end.

A large number of troops and police are taking part. The biggest success occurred in the Batang Kali area when a patrol of police and Scots Guards numbering 11 men shot dead 25 Chinese they had surprised yesterday morning and rounded up and who then attempted to escape early this morning.

Moving through the jungle yesterday afternoon the patrol spied two armed Chinese in uniform but lost them.

Food Lorry

A large quantity of food.

As the lorry was brought towards the kongsi guards were once again put out at strategic points.

Most of the guards were hiding from view of the men in the kongsi.

They could see only three sentries.

Suddenly the 25 men made a break running in all directions.

A police officer said: "The guards had been well placed and the running men just ran into their guns. Every man was killed."

On The Trail

A few men ago, a second column of Scots Guards was rushing towards an objective when it saw and challenged an armed Chinese, who was shot dead.

Down in the Rawang area further south more police and Scots Guards were on the trail of men of the Eighth Regi-

4 BANDITS KILLED IN KEDAH

From Our Staff Correspondent
KUALA LUMPUR, Sun.

IN the Baling area of Kedah, anti-terrorist operations have now been completed. Four bandits were killed and 31 bandits or collaborators arrested.

Eleven fire arms, 100 rounds of ammunition, two handgrenades and three detonators were recovered. Eleven bandit ramps or hide-outs, together with a few isolated huts, were destroyed. Two thousand persons were screened.

Air strikes took place on Dec. 10 and 11 and aircraft were mortared on the 2nd and 6th. There were no casualties to Security forces.

BANDITS RAIDED

THESE men have been described as "mass murderers" by the Republican Government in Indonesia. They are said to have taken part in atrocities among the civilian population. Now they are in captivity.—A.P. picture.

Washington Concern Over Indonesian Crisis

WASHINGTON, Sunday.

THE U.S. State Department was today reported to be seriously concerned over the Netherlands' decision yesterday to break off negotiations with the Indonesian Republic.

Department officials spent several hours discussing the matter, although today is generally a holiday at the State Department.

TANKS IN EGYPTIAN ATTACK

THE United Nations

Japan's P.M. Now Named

An official spokesman said that the breakdown "must be assessed in relation to possible effect on South-East Asia." Clari-

ANTI-CHIANG LEADERS TALK OF COALITION

HONG KONG, Sunday.

TEN delegates, representing anti-Chiang Kai-shek groups, have left Hong Kong for Harbin, Manchuria, for talks with Chinese Communist leaders on the formation of a coalition government if Nanking falls, it was reported in Hong Kong yesterday.

The report added that talks were going on between Leftist groups and the Communists in Harbin. It said that the possibility of a coalition government being formed should Peking be captured by the Communists, or Chiang resign, was also being considered.

In Washington yesterday, the White House refused to comment on Chinese reports that the United States, was trying to persuade the Nanking Government, through Madame Chiang Kai-shek, to reach a settlement with the Communists.

President Truman, meeting the Chinese President's wife for the first time on Friday night, said afterwards he had given a "sympathetic" hearing to her appeal for increased American aid.

It was unlikely that Mr Truman and Madame Chiang had anything like an extensive discussion.

No plans for a further meeting were announced, though a Chinese Embassy spokesman said yesterday the possibility should not be

"Stay At Work." Say Reds

PEKING, Sun.

THE Communists today broadcast to Nationalist China their policy from a regional station in Hantan, Southern Hopei, they voiced a seven-point programme on a follows:

Stay at your jobs: Government employees are not to be dismissed if their work is satisfactory; schools will remain open; Government-owned enterprises will be confiscated but work will continue;

Anyone destroying factories, railways, mines and other projects will be classified as war criminals and executed or imprisoned; free enterprise will be allowed, but Government shares in various concerns will be confiscated; all inhabitants except the Kuomintang agents will be protected.—A.P.

Surely, remarks by Foreign Secretary Ernest Bevin, speaking to the same parliament 24 hours earlier, had more accurately reflected reality. Great Britain, the Foreign Secretary declared, had advised Chiang Kai Shek's nationalist government that 'our financial and economic position precludes us from doing anything material for China'. Sobering words indeed, to which he added: 'Inevitably, as the result of war-time strategy of the Allies and post-war circumstances, the United States Government has been more directly concerned with assistance to China than this country.'

The impact of these remarks was only multiplied when, a few hours later, the commander of the United States Western Pacific Fleet, Admiral Oscar C. Badger *11*, gave a press conference on the other side of the world to announce that US Marines would shortly be moving to Shanghai to protect American lives and essential property. 'But,' the Vice-Admiral pointedly added, 'there is no intention of any intervention whatsoever in China's civil war.'

So when Kuala Lumpur and Singapore editions of *The Straits Times* newspaper on Monday, December 13, carried the front page lead headline POLICE, GUARDS KILL 28 BANDITS IN DAY, with the sub-head – *Biggest Success For Forces Since Emergency Started* – here, finally, was something positive, something to crow about, something worth celebrating.

The accompanying story explained that the kill total of 28 in the headline was a collective figure derived from the results of four separate Scots Guards actions the previous day. Single kills were claimed by each of three patrols operating with police. Two of those were in the Rawang district and the other near Batang Kali. But it had been yet another separate action on an unnamed estate, again in the Batang Kali area, that had produced the spectacular total of 25 dead bandits. 'This constitutes the biggest success in any one day's operation in one area since the Emergency began,' proclaimed the newspaper triumphantly.

A Rawang tin miner's reaction to the news was quoted high in the story: 'It's wonderful. It's the best news I've heard for many weeks.'

Written under a Kuala Lumpur dateline, indicating the reporter had not been to the scene, the account had been based on information supplied in a brief statement issued by the colonial authorities. The Scots Guards unit involved, the story explained, had been moving through the jungle during the day when two armed Chinese in uniform were spotted. Both managed to escape. Soon afterwards the patrol members found a *kongsi* inhabited by men and women. Before any alarm could be raised, the Scots Guards had surrounded a large hut and all the men in it had surrendered.

A police spokesman was quoted as saying: 'The *kongsi* was searched and under a mattress was found a large quantity of ammunition.' One Chinese attempted to escape and was shot dead. When the Scots Guards learned food was expected at the *kongsi* early the following morning, they decided to wait.

At 5.30 am the sound of a motor was heard and very soon a lorry came into view. It was halted, surrounded and discovered to be carrying a large quantity of food.

The newspaper account continued: 'As the lorry was brought towards the *kongsi*, guards were once again put out at strategic points.

'Most of the guards were hidden from view of the men in the *kongsi*.

'They could see only three sentries.

'Suddenly, the 25 men made a break running in all directions.'

The story then quoted a police officer as saying: 'The Guards had been well placed and the running men just ran into their guns. Every man was killed.'

Coming as it did from an official source, the government's statement would present a whole array of problems for the authorities once newspaper reporting staff and informed members of the public began fitting together the pieces of the Batang Kali puzzle. If the 'fleeing' plantation workers had run 'into' the Scots Guards fire, the majority of wounds would naturally have been inflicted on frontal features of torsos, heads and legs. In the same circumstances, sentries discharging their weapons at suspects running at them would have been firing automatic weapons into the clearing area still occupied by the remainder of the Guards patrol along with the three police guides.

Interestingly, Selangor's Police Chief H. G. Beverley, the man behind the original government account, announced later the same night that no further details were available. He explained that the report of the military action had been 'flashed by radio' from the jungle to tactical headquarters. He went on to say that the operation was continuing and not until it was completed could the scene of the shooting be identified.

Only two British newspapers then had staff correspondents operating in South East Asia – *The Daily Telegraph* and *The Times*. Both men were based in Singapore. With the time difference between Singapore and the United Kingdom working in their favour, each was able to file stories on the Batang Kali killings and make their respective London newspapers on the same day *The Straits Times*' account appeared.

The Daily Telegraph report, headlined '*Guards kill 28 bandits*' ran a mere five paragraphs in length and was tucked away on an inside foreign news page. It concluded with the police quote describing how those fleeing from the Scots Guards 'just ran into their guns'. *The Times* coverage, longer by a few column inches, was given slightly more prominence in the paper's *Imperial and Foreign* news section. Its

Selangor Police Chief H. G. Beverley releases the first official account, albeit sketchy, of the Scots Guards Batang Kali action. When the official line starts losing its gloss, Beverley becomes linked to a so-called 'police inquiry' into the Sungei Remok killings – an inquiry, as it turns out, that never takes place. Beverley well understands the intricacies of colonial control. He has previously held the post of Assistant Commissioner of the Federated Malay States Police Force and, prior to the Japanese occupation of Malaya and Singapore (1942-45), had served as ADC to the Governor of Singapore, Sir Shenton Thomas.

For all the public enthusiasm initial Batang Kali headlines are generating in Malaya and Singapore, the same cannot be said about press reaction in Britain to the Scots Guards 'success' story. The Daily Telegraph account (below) amounts to five short paragraphs on an inside foreign news page in the paper's December 13, 1948, edition. Three weeks later The Times, again giving modest coverage, publishes a story (right) reflecting the colonial government's calculated reassessment of the Sungei Remok raid.

GUARDS KILL 28 BANDITS

◆

PATROL ACTION IN MALAYA JUNGLE

FROM OUR OWN CORRESPONDENT
SINGAPORE, Sunday.

Operating in the Batang Kali and Rawang areas of Selangor, Scots Guards and police have killed 28 bandits in the last 24 hours. In one operation a patrol of 14 men killed 26 Chinese, the biggest success in any one day's operation in one area since the declaration of an emergency.

In addition a Chinese bandit leader has been seriously wounded and five bandits have been captured. The security forces opened an offensive round Rawang, in the tin fields north of Kuala Lumpur, at the week-end.

The 26 Chinese who were killed had been surprised and captured yesterday in a jungle hut in the Batang Kali area. One who attempted to escape was shot dead.

Learning that food was expected to arrive, the patrol waited, and a lorry was escorted to the hut, from which the captured bandits could see only three sentries.

The remaining 25 men made a sudden break, running in all directions. The police officer said: "The Scots Guards had been well placed, and the bandits just ran into their guns. Everyone was killed."

SCOTS GUARDS AND SHOT CHINESE

MALAYAN INQUIRY
FROM OUR CORRESPONDENT
SINGAPORE, JAN. 3

The Government of the Malayan Federation has decided to take no action after investigation into the shooting near Rawang, Selangor, on December 12 of 24 Chinese by Scots Guards and a police patrol.

An official statement issued at Kuala Lumpur to-day says that the Guards section concerned was commanded by a sergeant under general orders that if any detained person tried to escape he was to be chased and recaptured, but in no circumstances was he to be allowed to escape. The section patrolled an area which included rubber estates and jungle, and bandits were seen and fired on. The sergeant feared that these bandits would carry the news to others and decided to press on. He eventually arrived at a clearing of *kongsi* (communal living) houses, huts, and shacks, in one of which ammunition was discovered. The statement continues: "·Information from interrogation was that armed bandits were in the habit of visiting the area and used it for obtaining supplies, which were brought in every morning by the lorry which brought food for the tappers and others who occupied the clearing. If attacked the clearing was a death-trap, and the sergeant therefore posted three groups to cover the entrances. These groups were out of sight of persons in the clearing and were posted on the afternoon of December 11."

PREARRANGED PLAN

The interrogated men were placed in a *kongsi* house for the night under guard, and in the morning, seeing only the sergeant and two sentries, they made a break in three parties in accordance with what was obviously a pre-arranged plan. The sentries and the sergeant called upon the men to stop, but could not use their arms because their hidden comrades were in the line of fire. These three groups heard shouting, but did not know what was happening until they saw Chinese running through the jungle past their posts. The soldiers called in the Malay language upon the fleeing men to halt, gave chase, and finally opened fire.

From June 16, when a state of emergency was declared, until the end of the year 409 bandits have been killed and 268 captured. Police, service, and civilian casualties were 482 killed and 404 wounded. Civilian casualties, of which more than two-thirds were Chinese, were 330 killed and 194 injured.

headline: 'Forces' success in Malaya'. Like *The Straits Times* and *The Daily Telegraph*, *The Times* quoted the police as saying those attempting to escape at Batang Kali had run 'into' the soldiers' weapons.

The lukewarm interest shown by Britain's mainstream press in the seemingly amazing results at Batang Kali that weekend was symptomatic of the period. That British newspapers in late 1948 seemed indifferent to events taking place in Malaya and Singapore had incensed colonial planters, tin miners and businessmen alike since well before the Emergency's declaration half-a-year earlier.

Britain's war-weariness was partly to blame. There had been too much fighting, too much misery. Events around Europe and behind what Churchill in 1946 had defined as the 'Iron Curtain' presented as far more relevant to the average Briton in the street. Adding to the problem of projecting developments in Malaya to the outside world was a running dispute between the Foreign and Colonial offices in Whitehall over the best propaganda line to adopt towards the communist guerrillas in Malaya. Top echelon civil servants disagreed over the definition and interpretation of 'terrorism' as it applied to Emergency conditions. Equally significant, they disagreed over whatever relationship existed – if any at all – between the CPM and the Communist Party of China (CPC), on the one hand, and the CPM and Moscow, on the other.

A dominant concern in both ministries was that the Malayan 'bandits' might end up being portrayed as 'true patriots'. In a classic civil service reaction throughout most of 1948, it was deemed better to say nothing and discourage publicity and discussion than become enmeshed in any complex propaganda effort.

It was not until August that year that the Foreign and Colonial offices appeared finally to have reached a common line of approach. They decided, as Colonial Secretary Arthur Creech Jones noted at the time, on a joint campaign geared to undermining any suggestion that 'present troubles in Malaya arise from a genuine nationalist movement of the people of the country'. Directives outlining what the Colonial Secretary anticipated would be a 'vigorous counter-attack on Communist propaganda both at home and abroad' were dispatched to all relevant offices. But it would be well into 1949 before campaign teething troubles were overcome and colonial authorities in London, Kuala Lumpur and Singapore began speaking in vaguely compatible tones when it came to describing CPM activities.

～∾～

Packed with the casual hired tappers and Sungei Remok Estate's women and children, the contractor's lorry lurched to a stop in the Ulu Yam Bahru main street. There it disgorged its hapless load of shocked passengers. For a while they stood on the roadside, their faces drained of all expression. Tappers who lived in the village returned to their homes. As far as the plantation's women and children were concerned, they were now homeless. They had no money and – but for the paltry items snatched at the last minute from *kongsi* rooms – possessed only the clothes on their backs. As word of their plight spread through the village, locals began organising relief. In an abandoned shophouse someone provided biscuits and drinks. This was the first sustenance for the adults since lunch the previous day.

As they sat sipping tea and coffee, more villagers trickled in to hear for themselves what had transpired overnight. Among the women, numbness had replaced terror. A few had relatives in the village from whom they could seek succour. Some would be sheltered by kind acquaintances. The rest would remain in the shophouse.

Among those with no alternative but to share this communal space was 30-year-old mother of four, Foo Moi. She had watched from the back of the lorry as the soldiers separated the men into groups and began escorting them at gunpoint in different directions. She had recognised her husband at the head of six or seven captives walking first towards the lorry, then away down the nearest track to the stream. Transfixed by dread, she had seen the father of her children amble to the bank, then collapse to the ground as the soldiers fired.

Foo Moi spent the rest of the day taking care of her children. As she did so, she agonised in her mind whether she should attempt to go back to the estate. Instinctively, she knew she had witnessed her husband's death. In fact, Foo Moi was convinced that the soldiers had killed all the detained labourers at Sungei Remok that morning. In this, as it happened, she was not quite right.

———∿———

Back on the estate, the three *kongsis*, two smokehouses and rubber storage shed were being gutted by fire. The Scots Guards had gone, satisfied they had met the objectives of their mission.

By the stream, at the end of the track nearest the first *kongsi*, a body stirred. Chong Fong, the young tapper who late the previous afternoon had been bathing at the same spot, regained consciousness. He opened his eyes and found himself surrounded by felled bodies. The realisation that he had fainted and survived unscathed a mass killing was almost too much to bear. The sound of water surging over stones and around boulders escaped him, blotted out by the wild beating of his heart. His temples throbbed. All he wanted was to get away, to run for his life.

Britain's Secretary of State for the Colonies Arthur Creech Jones serves in this capacity from 1946 – 1950.

Pushing aside the bloodied limbs of the dead who had fallen across him, he struggled to his feet, his body shaking violently. Marshalling all his strength, he set off downstream. Where possible, he walked along stretches of the bank. Where necessary, he diverted and waded down the course of rushing water. At a point where the stream ran beneath a familiar bridge, Chong Fong decided to clamber onto the road above and from there make directly for his father's coffee shop in Ulu Yam Bahru.

The old man listened to his son's account in silence. He asked no questions. Even when the youth blurted that he'd seen his brother, Chong Sip, in the *kongsi* room the previous night, but knew nothing of his fate, the father remained calm. He told his son he would personally handle all matters concerning Chong Sip. He further advised his deeply agitated boy to keep quiet about the killings.

Scared that the soldiers would track him down should they discover he had survived, Chong Fong at first did as he was told. He surmised his own mother, who had been with the women and children on the lorry, would have seen much of what had happened. He would learn about Chong Sip's death from his father the next day. And that was when he discovered he was the lone survivor. The young tapper was anything but elated. Indeed, it would leave him all the more confused and bewildered about life. He started talking to his friends. Two days later a police van pulled up outside the coffee shop and Chong Fong, under escort, was taken away.

On the morning following the mass killing, another patrol from 7 platoon, G Company, was dispatched to the estate on a reconnaissance mission. The lone body still lay on the estate road approaches, putrifying in the midday heat. Whiffs of smoke curled upward from the remains of a quietly smouldering smokehouse. All three *kongsis* had been reduced to charred ruins. As one of the follow-up Scots Guards patrolmen would recall many years later, the sights that confronted him and his colleagues on the plantation that day 'weren't pretty'.

At the bottom of the first track leading to the stream lay seven bodies in a tight group, all showing signs of having been shot from behind. One was headless. A short way upstream, at a point where a second track led down from the *kongsi* area, another seven bodies were located, all similarly showing signs of multiple wounds inflicted by weapons fired from behind. Once again all bodies in this location lay in a tight grouping.

Behind the burnt-out third *kongsi*, at the foot of the hill, where the plantation tree rows began, the reconnaissance patrol discovered another clutch of bodies –

this time numbering four. Finally, in the space between the second *kongsi* and what was left of a storeroom, further on down the estate road, lay more bodies – five of them. Again, they were tightly clustered.

The follow-up patrol made careful body-counts at the four separate group killing sites and added the single body on the estate road approaches. Their reported assessment of enemy killed: 24, one short of the 25 figure released by the authorities. The original total of 25 dead had derived from the patrol's count of those detained overnight, the addition of two men from the morning lorry and the single body lying on the estate road. Neither police nor Scots Guards, at this stage, had any knowledge of Chong Fong's escape.

—⁓—

Later that Monday morning a group of four women, including Foo Moi, decided to return to the estate and confirm, once and for all, the fate of their menfolk. They set out on foot and had covered less than half the distance when they met a Malay man, an acquaintance from a nearby *kampong* (village). The Malay urged them to turn back. He claimed he had just come from the estate's outskirts and had seen a batch of soldiers in the clearing. The women were undeterred and pushed on.

There were no troops about when they eventually reached the plantation. There, in the centre of the approach road, they identified the corpse of Loh Kit Lin, the 19 year-old tapper who had so doggedly insisted he had never gathered durians for the communists. Thirty-four year-old Wong Yen, one of the four women, shook her head in despair as she squatted by the mangled, lifeless body of her brother-in-law. Until two days earlier, the youth had been helping support Wong Yen and her two sons, aged seven and four. She had been forced to accept his charity, and that of her mother-in-law, when her husband deserted her for another woman a year earlier. She wondered how she could break the devastating news to the old woman who was waiting back in Ulu Yam Bahru.

The smokehouse was still smouldering. The three *kongsis* that had been home for the four women presented little but charred stumps. Unaware of the risks they might be taking, all four then went ahead to conduct their joint search of the killing field. Foo Moi led them to the stream where she had seen her husband drop to the ground when the firing began. She let out a tearless wail when her worst fears were confirmed. The body of 42 year-old Wong Yan, father of her children, lay face down, spread-eagled over rocks and half submerged in the water. She could identify him only by the shirt he had been wearing. Six other bodies lay close to him.

By this time the four women felt certain all the men had been similarly executed. But, something made them continue their search. They needed verification. Filled with grief and anger, Foo Moi, who had paused to pray, rejoined the others as they negotiated the short distance upstream to where all were convinced another grisly scene awaited them.

They were right. Seven more bodies, just like the others downstream, displayed similarly horrendous bullet wounds to backs of torsos, napes and heads. So far, they had confirmed 15 dead. Between the second *kongsi* and a storehouse, not far from the estate road, they discovered five more. Walking towards the hill behind the third *kongsi*, from where they recalled the sound of firing had come the previous morning, the women stumbled onto yet another four dead. There were now 24 corpses.

The women pressed on. When further searching yielded nothing more, they trudged back to the estate road. Giving Low Kit Lin's body a wide berth, they moved out of the plantation, over the bridge and onto the road along which they had earlier walked from Ulu Yam Bahru.

Back at the abandoned shophouse, estate refugees were waiting desperately to hear what the four women had to say. They listened in silence to descriptions of body numbers, where the dead were lying and the extent of their mutilation. Of far less concern was what the women said about the utter destruction of the *kongsis* and associated plantation structures.

They would abide by their earlier decision to stay clear of contacts with the police. The women were oblivious to the reported 25 deaths making headline news in Kuala Lumpur and Singapore.

Paramount was the need to retrieve the bodies for burial. Local religious rights demanded nothing less. Surely, the one man who could help with this task was the plantation contractor, Lim Chye Chee? But initial attempts to contact him had already failed. Had he absconded? The contractor had a nephew who taught at the local school. He willingly helped the women draft a letter seeking formal permission to enter Sungei Remok Estate and collect the dead.

A day or two later a shaken Lim Chye Chee re-appeared – released by the police who had arrested him on the morning of the shooting. To each family the contractor immediately offered $30 (Straits currency) as a contribution towards burial expenses. He also made tentative arrangements for the transportation of corpses once permission to proceed with their recovery was granted.

Official consent came in the form of a police letter and individual recovery chits. These were issued late on the fourth day after the shooting. Throughout those four days no attempt was made by the authorities to visit the scene – apart

A formal Chinese gateway (above) today stands across the entrance to the Ulu Yam Bahru cemetery where all 24 shot dead at Sungei Remok Estate were ultimately interred. Each year surviving kin of those killed by the Scots Guards gather here on Cheng Beng day for the ritual cleaning of the gravesides and prayers for the departed.

from the Scots Guards follow-up reconnaissance mission. Nor had there been any offer by the same authorities to assist with the recovery of bodies or related burial requirements.

On the day set aside for the retrieval, the lorry driver tasked with the job was the same man who had driven the frantic families out of the plantation as the mass killing was in progress. In addition, estate contractor Lim provided a team of men for the gruesome recovery duties. It took all day and three separate lorry trips before the 24 now well decomposing bodies had all been removed. Four or five families were able to afford proper Chinese coffins. For the rest, corpses were confined to crude boxes made of planks.

It was dark by the time the recovery concluded, too late for the required prayers and rituals. So the coffins were left in rows overnight at the Ulu Yam Bahru cemetery, located directly opposite the local police station. The following morning – December 19 – the Sungei Remok Estate victims were interred.

After chanting their prayers and watching the last shovels of earth drop into the freshly dug graves, the women, their cultural obligations met, shuffled off to face what was left of their lives. Adjustments had to be made. Expedient decisions only added to the women's bereavement. Children were given away. Some siblings were never to meet again. To earn their meals, older sons and daughters – aged nine or ten – were sent out to help collect latex on neighbouring plantations. For most of the women, fending for themselves meant begging for weeks on end. It would take months for them to wobble out of the surreal predicament that followed the mass killing of their men. Still bereft, they would emerge and slowly return to exploited lives of more rubber tapping and more grass cutting.

Chapter 3

Explaining away the inexplicable

On Friday, September 7, 1945, the first post-war issue of *The Straits Times* newspaper in Singapore – a limited four-page tabloid edition – hit the streets. Its headline: SINGAPORE IS BRITISH AGAIN.

For several years thereafter, the morning daily became regarded as an extension of the returning colonial administration. An 'in' joke among expatriates during this post-war phase told of the island's Tanglin Club, its Singapore Swimming Club, its Singapore Cricket Club and *The Straits Times* as being bastions of the crumbling empire's remaining 'whites only' enclaves.

In the newspaper's Cecil Street headquarters, the expatriate editors and management occupied private offices while Asian staff had desks. Pay and perks were such that a number of the expatriate journalists jointly owned race horses. Most lived in company-provided bungalows in an exclusive residential area – a development fondly referred to by the occupants as '*The Straits Times kampong*'.

Some of the senior editorial staff had been prisoners during the 1942-45 Japanese occupation. With the establishment of the interim British Military Administration (BMA), precursor to full colonial control, the released 'old hands' quickly rejoined the newspaper and helped it regain its pre-war footing. Other staff were hired directly from the Colombo-based South East Asia Command (SEAC) headquarters, headed by Admiral Louis Mountbatten. There they had functioned essentially as war-time propagandists. One or two more would transfer to the paper from the re-established British Malaya Broadcasting Corporation (BMBC) located at the island's Caldecott Hill radio complex.

Once ensconced, expatriate staff on *The Straits Times* found themselves in unquestionably privileged positions. They enjoyed far greater access to senior colonial figures than their local Asian counterparts. It was a most convenient environment, both professionally and socially. It revolved around a racially determined concept of who was considered more reliable and more trustworthy. In such an environment it became accepted that all major local stories featured in the paper were handled by a select circle of expatriate journalists.

So it was that the man chosen by *The Straits Times*' editors to follow-up the action being touted 'the biggest success in any one day's operation in one area since the Emergency began' was Harry Miller. One of three sons of a retired Boer War

The Straits Times

MALAYA'S LEADING NEWSPAPER—ESTABLISHED 1845.

SINGAPORE, FRIDAY, SEPTEMBER 7, 1945.

2 PAGES

SINGAPORE IS BRITISH AGAIN!

OUR DAY OF LIBERATION

Reoccupation Proceeds In City Ablaze With Allied Flags

The reoccupation of Singapore by British forces, following the formal surrender of Japan and her acceptance of the terms of the declaration at Tokio last Sunday, thus bringing to an end the Japanese occupation which began on February 15, 1942, and which had thus lasted 1318 days.

A large convoy of transports, mechanical transport ships and other vessels steamed into the Singapore roads under the lowering clouds of a monsoon. The cruisers Sussex and Cleopatra, destroyers and the minesweepers which swept a path through the heavily mined Straits are already here

First to land were the vanguard... correspondent representing... press and news agencies of the world...

Japanese Guard Route

all important street junctions... Japanese soldiers who also kept... from the docks along Collyer...

Quickly revived and functioning, The Straits Times, in its first publication following Japan's Pacific War defeat, sets the tone for the British return to the region as colonial rulers.

Supreme Allied Commander South East Asia, Admiral Mountbatten, flanked by senior military officers on the steps of Singapore's then Municipal Building, formally proclaims the re-establishment of Britain's colonial presence.

January 6, 1946. A grateful Britain chooses to acknowledge publicly the local communist movement's services in Malaya and Singapore on behalf of the anti-Japanese war effort. Among those to receive medals and thanks personally from the Supreme Allied Commander is one Ong Boon Hua who, 30 months later, emerges as Chin Peng, leader of the Communist Party of Malaya's anti-colonial rebellion.

British military officer who had demobbed in Singapore, Miller and his siblings had all been educated at the local St. Andrew's school. Immediately on leaving St. Andrew's, Miller moved to the paper's reporting staff. The Japanese invasion saw him incarcerated in Singapore's Sime Road internment camp. On his release, the then 27 year-old rejoined the newspaper's staff and was quickly appointed chief reporter. At the outbreak of the Emergency, he was transferred to Kuala Lumpur in a switch calculated to beef up the newpaper's Malaya coverage.

Miller received his Batang Kali assignment late in the evening of December 12 as sub-editors in Singapore were laying out the initial report of the killings based on the statement provided by the authorities. The following morning he drove north from Kuala Lumpur along the trunk road, choosing Kuala Kubu Bahru as his prime destination. Probably because of police unwillingness to identify the exact location of the Sunday morning action, Miller failed to visit Sungei Remok Estate where the bodies of the slain still lay exactly where they had fallen. Neither did he drive to Ulu Yam Bahru where the refugee families of the dead were seeking shelter.

Instead, he concentrated on stopping by the Scots Guards operational headquarters and the nearby police Special Branch offices at Kuala Kubu Bahru. There he was given security briefings as well as ready access to patrol members. He took the opportunity to conduct an interview with the 22 year-old sergeant in charge of the platoon claiming the extraordinary kill-rate.

Miller's story led page seven of his paper's December 14 edition. It appeared under an impersonalised 'From Our Staff Correspondent' by-line, and beneath the headline: HUSSARS PATROL TROUBLE AREA'. The sub-head read: *Big Offensive By Guards Continues*. Either Miller himself, or his editors, had decided that the interview with the man who had led the acclaimed action – the subject of the previous day's front page banner headline – was less significant than a general report angled on the continuing anti-insurgency effort underway across Ulu Selangor. From a professional journalistic viewpoint this was a curious approach.

The downplayed aspects in Miller's story would soon assume special importance as senior government and military officials realised they would need to provide key answers to most unwelcome questions centred on the killings.

Forming the second half of his overall account, Miller's interview with the patrol leader conveniently left the man unnamed. But it quoted him at length. After spotting two armed men in jungle green, 300 yards away on a hill, the patrol leader had decided 'the best thing we could do was to get to our specific objective'. Miller went on to explain that the 'specific objective' comprised three large *kongsis*, a smokehouse, a rubber store and other sheds – in other words, Sungei Remok Estate. As with the identity of the patrol leader, Miller's report left the estate unnamed.

Tuesday, December 14, 1948.   THE STRAITS TIMES   Page 7

HUSSARS PATROL TROUBLE AREA

Big Offensive By Guards Continues

From Our Staff Correspondent
KUALA LUMPUR, Monday.

MORE than a battalion of Scots Guards and Grenadier Guards and a force of Police are being used in the big offensive against terrorists in Ulu Selangor.

Meanwhile, the 4th Hussars have begun a 24-hour patrol with armoured vehicles on the 51-mile stretch of road between Kuala Lumpur and Tanjong Malim, on part of which the 8th Regiment of the MPABA proclaimed a "curfew."

Up to six o'clock this evening there were no more reports of ambushes, or further details from the Security Forces trailing the bandits in the jungle and tin and coal mining areas in Ulu Selangor.

Today, at Kuala Kubu Bharu, I met a 22-year-old sergeant of the Scots Guards who led the patrol which on Sunday morning shot dead 25 Chinese who tried to escape as they were about to be brought back to Kuala Kubu Bahru for interrogation.

His patrol—14 men, plus an Indian police sergeant and a Chinese detective were led by guides to bandit territory in Batang Kali, at a point roughly three miles from Ulu Yam Bahru.

Surrounded

They were examining one kongsi, when his sentries fired at two armed men, in jungle green on a hill 300 yards away.

"I decided the best thing we could do was to get to our specific objective," said the sergeant.

They reached their destination at about four o'clock on Saturday afternoon. There were three large kongsis, a smokehouse, a rubber store and other sheds.

Men were working and women cooking. They did not notice the patrol and were surrounded.

There were 78 men. They were separated from the women and put in a large hut. Interrogation began. During the evening, one Chinese tried to escape and was shot dead.

Food Lorry Ambushed

A search of the kongsis revealed 13 rounds of Sten ammunition in a kepala's bed. The patrol heard that bandits had visited the kongsi, where they collected food and money—and food was carried by lorry ... morning

rounded, and brought back to the kampong. On it was a Chinese, said to be a kepala, and several other men and women.

It was fully loaded with food.

The kepala was put in a separate hut, and the screening of the new arrivals was carried out.

"It was decided that they were free from suspicion," said the sergeant.

"The men were put back into the lorry and so were all the women and children from the kampong, who were told that they were to leave with as many belongings as possible.

"We sent the lorry off and made preparations to bring the 25 suspects and the kepala back with us after burning some of the huts.

"They Started Running"

"We brought the men out of their kongsi and the kepala from his shed at the same time, with the intention of having him identified.

"As we did so, one of the Chinese shouted and every man started running.

"We called out to them to stop but they continued.

"When the men started running, they went into the direction of our sentries, who were in position.

"There was a terrific amount of firing."

Only one man came out alive. He was brought back to Kuala Kubu Bahru.

The company comman... said that the bandits ... were ... 12 ...

Payments To Bandits Must Stop

KUALA LUMPUR, Mon.

FIVE officials of the All-Malayan Chinese Miners' Association and the Perak Chinese Miners' Association met the High Commissioner (Sir Henry Gurney) today to discuss the position of Chinese miners and the question of extortion payments to terrorists.

An official statement stated that the deputation outlined various suggestions which would contribute to an immediate cessation of such payments.

Sir Henry welcomed these suggestions and said he would see that those which appeared likely to be effective would have the fullest support of Government.

He also made it clear that the Government was determined to put a stop to extortion payments and would not relax its own efforts in the meantime.

Nine Arrested

Nine Chinese bandits were arrested by Perak Police at Shanghai Klabang Estate, near Ipoh, yesterday. They were picked out when police screened about 200 people in the area.

In the Kajang and Selangor, Police and Grenadier Guards yesterday ... a kongsi at Kajang ... graphed.

SUCCESSFUL students of the Singapore Chinese Mandarin School who were presented with graduation certificates issued by the Chinese Consul-General, Singapore, on Dec. 11.

Jewellery Not In Xmas Favour

By Our Woman Correspondent

SINGAPORE jewellers cannot tempt husbands and fathers into buying expensive jewellery as Christmas presents.

Neither can many women be prevailed upon to buy for the men gold cuff links or onyx and gold dress studs costing well over a hundred dollars.

Christmas sales of small and valuable ... leading jewellery ... views ... look ...

NEW SHIP BRINGS IN 44 CARS

FORTY-FOUR new motor cars were brought to Singapore yesterday by the 10,000-ton Glen Line Glenorchy, which made her maiden voyage to the East.

The new vessel, after her arrival here, was built ... 1937 ...

Singapore Firm Charged With Holding Dollar

A TOTAL of U.S. $205,816, was brought to Singapore by the firm of Montou... between September, 1946, and October ... was stated yesterday in the First Di...

The statement was made dur... day's hearing into the case again... alleged infringement of the Finan...

The company is on two ... charges of having failed ... to offer for sale United ... States currency alleged ... have been credit... their account ... firms in Americ... 1947.

The firm is al... allowed comp... agents of ... to acc...

Two days after the slaughter at Tom Menzies' plantation, The Straits Times publishes a general report on anti-insurgency action. It includes a somewhat down-played interview with the unnamed leader of the Scots Guards patrol responsible for the much heralded killings.

The Straits Times story went on: 'The men were working and women cooking. They did not notice the patrol and were surrounded.

'There were 25 men. They were separated from the women and put in a large hut. Interrogation began.

'During the evening, one Chinese tried to escape and was shot dead.'

Miller wrote that a search of the *kongsis* had uncovered 13 rounds of Sten-gun ammunition in a *kepala's* bed. The patrol had been informed bandits had visited the *kongsis* where they collected food and money. Food was expected by lorry the following morning. In view of this, the patrol had decided to stay on the estate and ambush the lorry.

Much of Miller's interview closely resembled the police account provided the previous day. When it came to the killing action itself, though, the sergeant volunteered some interesting elaboration.

He told Miller: 'We brought the men out of their *kongsi* and the *kepala* from his shed at the same time, with the intention of having him identified.

'As we did so, one of the Chinese shouted and every man started running. We called out to them to stop but they continued.'

Then came the critical aspect of the patrol leader's remarks: 'When the men started running, they went in the direction of our sentries, who were in position.

'There was a terrible amount of firing'.

Only one man came out alive. He was brought back to Kuala Kubu Bahru, continued the report.

By the patrol leader's calculations, the one man who came out alive was Chan Loi, the estate worker who had collapsed during interrogation and had been transported by lorry, along with the women and children, back to Ulu Yam Bahru. Significantly, at this point neither military nor police had any knowledge of Chong Fong who, alone and undetected, had walked to his father's coffee shop.

Miller's penultimate paragraph quoted the Scots Guards company commander, again unnamed, remarking that his unit's total 'bag' – a popular British hunting term normally reserved for rabbits and other game – had been 26 killed and 12 captured.

The Straits Times report concluded: 'A police release this evening said that the patrol was searching for bandits believed responsible for burning Sungei Tempayan and Ulu Yam Lama railway stations and for the attack in which Inspector Harnum Singh was wounded.'

The Sikh inspector identified in this account would re-emerge many years later to provide important information on the whole Batang Kali affair.

Police at Ulu Yam Bahru, required to deal directly with relatives of those killed by the Scots Guards, quickly came to realise there had been a discrepancy in the official body-count figure.

If 25 alleged communist sympathising plantation workers had been shot dead on Sungei Remok Estate, how come officers were being required to issue 24 retrieval chits for corpses?

Reports of the numbers' discrepancy quickly reached Selangor Police Chief Beverley and, by association immediately thereafter, top military and civil colonial authorities. With these came other reports indicating the existence and rapid detention of lone survivor, Chong Fong. At this point those in charge of instigating the cover-up were faced with a major credibility predicament.

Additional action, in parallel with the apprehension of Chong Fong, would clearly be mandatory. If the cover-up was to be maintained, a revised kill total had to be quietly and effectively fed to the press along with suitable 'height of battle' explanations as to how such confusion had come about. Otherwise, awkward questions could be asked and these might well lead to a revelation of the lone survivor. Four days after the slaughter, local newspapers began using the corrected figure – 24 dead. Pointedly, there was no mention of a lone survivor.

Two Singapore-based newspaper organisations competed for the local English-language readership market in the late 1940s. *The Straits Times* printed exclusively in Singapore but flew copies daily to Kuala Lumpur in two chartered aircraft for circulation throughout the peninsula. Its main competition came from a publishing group known as Tribune Newspapers. Owned by the renowned Chinese philanthropist, S. Q. Wong, this had begun operations in 1915 and in pre-war years had cut drastically into *The Straits Times'* readership by offering subscription rates half those of its competitor. The Tribune organisation produced two dailies – *The Morning Tribune* and an afternoon edition called *The Malaya Tribune*. The latter boasted 'larger sales than any afternoon paper in Malaya' and printed simultaneously in Singapore and in the peninsula's three main population centres – Kuala Lumpur, Ipoh and Penang.

Unlike *The Straits Times*, the two Tribune dailies had set out specifically to tap an English-speaking Asian readership. Part of this successful endeavour involved the hiring of budding young Malay and Chinese journalists. It was not until 1956 that *The Straits Times* adopted a 'Malayanisation policy' resulting in Asians being appointed to top editorial positions. Again, unlike *The Straits Times*, the two Tribune papers in the late 1940s harboured no qualms about criticising colonial authorities. An editorial in *The Malaya Tribune,* four days after the Batang Kali incident, stunned colonial officialdom in both Kuala Lumpur and Singapore.

'The shooting of twenty-four Chinese who attempted to escape from a patrol of police and Scots Guards,' declared the paper, 'requires more explanation if the public conscience is to be satisfied that such drastic action was unavoidable.'

The editorial went on: 'The brief official report, which is the only information so far made available, raises many uneasy questions that should be answered as quickly as possible. For much is at stake.'

The paper acknowledged the bandit war was 'grim business'. The public had no wish to hamper the men in the field by expecting them to fight in kid gloves. 'But,' the editorial went on, 'at the same time, they wish to be reassured that when blood is shed it is the blood of the guilty and not of the innocent. They wish to be satisfied that when men are killed they are killed for good reason, and not for the sake of killing. It is all too easy, under the strain of jungle fighting, to assume that every Chinese found in the jungle is a bandit, and to shoot first and to ask questions afterwards.'

It suggested that the mass killing by the Scots Guards had 'the macabre air of an execution – an execution without trial.'

'Were all the dead men proved bandits?' asked *The Malaya Tribune*.

'The report does not say. It merely states that one man spoke against his fellows.

'Is one man's word enough evidence to justify the killing of twenty-four?

'By attempting to escape, the dead men suggested guilt. But innocent men have run from the police before now. Fear and ignorance can make men do foolish things.

'To prevent the escape, was it necessary to shoot to kill? The marksmen who hit twenty-four out of twenty-five moving human targets, could surely have shot to lame.' The editorial's reference to a survivor at this point was another reflection of the Scots Guards version of the action. It incorporated again the predicament of Chan Loi.

The publication continued: 'Where were the women and children while the shooting was going on? Did they witness the death of their menfolk?

'Surely the patrol, outnumbered two to one, must have anticipated that an attempt to escape would be made? Could they not have bound their prisoners?'

The editorial concluded: 'These are some of the questions that people are asking. They are asking them not only because they place a high value on British justice, but because the Kuala Kubu affair will be used as powerful propaganda by the bandits.'

The Malaya Tribune's blunt rebuke forced both civil and military leaders into damage control mode. After two days' preparation, Malaya's Police Commissioner W. Nicol Gray and Major General Boucher called a joint press conference in Kuala Lumpur. Both men began by providing general appreciations of anti-insurgency activities thus far. Gray talked about the arrest of a number of tin-mine owners in Malaya who were reported to have been paying protection money to the communists. Boucher followed with a state-by-state review of the insurgency situation.

During his discourse, the general was interrupted by a local reporter who pointedly asked for the commander's reaction to *The Malaya Tribune* editorial. In raising his question, the journalist insisted the editorial had reflected the views held by many people in Malaya and Singapore. He requested an official reply.

A visibly irked commanding officer responded that he was surprised the newspaper could 'write like that'. He was also amazed at the claim that the views reflected were held by many people. He had no wish to add anything further to the record. It was not proposed to issue a more detailed account of the events that had taken place at Batang Kali. With considerable emphasis, Boucher added, *The Straits Times* account published on December 14 was 'extremely accurate'.

In short, the military high command was relying on Harry Miller's interview with the 22 year-old unnamed patrol leader as being the ultimate word on the issue. Boucher made one more observation. The sort of insinuations carried by *The Malaya Tribune*, he said, were bad for the morale of his troops.

That paper's response the following day was scathing. It declared in an editorial that the general had made no effort to reply to the public's questions. He had not explained why one man's word was considered good enough to justify the deaths of 24.

'We appreciate the general's concern for the morale of his troops,' pursued the paper. 'We have not the same appreciation for his concern for the morale of the people.'

***

Left entirely to their own devices, the same four women who had carried out the first search for bodies the day following the killings, decided they must travel to Kuala Lumpur and appeal personally to the government. They scrounged together $6 from sympathetic villagers to pay for their round-trip taxi fare. But the government official they thought might come to their aid promptly refused to meet them. Frustrated, the women called by the diplomatic residence of Chinese Consul General Li Chin.

Official embarrassment over Batang Kali quickly compounded when word of the visitation to the Chinese Consul's office was relayed to the colonial authorities. Now they were confronted with a decidedly dispiriting and conflicting picture. The government was insisting those killed on the plantation had been communists caught in an escape attempt. This was a key pillar to its justification of the mass killing. How could it possibly explain away the image of the kin of communists seeking assistance from the chief representative in Malaya of China's nationalist Chiang Kai Shek regime? And this after being firmly denied access for appeal to colonial sources.

The Consul General spent some time speaking to the women, made notes and assured them he would personally take up their grievances with the local authorities.

Li Chin kept his word. He took action immediately, dispatching a letter to the Chief Secretary, Sir Alec Newboult, requesting comprehensive details of events that had transpired on the plantation. He went further. The Consul General then held a meeting with the press on December 21. At this, he outlined in brief the contents of his letter to the government.

'I want to find out what actually happened in that locality on that occasion,' said Li Chin. 'I told the Chief Secretary that representations had been made to me by the families of the dead men.

'I personally feel that the killing was out of all proportion as the men were not armed. I feel that they should have been shot in the legs and lamed instead.'

The Consul General went on to emphasise that he, of all people, would not wish to hamper any anti-insurgency exercise. Elaborating, he explained: 'I admit it is difficult to know whether a running man is armed, but in this affair at Batang Kali the evidence would appear to be that they had no weapons.'

It was now nine days since the Sungei Remok Estate operations had wound up. For the first time the correct figure for the death toll had been presented and it had come via the families of the victims. Even more telling had been the emphasis placed by the Consul General on the fact that the men cut down by the patrol had been unarmed. None of the press reports or official pronouncements thus far had even referred to, let alone accentuated, this critical aspect. By now, the rising pressure of public opinion was something the government could not ignore.

Doubtless prompted by apprehensions that factors outlined in the Consul

General's letter would enter the public domain and fuel further misgivings, the government decided to let it be known quietly – on the 'old boys net' and exclusively to *The Straits Times* – that 'a full inquiry' into the Batang Kali incident was in hand. Having re-thought their strategy, the authorities now wanted the general public to be told that this inquiry had been ordered two days after the plantation shooting. The senior officer responsible for launching the investigation was named as Selangor Police Chief Beverley. The government wanted it publicised that statements had already been taken from Chinese, police and Scots Guards witnesses.

Details of the Chinese Consul's formal letter to the Chief Secretary together with the leaked story on the 'full inquiry' being underway received inside-page treatment in *The Straits Times* on December 22. But if government officials responsible for manipulating public information thought indications of a 'full inquiry' would silence the critics, they were mistaken. Later that same day, Sungei Remok Estate owner, Thomas Menzies, felt compelled to come forward with highly relevant information about his property and what had occurred there.

All those killed by the Scots Guards had been employed through 'all-in' plantation contractor, Lim Chye Chee, with whom Menzies had been associated for 20 years. The permanent labour force living on the estate, he said, had totaled 26 males. Nearly all were Cantonese. Menzies emphasised that the labourers had established a long record of being well-behaved. There had never been a strike nor had there been labour problems of any nature. Of the victims, four had been on the estate for 18 years, six for 14 years, ten for ten years and the remainder for at least three and a quarter years each. Menzies identified one of the dead as his plantation *kepala* and another as his estate clerk.

He blamed the police for the five-day delay in retrieving and burying the bodies. It had taken this long for the Ulu Yam Bahru police station to issue the necessary permits. Funeral expenses totaling $1,400 had been met by the contractor.

Menzies was anxious to clarify official innuendoes that his plantation was being used as a supply point for communist guerrillas. He declared that the lorry the government was alleging carried food for the bandits was indeed his estate vehicle. It had never been involved in supplying the enemy. On the day in question it was engaged in the delivery of rationed food for the estate labour. He then enumerated the food list transported from Ulu Yam Bahru by the vehicle on the morning of the shooting: 60 katties of rice and 10 katties of sugar. These quantities were in strict conformity with Emergency rationing laws.

Menzies' remarks on this occasion struck at the very foundations of the

Colonial Chief Secretary Sir Alec Newboult becomes intricately involved, along with Command top brass, in preparing and delivering a progressively revised and doctored official line on the Batang Kali killings.

The Straits Times

Singapore, Fri., Dec. 24, 1948.

BATANG KALI SHOOTING

We had hoped today to be able to publish an official statement by the military authorities on the attitude they are taking regarding the Batang Kali incident, in which 24 Chinese, suspected of complicity with the bandits, were shot dead when they attempted to escape. No statement, however, has been made, perhaps because it is preferred that nothing should be said until the conclusion of the enquiry which the police began two days after the incident.

We feel that in the exceptional circumstances of the case, an immediate statement of the army's attitude would be in the public interest. Normally it would be undesirable, even although such a police enquiry does not have privileged status, for any authority to say anything likely to prejudice the finding, or to anticipate it. The essential fact is that the enquiry was begun on the initiative of the local civil authorities, at the earliest possible moment. But the shooting was not an ordinary incident. It has caused serious concern among all communities, and has brought from the Chinese Consul-General in Kuala Lumpur representations on the basis of information laid by relatives of the dead men. There are two issues: the circumstances in which the men were shot, and the wider question of the instructions under which troops and police operate.

An assurance by the military authorities that they are associated with the enquiry, and will act in the light of its findings, is all that is necessary.

BATANG KALI REPORT

The meagre official report of the enquiry into the shooting of 24 suspects who attempted to escape from military custody at Batang Kali is not likely to end public concern over this incident. The enquiry was held on the instructions of the Attorney General, and was conducted by a Federal Counsel. After "careful consideration of the evidence" and a personal visit to the place where the incident occurred, the Attorney General has expressed the opinion that the suspects would have made good their escape if the security force had not opened fire. In view of this, and in the light of certain information regarding the suspects, "it is not proposed to take any further action," adds the official statement.

No-one will question the affirmation that it is the duty of a security force to fire on prisoners who attempt to escape. It is the fact that all 24 of the men who ran were killed which has aroused concern, a concern that can be ended only by publication of the relevant parts of the evidence given at this enquiry. It would be impertinent to suggest that what has satisfied the Attorney General will not satisfy the public, whose interest in the suppression of Communist banditry and the complete restoration of law and order is not less than the Government's, and it would be still more impertinent to suggest that any of the evidence given at the enquiry is not fit for publication. There remains, however, the fact that none of the evidence is being published. The Government must expect that the concern already shown will now be deepened.

Twelve days after the mass killing, The Straits Times' leading editorial (above) indicates the paper has begun re-evaluating official explanations of the Scots Guards action. A week later the same editorial page (right) reflects deepening suspicions that the authorities are withholding important information and that a cover-up is underway.

military's stand on Batang Kali. The killing was being justified by the Army on the basis of the estate labour force's pro-communist sentiments and activities. The supposedly deciding factor had been the arrival of the lorry with its illegal supplies. That such contradicting facts were now coming from a leading planter, renowned for his anti-communist political persuasion, his enthusiasm for effective anti-insurgency measures and a Scotsman to boot, could not be dismissed lightly.

～๑๑๑～

With three days to go before Christmas, international news dominated the front pages of local newspapers in Singapore and Malaya. Agency reports disclosed that the United States had halted all Marshall aid to Dutch Indonesia. The cessation of US assistance would remain in force until hostilities between the Dutch and the Indonesian Republic got resolved. Thursday, December 23, editions headlined news out of Tokyo that Japan's wartime Prime Minister, Hideki Tojo, and six other 'war lords' had been hanged. Among the executed was General Seishiro Itagaki, who had commanded the Japanese army in Singapore in the latter stages of the Pacific conflict. Also hanged was General Iwane Matsui, commander of the Japanese army at the 1937 'Rape of Nanking'.

On the lighter side, readers of *The Straits Times* were treated to two front-page pictures taken at Buckingham Palace shortly after the christening of one-month-old Prince Charles.

However, the Batang Kali issue would not go away. It was back in the news on Christmas eve when *The Straits Times* featured it in a critical opinion column – the first such attempt on the subject by this publication. The editorial began: 'We had hoped today to be able to publish an official statement by the military authorities on the attitude they are taking regarding the Batang Kali incident. . . ' Noting that the police investigation was underway, the newspaper observed that the shooting was 'not an ordinary incident' and had caused serious concern among all communities.

The editorial concluded: 'There are two issues; the circumstances in which the men were shot, and the wider question of the instructions under which troops and police operate. An assurance by the military authorities that they are associated with the inquiry, and will act in the light of its findings, is all that is necessary.'

A week later the same newspaper took up the cudgels once again. The government had, in the interim, issued a three-paragraph report on what it described as 'the shooting of 24 suspects who attempted to escape from military

55

custody at Batang Kali'. The report, it said, had been based on the findings of the official inquiry. This time *The Straits Times* editorial writer made no attempt to pull punches. He described the report as 'meagre' and castigated the authorities for not making public far more of the evidence thus far gathered. Intentionally or unintentionally, the paper's editorial suggested that much of the information on the investigation leaked 11 days earlier had been erroneous. It had not been a police inquiry after all. And it had not been launched, as reported, by the Selangor Police Chief. The inquiry was now being portrayed as having been initiated by the colony's Attorney General. The Attorney General was a prominent figure, widely identified as Stafford Foster-Sutton, formerly a leading London lawyer.

'No-one will question the affirmation that it is the duty of a security force to fire on prisoners who attempt to escape,' said the editorial. 'It is the fact that all 24 of the men who ran were killed which has aroused concern, a concern that can be ended only by publication of the relevant parts of the evidence given at this inquiry.'

It ended with the observation: 'The government must expect that the concern already shown will now be deepened.'

Under intense public pressure, the Kuala Lumpur government, obviously with the agreement of Boucher, then decided to issue additional information to the brief official statement *The Straits Times* had disparagingly dismissed. Released on January 3, 1949, this second pronouncement, headed 'Supplementary Statement', would stand from then on as the authorities' final position on what happened at the Sungei Remok Estate.

It declared:

'Police had reliable information that there were concentrations of communists in the area west of the main road between Rasa and Sungei Tempayan.

'After discussion with the military it was decided to send in a platoon, divided into two sections – one commanded by an officer and, no other officer being available, the other commanded by a sergeant. Each section was accompanied by guides and some police personnel.

'The object of the patrol was to obtain information, search for arms and ammunition and to detain and bring back to Kuala Kubu Bahru for interrogation any suspicious characters.

'The general order was that if any detained person tried to escape, he was to be chased and recaptured but under no circumstances to be allowed to escape.

'The section in question consisted of a sergeant in command and 13 other ranks. It had no vehicles and no wireless or other easy means of communication with headquarters, which was a considerable distance away from the area of operations.

'The Section patrolled a wide area, including rubber estates and jungle, during which bandits were spotted and fired at.

'The sergeant feared that these bandits would carry information regarding the section to other concentrations of bandits and his section might be trapped.

'He decided to press on, eventually arriving at the clearing where shooting took place on the following day.

'In the clearing were three kongsi houses and a few other huts and shacks. The occupants of the kongsi houses were interrogated and some Sten-gun ammunition discovered hidden in one of the houses.

'Information from interrogation was that armed bandits were in the habit of visiting the area and used it for obtaining supplies and that such supplies were brought in every morning by a lorry which was employed to bring in food for the tappers and others who occupied the clearing.

'If attacked, the clearing was a death-trap to the section and the sergeant therefore posted three groups to cover the three entrances to the jungle.

'These groups were put out of sight of persons in the clearing. This took place on the afternoon of December 11.

'The Chinese men found in the clearing were placed in a room in one of the kongsi houses for the night, under guard.

'The following morning they were brought out of the room by two sentries who were on the verandah of the kongsi house in which the room was situated. The only other soldier in sight was the sergeant in command who was standing on the ground a little beyond the kongsi house, ready to receive the Chinese as they came off the verandah.

'When all the Chinese had reached the ground from the verandah, one of them shouted and they thereupon split up into three groups and made a dash for the three entrances to the jungle.

'There is no doubt that they were then under the impression that the only troops that they had to compete with were the two soldiers on the verandah of the kongsi house and the sergeant.

'The attempted escape was obviously pre-arranged because there was no hesitation in the formation of the three groups and the shout was no doubt the pre-arranged signal for putting the plan into effect.

'The sergeant and the two soldiers on the verandah immediately shouted, calling upon them to halt. They could not use their arms because to do so would have endangered the lives of their comrades who were posted out of sight but in the line of fire. The men in the three groups covering the entrances heard shouting but did not know what was happening until they saw the Chinese running through the bush and jungle past where they were posted. They thereupon shouted the Malay word for halt to which *no attention was paid by the escaping Chinese.*

'The men of the three groups gave chase, continuing calling upon them to halt and, as they failed to do so, the soldiers opened fire.'

The 'supplementary' information contained glaring contradictions and one outstanding omission – mention of the women, children and other contract labour who had been present at the time of the shooting. The report could never have withstood scrutiny by anybody who had inspected the plantation clearing or spoken to those who had departed on the lorry. Had any pressman, an independent Scots Guards investigator, a member of the first asserted police inquiry, or a representative of the claimed probe by the Attorney General's office gone to the estate, or to nearby Ulu Yam Bahru, such a statement could never have been released. The problem was that nobody with influence or authority had been near these areas.

Stuck with the unsustainable initial pronouncement that the intended escapees had 'run into' the Scots Guards gunfire, the authorities chose their Supplementary Statement to slip in an alternative and totally revised explanation on the 'line of fire' question. The latest claim at this point was that the running men had passed the Scots Guards sentry positions before they were gunned down. If post mortems were ever held this, it was hoped, would explain the conflicting location of wounds.

A further critical contradiction remained unaddressed. The Supplementary Statement was now claiming the Scots Guards patrol had no means of communicating with headquarters at Kuala Kubu Bahru. This clearly clashed with the information given by Police Chief Beverley on the night of the killing, three weeks earlier. Beverley had then revealed that first reports of the shooting had been 'flashed by radio' from the jungle. If the claims of the authorities were to be accepted, it was essential to the overall cover-up that the patrol concerned be portrayed as having been isolated in the jungle without any means of communication. Nobody questioned this contradiction.

If it was, indeed, the intention of the patrol leader, as asserted, to escort 'suspicious characters' back to base headquarters for interrogation, why did he overlook the choice of transporting the detained men via the lorry that stood in the clearing? As pointed out in the supplementary information, the broad operational area was believed to contain 'concentrations of communists'. Furthermore, as noted, the estate was situated 'a considerable distance' from headquarters at Kuala Kubu Bahru. Yet a patrol leader, in fear of 'being trapped', supposedly preferred the alternative of escorting 25 suspects with a 14-man squad on a trek through alleged enemy-controlled territory, a manoeuvre that would have taken hours, rather than sending them via road, a journey that would have taken minutes.

The additional claim that Scots Guards sentries had been posted on 'the three entrances to the jungle' was particularly deceptive. Here it was being suggested that the clearing was surrounded by jungle and anyone fleeing from the *kongsi* area had the choice of only three escape routes. For this reason, sentries had been posted 'out of sight' covering all three claimed departure points. If the official version of events was to be believed, it was essential for the authorities to establish one other factor. This was the existence of a surreptitious escape plan devised by the detainees which, on a given signal, would have them forming into three pre-arranged groups which then conveniently headed independently to the three pre-determined jungle entry points.

The clearing, as it happened, was situated within a rubber plantation entirely surrounded by rubber trees. Rows of rubber had been planted down to the river in front of the *kongsis*. Similarly, the tree rows began immediately behind the clearing and ran up the side of a steep hill. The nearest jungle was that fronting the plantation's eastern border, a considerable distance away. Anyone choosing to make a run from the clearing would certainly not have been restricted to the three escape routes fortuitously guarded by patrol members.

Equally spurious was the quite extraordinary allegation in the latter part of the government statement that a period of shouting and chasing 'through bush and jungle' had preceded the shooting. Had officials taken the trouble to visit the plantation, such claims could never have been made. The supposedly fleeing men had been shot in tight groupings in four separate locations. Claims that 'rushing through bush and jungle' had taken place before the shooting were not only implausible, they were false.

By this time, the military was well aware that the Batang Kali corpses had been widely viewed by relatives, contracted labour involved in body retrieval work, not to mention local police. All had seen for themselves the massive wounds that had been inflicted. They would have to be kept silent. One other serious problem presented itself to the authorities. If ever post mortems were to be conducted, original descriptions of the mass killing, so carefully presented by the military, would be demolished as fiction. That possibility would have to be eliminated.

Tell The People
KUALA KUBU

THE story of Kuala Kubu, where twenty-four out of twenty-five Chinese were shot dead while attempting to escape from a patrol of police and Scots Guards, grows less satisfactory with every account issued by the Federation Government.

The attitude of the Federation Government also becomes increasingly difficult to understand.

When the Tribune Newspapers first expressed concern at the shooting and voiced the public's uneasiness at such a wholesale killing, the Federation Government had nothing to say.

The next development took place at a Press conference in Kuala Lumpur on December 18, when Major-General C. H. Boucher, G.O.C. Malaya, expressed surprise at a Malaya Tribune editorial on the matter, and said that he did not propose to volunteer any further information.

Again the Tribune newspapers protested, and five days later it was announced that an inquiry was to be held by the Attorney General.

The result of that inquiry was made known on New Year's Eve. It consisted of three paragraphs, which made no attempt to answer any of the public's questions, and which announced the Government's intention to take no further action in connection with the incident.

Again the Tribune Newspapers protested at this indifference to public opinion, and stated bluntly that although the Federation Government might be satisfied the public were not.

Yesterday a further official statement, (on the back page) was issued from Kuala Lumpur.

Now the Tribune Newspapers voice their protest for the fourth time.

While certainly shedding more light on what happened at the Batang Kali estate, Kuala Kubu, Selangor, on the grim morning of December 12, the statement will do little or nothing to remove the doubts caused entirely by the Federation Government's reluctance to take the people into their confidence.

What kind of people do they think we are? Do they think we are children that we must

See Back Page ☛

The Malaya Tribune on January 4, two weeks after the first published reports of the Batang Kali raid, launches a stinging attack on the colonial administration's handling of the mass killing aftermath. It is prominently placed at the centre of the front-page layout, rolls onto the back page and reads far more like a hectoring editorial than news coverage.

Chapter 4

Securing the cover-up

A fortnight after the Emergency declaration in Kuala Lumpur, Colonial Secretary Arthur Creech Jones was telling the Cabinet in London: 'During 1947 the total value of exports of Singapore and the Federation together was £151 million, of which dollar exports accounted for £56 million.'

He added: 'It is by far the most important source of dollars in the Colonial Empire and it would gravely worsen the whole dollar balance of the Sterling area if there were serious interference with Malayan exports.'

Creech Jones' report to Cabinet was notably devoid of any lofty plan, short or long term, for the establishment of independence in its money-making 'jewel in the crown'. What Britain wanted for Malaya, he told his colleagues, was the 're-establishment of stable, prosperous conditions'. In blunt terms, Britain needed continuing access to Malaya's exploitable wealth to meet her post-war debts and ever-expanding obligations on the home front.

It was not that mounting press criticism in Malaya following the Batang Kali killings had been dismissive or ignorant of Britain's massive and mounting post-war problems. Nor was it unappreciative of the men she had sent to fight the Emergency. Sympathetic remarks along these lines were being made repeatedly and publicly by observers in both Singapore and Kuala Lumpur.

On January 4, 1949, though, *The Malaya Tribune* in a blistering front page commentary on the incident argued that locals had been through an invasion, an occupation and a liberation. 'They know the rules of war are harsh, that men under tension and in fear of their lives make mistakes, honest mistakes, which cause the innocent to suffer along with the guilty.' The newspaper went on to emphasise it had no wish 'to pillory' the Scots Guards sergeant and his patrol. But 'the way this matter has been addressed by the Federation authorities' was of primary concern.

'It is an example,' the editorial thundered, 'of blundering folly almost without equal. Every official who has had a hand in it, from Major General Boucher downwards, should regard this as a lesson to take the people into his confidence. They should never again forget they are the servants of the people and the people are best served by the truth.'

It was now just over three weeks since the Scots Guards had killed the 24 estate labourers. In contrast to the vehemence of the local public outcry and manipulative

NO MORE
BLACK LEADING
ONE COAT OF
BLACK FORT ENAMEL

Daily Worker

(5391) 1½d ★

TUESDAY JANUARY 4 1949

THE ONLY DAILY
PAPER OWNED
BY ITS READERS

COMMUN|
RE-ELEC
—in bigg
of the

MALAYA AROUSED BY MASSACRE

Unarmed workers were shot down in cold blood

Daily Worker Special Correspondent

KUALA LUMPUR (by mail).

I HAVE spoken with the widows and other relatives of 24 unarmed Chinese plantation workers who were shot by British troops on December 12.

This assassination of peaceful citizens has provoked a veritable storm of indignation throughout Malaya. It is only the latest in a long series of acts of terrorism which have nothing to do with genuine military operations.

This particular mass execution took place at Kuala Kubu Bahru, in Selangor State. When I first reached the scene of the events I narrowly avoided arrest by the military still on the spot.

With some difficulty I found Wu Mei, the wife of Hwang Leing, one of the murdered men. She had with her their four children—King Swee aged 11, Moet Sing nine, Da Mei six, and King Chew, a little girl of three.

She told me that her family was one of several, numbering nearly a hundred souls, who lived in three houses on a European estate just outside Kuala Kubu Bahru village.

They were employed by the Lim Chai Cheg Company, contractors. In the little community were 30 men and some 70 women and children.

At 3 p.m. on December 11, after most of the men had returned from work in the fields, they were suddenly surrounded by a strong force of military.

'Inform or . . .'

A British officer, speaking through a Chinese interpreter, demanded to know whether they seen any Communists vicinity.

The officer refused to their statement that they all they wo refused to gi Then the from the according kept un

EDITORIAL

Nuts and Flies

LAST week a number of newspapers loudly announced on the authority of the Colonial Office, that the end of our meat shortage was in sight and that a new drug for combating the tsetse fly would enable colonial Africa to be turned into a new Argentine. The Daily Worker printed the official statement but displayed no enthusiasm for the new beef paradise.

It is now quite clear that although the Colonial Office has an undoubted aptitude for organising a war in Malaya and for shooting down native demonstrators on the Gold Coast, it is utterly incapable of bringing about prosperity in the vast areas under its control.

The tsetse fly stunt will probably be as effective as the groundnuts stunt, the monumental failure of which is now being shouted from the housetops.

Let us acclaim scientific achievement but beware of the deceptive, political tricks to which the production of wonder-drugs is put.

Big flop

In the case of antrycide, it is the scientists who have been the first to warn that premature claims are being made on its behalf. Dr. S. Davey, one of the discoverers of the new drug, warns against exaggeration and the Director of the Southern Rhodesian Veterinary Service states that adequate tests have not yet been made under varying conditions.

And even if antrycide should turn out to be a great success there is no possibility of getting beef out of Africa until vast economic change been brought about the settling of the land ownership vision of

Keep it up! £854 wanted

A REALLY heart-warming postbag of hundreds of letters, containing £345, swamped my desk yesterday.

All day, visitors were bringing gifts, and even outside the building I met them on the way.

We had £85 to add from our Birthday Meeting in Lewisham.

John Stewart Gs keep on arriving: £21 6s. 6d. more from 43 friends brings us £78 6s. 6d.

Make this u
will wip
TODAY
of

EROS HAS A PARTY

ROADS ARE BLOCKED BY SNOW

FOURTEEN passengers were injured when a double decker bus overturned on ice-bound Burnley-Todmor road yesterday.

The bus skidded, cras a hedge and overturn (1 feet below the r
One woman was d
pical.

TOBOG
Many roa
bound

Bus leaders
will see
Isaac

Daily Worker Indu

LONDON TRANSPORT
within 24 hours of
place between Transpo
Union leaders and M

This move I
the purpose,
the visit t
be held

Mr
be pr

---

gyrations by colonial authorities, the issue in London had failed to resonate as a subject of significance, let alone one demanding prompt attention. But on the same day as *The Malaya Tribune* was highlighting the 'blundering folly', Batang Kali finally elicited front page treatment in Britain.

The communist *Daily Worker*'s front page lead had been filed by airmail post. Twenty-three days after the shooting, the paper's banner headline screamed: MALAYA AROUSED BY MASSACRE. Beneath ran the sub-head: *Unarmed workers were shot down in cold blood.*

Prior to this, what little UK press coverage given to the Scots Guards action had portrayed, unchallenged, government claims of a resounding success by the security forces. The *Daily Worker*'s story was also noticeably angled – only from a staunchly pro-communist viewpoint.

'This assassination of peaceful citizens has provoked a veritable storm of indignation throughout Malaya. It is only the latest in a long series of acts of terrorism which have nothing to do with genuine military operations,' the paper's Special Correspondent wrote. The story claimed interviews had been conducted with 'the widows and other relatives of 24 unarmed Chinese plantation workers who were shot by British troops on December 12'.

It went on to highlight one particular interview with a widow, a mother of four children. Despite the story's strong pro-communist bias and somewhat muddled approach, it stands as the first attempt by anyone – press or government – to bother checking Batang Kali from any source other than the military, police and colonial authorities. The widow recalled a sequence of events that climaxed in the shooting. Overall, this correspondent's account was exhibiting a decidedly more humanitarian approach than any of the previous reportage.

Whether prompted by the *Daily Worker*'s front page story in Britain, *The Malaya Tribune*'s stinging editorial rebuke in Malaya, or a combination of the two, colonial authorities called a joint press conference in Kuala Lumpur the next day, January 5.

The objective: to reveal that the 'Supplementary Statement' released 48 hours earlier had, in the interim, been subtly re-defined. Civilian Chief Secretary, Sir Alec Newboult, accompanied by Boucher, now described the document as a 'narrative' prepared from statements taken from witnesses during the actual inquiry.

The adjustment in emphasis was devised to add extra weight to the previous government statement. Sir Alec's accompanying remarks underlined the importance the authorities were placing on this re-alignment of details.

'I would suggest,' he said, 'that, as we have gone to the trouble of putting a trained lawyer onto the inquiry, the narrative prepared from the statements he took should be accepted as fact.' The re-defined 'narrative' was, therefore, a reflection of the inquiry's ultimate findings. However, the Chief Secretary went on to stipulate there would be 'no public issue' of statements made at the inquiry. In other words, it had been a closed affair. Its specific findings would be classified, as would all the evidence presented to it.

There was a further disturbing aspect of Sir Alec's remarks. He had baulked at revealing the identity of the senior government official responsible for the claimed inquiry. The authorities were determined to conceal the fact that the officer concerned was none other than Colonial Malaya's Attorney General himself, Stafford Foster-Sutton.

After reading the new statement to the gathered press, the Chief Secretary reflected: 'I have no doubt at all that these men made an attempt to escape from legal custody, and having made that attempt, they had to stand the consequences.'

He went on: 'Let us be absolutely fair with the security forces. The point at issue is that, in starting the attempt to escape, the men were warned but continued to make their escape and the patrol opened fire.'

Boucher began his presentation to the same press gathering with a general summary of the first half-year of Emergency action. 'I think we are entitled to say that at the close of the year we are, at least, very much better off in every way than when operations started six months ago,' he said.

As he was speaking to an obviously sceptical group of reporters, he felt a need to deny any suggestion that security forces might be 'inadequate' for the task ahead. In support of this he gave a state-by-state review on how the military was performing.

It would be Boucher's later remarks, during the same conference, that would spark substantial long-term coverage, comment and heightened concern over Batang Kali. The first of these was his claim that he, too, had ordered an investigation – a military one – into the Scots Guards action. This brought the number of formal inquiries to three – police, civil and now military.

Boucher said his decision had been prompted by the first report he read on the matter. He said there were 'certain aspects of it about which I wanted to know more'. The military investigation had quickly demonstrated that people other than Army personnel were also involved. By this he could only have been referring to the three local police attached to the Scots Guards patrol. As a result, he added, he had requested the High Commissioner launch an inquiry by 'some impartial source'.

It was improper, he continued, for him to make any comment as to facts which may or may not have come out at the inquiry conducted by 'the Attorney General's department'. But, he remarked, there were 'one or two military aspects on which I would particularly like to enlist the help of the press in telling the people'.

Fundamental, said the GOC, was the need for wide understanding that those who consorted with or assisted bandits must automatically be viewed as enemies of the state. As such, they ran the risk of incurring military action in the same way as those killed at Batang Kali. He then proceeded to underline the dangers involved in running away from security forces – again as the Batang Kali victims had allegedly done. 'Usually, the only method of halting people who run is to shoot at them,' he said. 'If people have no guilty conscience, there is no need to run.'

Finally, Boucher sought the public's appreciation of the lethal effect of modern weapons. 'The single shot weapon, such as the rifle, is obsolescent nowadays. The armed forces use automatics which discharge a burst of fire, forming a considerable pattern. At close range, the effect is deadly.'

Even more controversial was his observation: 'I think the public should know that troops and police are trained never to open fire unless it is necessary, but when they have to fire, the fire is always intended to kill. It cannot be anything else.' At this point the GOC had alienated virtually the entire combined Chinese populations of Malaya and Singapore.

Boucher was regarded by his peers as small in stature and pugnacious by nature. Born in 1898, his military career began in 1916 when he was commissioned as a 2nd lieutenant in the 2nd King Edward's Own Gurkha Rifles, more popularly known as the Sirmoor Rifles. A transfer to the 3rd Queen Alexandra's Own Gurkha Rifles saw rapid promotion for the ambitious, young officer.

By 1940, at barely 42 years of age, he had already achieved General Staff Officer 1 status. During World War 11's North Africa campaign he commanded the Indian 10th Infantry Brigade and participated in the disastrous Knightsbridge Cauldron action, forerunner to the Siege of Tobruk. On June 6, 1942, while returning to his Brigade headquarters from forward troop positions he became lost in the desert and was finally captured by an Italian unit.

Boucher remained a prisoner of war until the following year when he was released under the Italian Armistice arrangements. Within a matter of months he was back in action, this time as Commanding Officer of the Indian 8th Infantry Division's 17th Infantry Brigade at the Battle of Monte Casino and the advance towards Rome. His appointment as General Officer Commanding Malaya District came in early 1948, prior to Britain's declaration of the Malayan Emergency. Boucher, now a Major General, would remain in this position until early 1950 when he returned to Britain. He would die prematurely in 1951 at the age of 53.

Not unexpectedly, it was the GOC's remarks about 'shooting to kill' that were singled out for immediate attention in the following day's headlines. Coverage was provided in all main local newspapers. *The Straits Times* headline declared: NEWBOULT AND GOC ON BATANG KALI. Below ran the sub-head: *Police, Troops 'Shoot To Kill': Boucher.* In the same vein, another local newspaper, *The Free Press* published its story under the headline: *Troops, Police shoot to kill.*

Once the various newspaper accounts had been read and digested, this latest attempt to justify what had happened at Batang Kali immediately backfired. On January 8, *The Straits Times* devoted the paper's entire two-column editorial space to a commentary tearing strips off the authorities for what was clearly regarded as blatant bungling of the shooting aftermath. Headed *Batang Kali lessons,* the editorial began with the observation: 'For much of the concern which the public still feels over the tragic Batang Kali shooting, the authorities have only themselves to blame.'

The paper noted Boucher's latest claim of having personally ordered a military inquiry into the incident as soon as he received the first report. 'Unfortunately, he did not say so at the time, although public concern was by no means less than his own,' was the paper's reaction. The editorial went on to lament the piecemeal manner in which the authorities had released conflicting bits of information about the shooting itself and about the way it had been investigated. 'This whole procedure has not been calculated to diminish concern.'

The editorial pointed out that the story now being made public by civil and military leaders differed from the original account gathered by the press from official sources. The 'large quantity' of ammunition that was claimed to have been found 'under a mattress' in the plantation's living quarters had 'shrunk to a handful of Sten-gun cartridges'.

'Nor did the men, in attempting to escape, run 'into the guns' of the sentries. They now ran past the sentries, and were chased, and were shot dead only when it appeared likely they would in fact escape. These discrepancies may not be important, although they are certainly interesting,' added *The Straits Times*.

Dealing with Boucher's accentuation of the deadliness of modern weapons and his command's 'shoot to kill' orders, the editorial posed the obvious question: 'Was it necessary, in this case, to kill?' The inquiry had 'furnished the assurance' that the sergeant in charge of the patrol had acted within his orders. Innocent or not, the 24 shot dead had been detained overnight and were in the legal custody of the Scots Guards who had orders to 'shoot to kill' if that was the only way of preventing escape. All this posed further questions. In the light of evidence heard at the inquiry, were the instructions given the security patrol right? Was there a need

Regarded as 'small in stature and pugnacious by nature', G.O.C Malaya District, Major General Sir Charles Boucher, is shown in this Army PR photograph of the day with C in C Far East, Sir E.J.Patrick Brind. To the centre and rear stands Commander R. Horncastle, Royal Navy Liaison Officer with Malaya District.

for every man who ran to be shot dead? Indeed, was it the soldier's view that a man without a guilty conscience had no need to run?

As far as the third question was concerned, the position declared by Boucher suggested the answer was unequivocally in the affirmative. Here *The Straits Times* was ready with a solid rebuttal.

A decision in the High Court of the Federation only three months earlier had demonstrated a very different view as far as legality was concerned. Mr Justice Laville, sitting at the Johore Assizes, had acquitted two Chinese who had faced charges of consorting with an armed terrorist. The terrorist concerned had been convicted and hanged. But the two men before Judge Laville had run from the hut in which the terrorist had been arrested. The judge ruled that flight from a house at the approach of police by 'uneducated people' in Malaya was far from being a conclusive or even probable indication that those running had a guilty 'knowledge or intention'. Recommending that the Federal authorities take note of Judge Laville's ruling, the newspaper added: 'The High Court which interprets the law does not agree with the Army, which is charged with preserving it.'

Strongly opposed to this and the now general press criticism of the authorities were the views of the influential planting community. With concern over the Batang Kali killings at its height, the Kuala Lumpur branch of the Incorporated Society of Planters called for the government to give greater 'pictorial publicity' to the hanging and shooting of terrorists. A meeting of the branch was convened in early January to discuss these matters. Members passed a resolution demanding far more ruthless action be taken against terrorists and that an expanded pictorial record of the punishment meted out be introduced to villages, estates and mines to show what law-breakers and bandit-helpers could expect.

On January 11, two letters from readers were published side-by-side in the Singapore press. One was signed *Veritas Sans Peur (Truth without Fear)*, the other, *A Planter's Wife*. They encapsulated the polarization of public opinion that had consolidated over the weeks following Batang Kali.

The first writer, probably a lawyer, took strong issue with both Boucher and Newboult on the legality of the 'shoot to kill' order and quoted Section 15 (iii) of the Criminal Procedure Code. 'Nothing in this section gives a right to cause the death of a person who is not accused of any offence punishable with death or penal servitude.' The writer went on to quote Section 86 (ii) of the same Code relating to action by the military and specifically to dispersal and arrest of unlawful assemblies. It stated: 'Every such (military) officer shall obey such requisition in such manner as he thinks fit, but in so doing he shall use as little force and do as little injury to persons . . . as may be consistent with . . . arresting and detaining such persons'. The writer then went on to ask how the GOC could therefore justify the wanton killing of Batang Kali victims. According to law, added the writer, the two sections of the Criminal Procedure Code he had quoted had not been abrogated. The argument was valid.

Veritas Sans Peur's letter then switched its attack to Newboult's insistence there could be no public issue of statements made to the official inquiry. 'Why not?' demanded the writer. 'That is just the point, the apparent hushing up of something which might be unfavourable to those responsible. Statements made to the police, or to Federal Counsel, by witnesses are not given on oath, and are not signed by persons making them.'

As far as the Chief Secretary's exhortation on the need to be fair with the security forces was concerned, the letter was in full agreement. 'And nothing could be fairer than a public inquiry, presided over by a Judge of the High Court, and at which witnesses would be required to give evidence on oath, and be subject to cross-examination. I am sure such an inquiry would be welcomed by the Chinese community, as well as by other members of the public. Suppression of evidence invites suspicion!'

In contrast, *A Planter's Wife* suggested that Boucher's comments at his recent press conference might have been reassuring to town-dwellers, but they had left planters and miners cold. 'It appears to many of them that the General thinks he is conducting a five-year war. What they want to know and what ultimately they will demand to know, is why sufficient force cannot be provided NOW to deal with this menace swiftly and effectively.'

If the GOC was confident he could finish the business quickly, she continued, he should say so. If he required more aid and had been refused it, the public ought to be informed. Bluntly, *A Planter's Wife* concluded her correspondence: 'Planters and miners want this finished whatever the cost. Without them Malaya is nothing. Government can take its choice.'

—⁓—

The Batang Kali affair now dominated discussions across Malaya and Singapore. Whether conducted in grimy coffee shops, or at the expatriate set's exclusive whites-only clubs, these were posing disturbing questions. Well recognised

were clear indications that the seven month-old Emergency regulations had serious flaws. They had failed, for one, to define the degree of force police or troops could legally apply in exercising an arrest, dealing with those in custody or thwarting an escape bid.

Whatever had been the Scots Guards orders on the plantation, the patrol may well still have violated the law. Due to oversights in the drafting of Emergency controls, it was eminently arguable that normal provisions of the Criminal Code still applied. After all, Britain had imposed the Emergency against the communists to avoid the formality of a war and all the financial encumbrances this would have involved. In an undeclared war the civil authorities remained paramount. Under such circumstances, part of the military's responsibility was to protect and uphold civilian law. And if the troops had flouted the law on this occasion, what about previous cases involving police and security force action in the territory?

From the very outset of the insurgency, there had been a number of highly controversial clashes with alleged communist elements. On each occasion, questions had been raised about the measures employed by British troops. Legal advisers to the colonial authorities had pushed strongly for amending legislation on what was widely referred to as the 'shoot to kill' and 'shout and shoot' issues. The critics were adamant. If ever-expanding public concern was to be effectively contained, new Emergency regulations simply had to be formulated.

With official documentation of that time so heavily manipulated, it is impossible to establish whether it was the advisers – or those being advised – who ultimately foresaw that the process of amending legislation might cleverly deflect the focus of public attention away from the Batang Kali killings. Instead of examining whether that action had been a massacre, debate might more conveniently centre on more prosaic explorations of legal limitations within Emergency conditions. In the event, that is exactly what transpired.

By the second half of January the amending documentation had been prepared and gazetted. An official statement by the Federation Government in Kuala Lumpur accompanied the notice of amendment. The purpose of the use of firearms when a person was known to be unarmed, it proclaimed, was 'not to kill, but to stop the person concerned'. So much for Boucher's earlier pronouncements on the matter.

In short, the thrust of the new legislation did not remove recognition of the fact that resort to firearms ran the risk of casualties, dead and wounded. The important clarification was that security forces, when using their weapons henceforth, were not covered by carte blanche licences to 'shoot to kill'. Different situations required different tactics.

The amendments provided details. Before security forces or police were permitted to use lethal weapons during an escape bid or to overcome resistance to arrest, they must call 'in a loud voice' upon those concerned to stop. Furthermore, the fugitive must be given 'a reasonable opportunity' to halt. Following any arrest procedure, there was a requirement for the arresting authority to inform anyone in custody that they risked being shot should they attempt to escape.

The grim realities of Batang Kali had entered a new phase. The incident itself now served as little more than a point of departure for local discussion of legalistic definitions, amended legislation and how all this would affect future operations. Ironically, as newspaper column inches talked of enhanced fairness and justice under the revised regulations, the issue of 24 corpses was relegated to the periphery.

So, too, was the fate of the destitute surviving dependants. Amid all the self-serving gloss, deflections and contradictions employed by the authorities, absolutely nothing was done by the government to console or assist the mothers, widows and children stranded in Ulu Yam Bahru. To have done so might have suggested that perhaps the dead weren't bandits after all. This, in turn, could have opened the legal floodgates, the likelihood of compensation claims, associated headline coverage and, in the end, the distinct prospect that the Batang Kali issue would continue for months, even years, to the great detriment of colonial interests.

Unresolved, Batang Kali has hung like a dark cloud through decades of modern history. As such it is an appalling testament to the actions of those in authority whose aim was to fudge the truth and then trust that carefully manipulated and protected documentation would effectively conceal it thereafter. Impossible to have foreseen in January, 1949, was just how many military, police and civil authorities in the decades to come, would prove more than ready to carry on the Batang Kali deception. It all amounts to a massive cover-up programme, rigidly maintained by British authorities and in operation to this very day.

⁓

On January 26, 31 days after the Scots Guards opened fire on the Chinese plantation workers, communist member of parliament in Britain, Philip Piratin, rose in the House of Commons to confront Colonial Secretary Creech Jones. Piratin wanted to know on what charges the 24 Batang Kali victims had been detained during the night of December 11-12. Furthermore, he inquired whether the Colonial Secretary was now prepared to make a formal statement on the shooting.

Replying, Creech Jones said: 'The Chinese in question were detained for interrogation under powers conferred by the Emergency regulations. An inquiry

Communist Member of Parliament for Mile End, Philip Piratin.

into this incident was made by the civil authorities and, after careful consideration of the evidence, and a personal visit to the place concerned, the Attorney-General was satisfied that, had the security forces not opened fire, the suspect Chinese would have made good an attempt at escape which had been obviously pre-arranged. A full statement was issued in Kuala Lumpur on 3rd January.'

The Colonial Secretary's reply, which in effect represented the British government's ultimate position on the affair, amounted to nothing more than a truncated version of the earlier final Kuala Lumpur statement. Significantly, Creech Jones chose to make no reference whatever to the widespread controversy in Malaya and Singapore that had been provoked by the shooting. Nor, apparently, did he feel it was pertinent – or advisable – to mention that the public debate that followed had forced the colonial authorities in Malaya to gazette legislative amendments incorporating new guidelines and firepower limitations to be employed henceforth by security forces handling detained suspects.

In answering the communist MP, the Colonial Secretary had provided planters with an indication of the effect their intense lobbying, post-Batang Kali, was having on overall policy. From his pronouncements, it was clear London was quite prepared to accept, at face value, whatever Kuala Lumpur wished to report on the mass killing and play down, or hedge, any aspect that threatened further scrutiny.

An even better indication of the impact planter organisations were having on policy would be provided by the very next series of inquiries posed to Creech Jones at question time that day. He was asked by a Conservative MP whether he was aware of Malayan planters' views that terrorist dangers in the territory had increased rather than decreased recently. Was he aware that the planters were seeking firmer action by the security forces if the situation in Malaya was not to deteriorate? 'What further steps are to be taken to apply effective action and when is it proposed to put into effect the recommendations of the planting community with regard to the squatter problem?' asked the parliamentarian.

Creech Jones began by reporting to the House on a meeting that had taken place in Kuala Lumpur earlier in the month between the newly arrived British High Commissioner, Sir Henry Gurney, and the United Planters' Association of Malaya. The meeting had occurred barely a month after the raid on Sungei Remok Estate. Seeking to portray to the House a generally satisfied planter viewpoint on the Emergency's progress thus far, Creech Jones admitted that some district planters thought the situation had deteriorated in certain areas. However 'the majority considered there had been no change as compared with December in the general situation'.

No progress on the war front, he seemed to be arguing, was, under the circumstances, acceptable enough for both government and planters. It was a curious reflection. When it came to dealing with Batang Kali in the context of this question, Creech Jones kept up the double-talk. Although there had been a number of tragic incidents in the campaign against the bandits, he conceded, there had been an overall improvement in recent weeks.

Then, finally, he uttered the words the planters wanted to hear. 'The campaign is being pressed with great energy, and strong measures which have met with general approval have recently been taken against persons who continue to give assistance to the bandits.' No names were mentioned but, in effect, it was London's further stamp of approval on the Batang Kali incident.

In case there might still be doubters of Britain's resolve to defeat communism in Malaya, the Colonial Secretary concluded his remarks with one further assurance. 'The High Commissioner will continue to use his powers to the utmost effect that the situation may demand. Steps have already been taken to deal with the immediate problem created by the squatters and the findings of a Federal Committee, appointed to make recommendations on all other aspects of this problem, are now under urgent consideration by the Executive Council.'

From the propaganda viewpoint, circumstances in 1949 – despite Batang Kali – were working in Creech Jones' favour. Many other world events were dominating the Fleet Street headlines. In Malaya and Singapore, the press ultimately proved malleable. This weakness was effectively masked by ever-evolving new issues and, like in Britain, readily available replacement headlines. The *Daily Worker's* stretched financial position could barely support a sustained publishing programme, let alone a campaign with a South East Asian focus. Additionally, the paper was permanently hampered by its unabashed ideological bias.

Most important of all was the ever-present fear along Westminster corridors that the CPM might one day emerge portrayed, locally and internationally, as a serious home-grown nationalist group fighting for independence. No one could have appreciated this point more than Creech Jones in his capacity as overseer of colonial interests. He was already acutely aware of the difficulties his office had encountered with the Foreign Ministry in drawing up a cohesive propaganda programme to portray the CPM in the worst possible light. Having finally arrived at the compromise epithet 'communist terrorist (CT)' – after the tag 'bandit' began losing its emotive ring – British officialdom saw a need to be extremely circumspect towards any in-depth examination of incidents such as Batang Kali. After all the CTs were the brutal ones.

Thus Creech Jones, by end-January, 1949, found himself in a perfect position to clamp a lid firmly on the Batang Kali cover-up mechanism. And there it would remain for more than 20 years.

Chapter 5

'Spectres in our cupboard'

It would take another ignominious episode in a much later conflict to dislodge the first protective lid clamped on the Batang Kali cover up.

On March 16, 1968, American soldiers, among them a platoon led by Lt William Calley, carried out a raid on the Vietnamese village of Son My. The associated hamlet of My Lai 4 was targeted. It was suspected of assisting guerrillas of the National Liberation Front's (NLF) 48th Battalion.

Calley and his men had been briefed to assume that genuine civilians left the village every morning and those who stayed were either communists or sympathisers. Although his platoon failed to uncover a single insurgent, Calley gave the order to kill the villagers, among them women and children. Their homes were destroyed by fire.

My Lai was initially heralded as a United States (US) military victory yielding a commendable enemy 'body count' of 128. Perfunctory investigations were carried out and a written report submitted a month after the attack. It pointed to 28 inadvertent deaths. The investigating officer's findings were based on interviews with soldiers who participated in the action.

In March, 1969, exactly a year after the My Lai killings, Ron Ridenhour, a 23 year-old who had served as a helicopter gunner in Vietnam, wrote to US authorities about what he had heard of the slaughter. Only one congressman of the 30 to whom he dispatched correspondence bothered to acknowledge him. All his other correspondence drew blanks.

Ridenhour's letters were written towards the end of a troubled decade crammed with diversities. The United States had stepped up its campaign in Indo China. The Beatles, a group from the northern English city of Liverpool, were inviting humanity to imagine a world of no possessions. It was the time of 'flower children' pleading for love, not war. Young men and women demonstrated their repugnance for arms by opting out and snorting their protests to premature oblivion. It was a fascinating, fearful, indeed, frightful world.

It was also, to its credit, a world that would not brook monumental untruths for very long. The Sixties were years given to questions and analyses. Nothing was sacrosanct; permissiveness was the rage. The role of opinion-maker ceased being the preserve of privileged men who, while swilling martinis in private clubs, dissected the tiresome difficulties of tawdry outposts. Both print and broadcast media were now accessible to those who had sentiments to convey. There was an abundance of opinion.

The whole aspect of mass communications had been vastly altered. Aided by more convenient modes of travel, many could readily pack their questions and seek answers for themselves.

Vietnam was a case in point. It was an unpopular war that became a magnet for those looking for a cause – the children of legends and heroes, people escaping their demons and those seeking something both grisly and exotic to tell, something that would earn them a scoop, perhaps, a headline to remember. And for those who didn't leave home there were the TV sets in the living rooms, the breakfast nooks and the rumpus rooms.

Vietnam became the first television war. Its horrifying images were relayed home at prime time, shocking families out of their peace-loving suburban platitudes. The American taxpayer woke up to footage of helicopters being emptied of body-bags. Parents sat by the fire and had grandstand seats to ambushes, pillaging and mindless brutality. Misgivings about the ongoing Vietnam conflict increased. More and more questions were being asked.

Behind scenes, the soullessness of 'search and destroy' missions, such as the one led by Calley, had to be re-examined and the offending men held culpable. Death-toll estimates for My Lai varied from 300 to 504. But there were no headlines when, in September, 1969, the man was charged with several counts of premeditated murder.

Seymour Hersh, a freelance investigative journalist writing for *The New York Times*, would first break the My Lai story to the American public, two months after Calley was quietly charged.

Hersh's exposé was carried in the November 12, 1969, edition of the paper. The real shock-waves, as far as public opinion was concerned, came eight days later by courtesy of *The Cleveland Plain Dealer*. The Ohio newspaper had obtained explicit pictures of My Lai from a demobbed military photographer. He had documented the incident. Early reporting on My Lai tended to refer to the village as 'Pinkville' – US military slang of the time that reflected the colour on operational maps used to designate more heavily populated Vietnamese regions. The term's usage was reinforced by the convenience of the colour pink representing an expression of the broad countryside's commitment to communism.

The photographs, published in the November 20 edition of *The Cleveland Plain Dealer*, would have their immediate searing effect across the Atlantic.

The following day, controversial British politician George Brown spoke on the BBC's *World At One* radio programme with renowned broadcaster William Hardcastle. Reports of the My Lai pictures' impact served as a major topic. Hardcastle asked Brown, then deputy leader of the ruling Labour Party and a former Foreign Secretary, for his views.

Brown replied: 'Terrible if it happened but, William, could you put your hand on your heart, and say in all the time that Britain has been playing a similar role, if one looked one couldn't find it?' He went on: 'Whether we could have turned up a Pinkville on the way if we had tried, I wouldn't know. I hope not but I just don't know.'

The politician's public gaffes were legendary. So was his propensity for over-imbibing. Was George Brown drunk again? His voice hadn't sounded slurred by alcohol and when he drank heavily it usually did.

Robert Edwards, editor of the popular UK Sunday paper, *The People*, heard the interview and decided to take Brown to task. It was a Friday afternoon and Edwards had already written his 'Voice of The People' column for the coming Sunday. Provided Fleet Street didn't make a meal of Brown's remarks in the days ahead, Edwards resolved to feature them as the subject of his column the following week. Brown's comments went unchallenged by the dailies and the editor had his next column prepared well in advance.

Edwards described Brown's remarks as an 'appalling slur' upon the honour of soldiers who had fought to keep Malaya free. Reflecting on Brown's sentiments about the possibility of Britain having committed a 'Pinkville on the way', Edwards wrote – 'This is akin to saying to the ex-war hero who lives next door : 'I don't know whether you did shoot women and children in cold blood, but you might have done'.'

The column went on to quote more of Brown's *World at One* comments. The politician had also told Hardcastle: 'People when they are fighting, when they are frightened, do terrible things and are terribly ashamed of them afterwards. I suspect there are an awful lot of spectres in our cupboard too.'

The People, wrote Edwards, did not believe that in either of the two world wars, or since, any such crime as Pinkville had been committed by British soldiers. 'If any such evidence was produced, we and other newspapers would search out the truth relentlessly.

'But Mr. Brown's chief offence,' continued the editor, 'is not the slur he casts upon honourable, brave men, but the excuse he unwittingly provides for those who committed such atrocities. The Nazis must never be allowed to excuse the wiping

US Army Lt. William Calley, circa 1970.

Former British Foreign Secretary, George Brown, the man whose radio remarks on the BBC's popular 'World At One' programme in November, 1969, serve to re-kindle the then 21 year-old Batang Kali controversy.

The BBC's popular but controversial 'World At One' anchorman, William Hardcastle.

Where's the evidence, George?

▲ **NOTHING CAN** now stop the truth emerging about the Pinkville massacre in Vietnam.

It can be extracted with honour by the American Government in a Nuremberg-style trial of the guilty.

Or it can be forced out into the open by such fine newspapers as the Cleveland Plain Dealer.

But out it will come.

There is, however, one appalling charge (or, if he does not like that word, smear or innuendo) that is not being examined at all.

This is the suggestion nine days ago by Mr. George Brown, M.P., that British soldiers might well have committed similar atrocities.

"Terrible if it happened," he said to radio interviewer Mr. William Hardcastle, "but, William, could you put your hand on your heart, could I put mine on my heart, and say in all the time that Britain has been playing a similar role, if one looked one couldn't find it?"

Mr. Brown made this appalling slur upon the honour of our own soldiers who fought for 10 years to keep Malaya free: "*Whether we could have turned up a Pinkville on the way if we had tried, I wouldn't know. I hope not, but I just don't know.*"

This is akin to saying to the ex-

VOICE OF The People

war hero who lives next door: "I don't know whether you did shoot women and children in cold blood, but you might have done."

As if this wasn't quite enough for one lunch-time performance by Mr Brown, he went on to say:

"People when they are fighting, when they are frightened, do terrible things and are terribly ashamed of them afterwards.

"*I suspect there are an awful lot of spectres in our cupboard, too.*"

The People does not believe that in either of the two world wars or since any such crime as Pinkville has been committed by British soldiers.

If any such evidence were produced we and other newspapers would search out the truth relentlessly.

But Mr. Brown's chief ━━ not the slur that he ━━

honourable and brave men, but th━ excuse he unwittingly provides ━ those who committed ━ atrocities.

The Nazis must never be al━ excuse the wiping out of Lid━ grounds that the soldiers of ━ nation might have done ━

The Americans must ━ to excuse the shame o━ the excuse c'est la g━ hope and believe that ━ make that excuse.

Some silly people ━ war is horror, ━ Dresden and the A━ is not rated a ━ Foreign Secre━ heeded.

He knows ━ vention. He ━ of civilized ━ try to fo━

Withd━

LE━ OF ━ FO━

The British Sunday newspaper, The People, reacts strongly to George Brown's radio remarks.

out of Lidice on the grounds that the soldiers of any other nation might have done the same. The Americans must not be allowed to excuse the shame of Pinkville with the excuse *c'est la guerre*. And we hope and believe that they will never make that excuse.

'Some silly people say that since all war is horror, since we bombed Dresden and the Americans Hiroshima, what's the difference? But Mr. Brown is not rated a silly person. He was Foreign Secretary. His words are heeded.

'He knows about the Geneva Convention. He knows about the standards of civilised behaviour that decent men try to follow even in war. Withdraw this slur, Mr. Brown. LET THERE NOT BE ONE TRACE OF MERCY OR TITTLE OF EXCUSE FOR THOSE WHO RAISED THEIR GUNS AND SHOT DOWN WOMEN AND CHILDREN IN PINKVILLE.'

Edwards' column was published on page 2 of the November 30, 1969, edition under the headline: *Where's the evidence, George?*

—◦◦◦—

Two days later, Tuesday, December 2, William Cootes, then a 40 year-old former national serviceman, walked into *The People's* Manchester office and spoke with the paper's northern news-editor, William Dorran. Details Cootes related about an incident in Malaya 21 years earlier involving a patrol of his old unit – the 2nd Battalion, Scots Guards – shocked the hard-bitten journalist.

Cootes, who lived in Manchester's Stretford area, explained he had decided to approach the paper after reading the previous Sunday's 'Voice of the People' section. Where was the evidence pointing to Britain's closeted spectres? Cootes maintained he could readily provide such evidence. What was more, he was fully prepared to have his story published.

By the following Saturday the tall, angular, one-time Scots Guardsman was sitting in *The People's* London headquarters, around the corner from Covent Garden. He recalled, in great detail, memories of his military service during the opening months of the Malayan Emergency campaign. What he had to say was quite obviously being delivered far too late for the paper's next edition due to go to press in a matter of hours. Indeed, Cootes' revelations were judged potentially so explosive they demanded extensive research and corroboration. This could take weeks, even months. Ultimately, it became a decision for editor Edwards. Was the paper prepared to devote extensive reporter time and funds substantiating what, on the face of it, seemed outrageous claims verging on the unbelievable?

British guilt revealed

The People

No. 4598   Sunday, February 1, 1970   8d.   ★ ★ ☆

HORROR IN A NAMELESS VILLAGE

...CEMBER 12, 1948, at a nameless village in a clearing ... Malayan jungle, a patrol of the 2nd Battalion, ...ds, shot and killed 25 suspected terrorists ...isoner overnight.

... Chinese plantation workers, died while ... years the memory of the massacre has ...ok part and today the truth can be told.

Why we are publishing this report

WE PUBLISH this report without any satisfaction, but in the certain knowledge that it is our duty to do so.

It arose because of a "Voice of the People" article in our issue of November 30, attacking Mr. George Brown.

Commenting on the Pinkville massacre in Vietnam, he had said: "I suspect there are an awful lot of spectres in our cupboard, too."

We called upon Mr. Brown to produce the evidence, or withdraw the slur. And we gave this pledge.

"The People does not believe that in either of the two world wars or since any such crime as Pinkville has been committed by British soldiers.

"If any such evidence were produced, we and other newspapers would search out the truth relentlessly."

After reading this Mr. William Cootes came forward and told us his story. We have, as promised, searched out the truth relentlessly.

It is not the story of another Pinkville. Women and children were not killed in cold blood. All of them in the village were spared. But what happened is appalling enough in all conscience.

Some people may believe that this unhappy story would be best left untold so many years after the event. But a newspaper has a simple duty to its readers which is best summed up in the Biblical phrase "Know ye the truth."

The truth, in this case, illustrates—as at Pinkville and elsewhere—the corrupting and fearful effect of war on otherwise decent men, and what can happen when the highest standards of discipline are allowed to fail.

That is the lesson, and it can never be taught too often.

There is nothing unusual about the men who took part in the crime. One after another they told us, in the most moving terms, how it had preyed on their minds ever since, and how relieved they are to get it off their consciences now by telling the truth. //

It is falsely said that the truth never hurt anyone. But at least in this case it may prevent such an act ever being committed again by British soldiers, with all the damage it did not only to the victims but to the soldiers themselves.

Robert Edwards,
Editor

After two months of research and interviews The People publishes its stunning exposé.

...older as he did so. I think ... there known he was ... shot.
...had gone about ...rdas dropped to ...his rifle and ...the back. He ...he, or go to ...he was dead.
...with on the ... and his ...upru by ...rd to see ...his head ...should ...that

... other waiting to see who was going to shoot first. I remember ... old man about 80 staring at ...stantly. Alan Tuppen ... them some matches to ...ast. we were going to ... village and ... A

...de must all be sick of our minds, morning, together with the ... to do a thing like we had just shocked man. done."

The huts of the village were then burned down, but the bodies of the Chinese were left where they had fallen.

"While we were ...

He also remembered that the guardsmen were told immediately before the shooting that the men and boys were to be shot.

They were also told ... has too

...nted al... ...him wh...

Two months would pass before *The People* felt confident enough to publish the results of their investigations into the one-time guardsman's original allegations. The front page lead story of the paper's Sunday, February 1, 1970, edition would have the effect of instantly and dramatically dislodging the Batang Kali cover-up lid put in place with such political skill and duplicity two decades earlier by Colonial Secretary Creech Jones.

The banner headline read HORROR IN A NAMELESS VILLAGE and the accompanying account spread across the entire front page, running additionally onto two inside pages. A sub-head in a black box prominently proclaimed: *British guilt revealed*. The by-line was shared between the paper's chief reporter, Ken Gardner and William Dorran.

Positioned directly beneath the headline ran a note of explanation from Robert Edwards.

'We publish this report,' wrote the editor, 'without any satisfaction but in the certain knowledge that it is our duty to do so.' Referring to his 'Voice of the People' column the previous November 30, Edwards explained how, as a result of that article, William Cootes had come forward. As promised, the editor emphasised, his paper had searched out the truth relentlessly.

It was not, he maintained, the story of another Pinkville. Women and children had not been killed in cold blood. In fact they had been spared. 'But what happened is appalling enough in all conscience.'

Edwards' observations concluded: 'There is nothing unusual about the men who took part in the crime. One after another they told us, in the most moving terms, how it had preyed on their minds ever since, and how relieved they are to get it off their consciences now by telling the truth. It is falsely said that the truth never hurt anyone. But at least in this case it may prevent such an act ever being committed again by British soldiers, with all the damage it did not only to the victims but to the soldiers themselves.'

Noble sentiments, indeed; and the following months would decide whether a public presentation of truth, no matter how horrifying the content, could be a match for politicians determined to replace the lid on a colonial military cover-up. After all, the British establishment had long decreed what happened at Batang Kali was best ignored in the national interest and had undertaken inordinate protective steps to ensure it remained that way.

The People's investigative report pointed out Cootes' recollections of events in the 'nameless' Malayan village were those of a patrol participant. He had been a member of the G Company, 2nd Battalion, Scots Guards unit responsible for the killings. In the eight weeks since Cootes first supplied his story to the paper and made a confirming sworn statement on oath, three other former Scots Guardsmen from the same unit had also signed sworn statements. All had agreed the male prisoners held overnight on the plantation by the patrol had, the next morning, been massacred. A fifth man, also a former patrol member, had made an oral statement. Holding out against making a sworn statement, he promised to tell the truth should any public inquiry be forthcoming. All five former Scots Guardsmen were adamant that none of the slaughtered plantation workers had been attempting to escape when the patrol opened fire on them.

Cootes' sworn statement was quoted first in the paper's coverage. Called up for national service, he had joined the Scots Guards in December, 1947. Following guard duty stints at Buckingham Palace, St James's Palace and the Tower of London he accompanied the battalion when it was dispatched to Malaya by sea in September, 1948. On arrival in the Far East, the battalion's G Company, had briefly undergone rudimentary jungle training before being packed off to Kuala Kubu Bahru in northern Selangor state.

Thereafter, Cootes and fellow guardsmen found themselves quickly deployed on daily patrols aimed at searching out and destroying CTs operating in Ulu Selangor terrain. They were told of atrocities reportedly carried out by the CTs against both European settlers and the local population. One of these concerned three British troops attached to the Hussars. The three were supposedly burnt alive by the communists. Cootes' statement noted that he and fellow patrol members had been angered by the 'Hussars incident' and, as the Sunday newspaper report put it, 'gathered they were going to wipe out a village that fed the terrorists.'

The paper then quoted verbatim from Cootes' sworn declaration:

'We arrived at the village mid afternoon on the Saturday. It was a small village comprising three *kongsi*s or houses, each about 60 ft long on stilts. Each *kongsi* had a verandah. The village was in a small clearing surrounded by dense jungle.

'A track ran through the village used by trucks carrying plantation workers.'

The quoted statement continued: 'I was posted on one of the verandahs so I could see what was going on in the village compound. I cannot remember if there was a Chinese liaison officer with us on this patrol. The sergeants and six men, I think, burst into the *kongsi*s with their arms at the ready and herded the villagers outside into the compound. I estimate there were about 80 men, women and children. I think there would be about 32 women and perhaps 16 young children.

'I caught some of the conversation between the sergeants and the villagers. The gist of the conversation seemed to be demands from the sergeants to know where the terrorists were and when they were coming back. The next thing which is clear in my mind is Sgt. Douglas walking below the verandah where I was with one of the young villagers. Beneath the verandah was a narrow path running to a stream nearby. Douglas and the youth were on this path . . .

'He (the youth) ran down the path, looking over his shoulder as he did so. I think he must have known he was going to get shot. When he had gone about 15 yards, Douglas dropped to one knee, aimed his rifle and shot the youth in the back. He didn't speak to me or go to make sure the youth was dead. I could see the youth on the path on his back and his stomach was ripped open by the shot. I was amazed to see him suddenly raise his head from the ground and I shouted to Sgt Hughes nearby that the boy was still alive.

'He walked over with his Sten gun and put a bullet through his (the youth's) head where he lay. Hughes had not been more than a few yards away when Douglas shot the youth in full sight of all the villagers.'

The newspaper report then referred to a part of Cootes' affidavit where he recalled being ordered to fire a shot behind a male plantation worker who was being interrogated. The intention had been to frighten the man into providing information about the communists.

Overnight, he explained, the villagers had been incarcerated in two *kongsi* rooms – men in one group, and women and children, in another. Still summarizing Cootes' statement , *The People's* story went on to record how, the following morning, a lorry carrying plantation workers into the village had been 'commandeered' to take the incarcerated women and children away.

At the last minute, the man who had been intentionally traumatised by Cootes' rifle shot during the previous afternoon's interrogation session was loaded onto the truck with the women and children. He was, it was noted, still 'in a state of shock'.

Patrol members were subsequently informed that the remaining prisoners – men and youths – were to be shot. Expanding on this the Cootes statement commented: 'None of us protested.'

His affidavit continued: 'We were divided into groups, four groups of three, I think. We had .303 rifles. There was one Bren gun in another group and a couple of Sten guns among the patrol. The Chinese were brought from their hut. Their ages ranged from about 16 to 80 years. We took our seven down to the edge of the stream just outside the village. We were looking at each other waiting to see who was going to shoot first. I remember an old man about 80 staring at me constantly.

'Alan Tuppen showed them some matches to indicate that we were going to burn down the village and motioned them to run away. A couple started to walk. The old man stayed still, and a youth about 16 was too terrified to move. We still hadn't fired and we were still looking at each other. Then we heard shooting from one of the other groups so, instinctively almost, we opened fire.

'Once we started firing we seemed to go mad. The old man died immediately from one bullet. The one that was farthest away at the time took about seven bullets before he finally stopped crawling. Apart from this one, the bodies were in touching distance of each other and quite near to the stream. I remember the water turning red with their blood.

'The incredible thing was that none of them spoke. They didn't shout or scream or anything. It was all over in something like half a minute. The man who kept crawling was shot in the head at point blank range. The man's brains spilled onto my boot.'

In recalling the reaction of patrol members after the mass killing, Cootes' statement noted: 'Some of the men were excited, some were delighted, some of us stayed quiet. It struck me we must all be out of our minds to do a thing like we had just done.'

The reference to the name Alan Tuppen in Cootes' statement was then quickly clarified by the newspaper under the sub-heading: *The Sworn Testimony of Alan Tuppen*. A 7 patrol member present on the day, Tuppen, by now a truck driver living in Portsdale, Sussex, readily confirmed Cootes' testimony. Pointedly, Tuppen's affidavit fully supported Cootes' claim that the guardsmen had been informed, prior to the killing, the male prisoners were to be shot. In this respect, Tuppen provided important additional detail. The patrol had been told that those feeling squeamish about such action could fall out.

The People's report continued quoting verbatim from Tuppen's affidavit: 'I did not want to kill anybody, but I was too frightened to move and make myself look a coward in front of the others. I was also aware of the strict discipline of the Guards.'

Tuppen's statement included the passage: 'The important point I wish to make is that none of the villagers was shot while trying to escape of their own free will or after being forced to run away by any action on our part.'

Further sworn testimony published by the paper, this time from Victor Remedios, a Liverpool taxi driver, provided substantiation of the testimony given by both Cootes and Tuppen. In particular, Remedios confirmed how patrol members had learned of the intention to shoot all prisoners. He also recalled how they had been instructed that those opposed to the killing plan could fall out. 'None of us did, but I found I need play no part in the killing if I went up the road to where the lorry with the women was parked and acted as a guard. I volunteered to do this with orders to shoot any of the women if they attempted to escape,' Remedios said.

The People then presented remarks by George Kydd, a farm worker from Arbroath, Scotland, the man who declined making a sworn statement but had promised to tell the truth should a formal inquiry be held. It quoted him as saying: 'It was murder – sheer bloody murder. Those poor blokes.'

When asked by a reporter whether those killed were at the time attempting to escape, Kydd had replied: 'The truth is what Cootes has told you – that these people were shot down in cold blood. They were not running away. There was no reason to shoot them.'

A close to identical story was told in the testimony provided by 40 year-old Robert Brownrigg, by then earning his living as a welder and residing in Manchester. He, too, remembered being told 'something to the effect that all the men and youths remaining were to be shot.'

Brownrigg's testimony, as quoted, went on: 'So far as I was concerned it seemed to be a matter of killing in cold blood and when the shooting started I fired into the ground or anywhere to avoid hitting any of the villagers. I don't know whether someone shouted an order, but suddenly firing started and all the villagers started running. As I say, I fired to miss them, but within a minute or two all the male villagers were dead. Some tried to escape in a stream but were shot. Looking back, I am quite sure in my own mind this was a needless killing that was like murder under orders. There was no reason to kill these people, although somebody might have had a reprisal in mind. There had been a lot of talk about atrocities to British troops.'

Continuing its exposé, the newspaper went on to recount a verbal exchange between one of its investigating reporters and a former Lance-Sgt Hughes who held a British Empire Medal for services in Malaya. Hughes had been on the same patrol as Cootes, Tuppen, Remedios, Kydd and Brownrigg and was now employed as a prison officer at Brixton Jail.

'I know why you have come,' Hughes told the reporter. 'You think this action was another Pinkville. That we murdered them. But I know what happened at that village in Malaya. I was in charge. I gave the order to shoot,' the former Scots Guardsman was quoted as saying.

When informed by the reporter there were sworn affidavits telling quite another sequence of events, Hughes abruptly changed his position. He then admitted he had, in fact, not issued the shooting order. He had only been a lance-sergeant. A Sgt. Douglas had been the man in charge of the patrol. According to the newspaper, Hughes then described how Douglas had shot a youth in the same village the previous day.

'This would be the first man Douglas had ever killed and he didn't make sure he was dead. A guardsman called to me that the man was moving and I went down the path. I turned him over and saw that he was still alive, but his guts were all shot up. I put my Sten gun to his head and finished him off. It was a humane act,' was how Hughes related these events.

Hughes told a substantially different account of the shooting than that revealed in the four sworn affidavits made available to the newspaper. Interestingly, it was almost identical to the coordinated line provided more than two decades earlier by both the colonial administrative and military authorities. Prior to the shooting, Hughes insisted, patrol members were on positions along three or four paths leading away from the estate clearing. 'Suddenly, there was a shout and all the men dived for the jungle. Naturally, we opened fire and killed them,' he declared to *The People*.

Insisting once more that he had never given the order to fire, Hughes provided further details of the terrible moment the killing commenced. 'There was a shout and shooting started. It (the shout) could have been Douglas or one of the Chinese interpreters,' he said. Was he convinced the dead were terrorists? 'How can you be sure?' was his reply. 'But we thought they were. I sensed danger in the village. I can always sense danger. It is better to be safe than sorry.'

As if this was not disturbing enough, Hughes was ready to provide a number of further observations for *The People*. 'If the women and children had made a break for the jungle, I would have given the order to fire,' he said. 'That's natural in war. If you can't shoot, you might as well pack up and go back to Blighty (Britain).'

When asked whether, as it was reportedly the patrol's intention to capture bandits, it would have been preferable to carry the men and youths back to camp on the lorry with the women, Hughes responded: 'We didn't want screaming women and kids around as we took the men away. In any case, if the men had been taken to the police station first they would not have got a fair trial. They would have just disappeared – and the Malayan police would have got rewards for killing them.' He was unsure whether anyone got a reward for the killings. However, reported the paper, Hughes remembered the police accompanying the patrol had looted the money belts of the dead Chinese.

The latter portion of *The People's* report dealt primarily with two specific interviews. The first of these was with the then Scots Guards' Regimental Sgt.-

Major (RSM) Charles Douglas who, as a young sergeant, had led the G company patrol onto Sungei Remok Estate on December 11, 1948. It was disclosed that arrangements for the interview, conducted at Hadrian's Camp, close to Carlisle, his hometown, had been coursed through official British Army channels. Douglas' account of events on the estate, like that of Hughes, was almost identical to the official military line.

He admitted shooting the young estate worker on the first day. 'He made a dash for it,' explained Douglas. 'I called upon him to stop in Chinese. It was just about the only word in the language that I knew. The youth did not stop so I shot him.'

When asked whether he had been the only patrolman to shoot the youth, Douglas affirmed this, claiming the victim had been felled with a single round. Told that the newspaper's information was that the first round only wounded the boy and that Hughes had admitted finishing him off with a shot in the head, Douglas had replied: 'I thought I had killed him. I had not killed a man before. I turned away and was violently sick.'

As far as the next morning's mass killing was concerned, Douglas claimed that the men and youths had 'made a dash for it' shortly after emerging from their overnight incarceration. 'The patrol opened fire from their defensive positions where they had been placed by Sgt. Hughes and that was it,' he declared. 'We went back to our HQ and reported the incident and that's all there was to it.'

The People then presented the following highly significant series of questions and answers between a staff reporter and Douglas:

Q. What, then, was the original intention of the patrol as far as the women were concerned?
A. I would think, if we had left the women behind in their village, they would carry-on feeding the bandits, so we would take them back with us with the men.
Q. Did you?
A. I don't remember.
Q. What briefing did your patrol receive before it set out?
A. As far as I remember, information was received that bandits were going to the village and feeding there and that perhaps some of the people who lived there were bandits. We had to go there and take the place tactically. The orders were to catch as many of the bandits as we could and bring them back.
Q. Were they bandits?
A. We were told they were.
Q. Were arms found?

A. They were found by the Chinese police afterwards.
Q. But weren't the kongsis burnt down?
A. No.
Q. What evidence did you have that they were bandits?
A. I was told at the briefing. We had little information. We were told for sure that they were bandits at the briefing by an officer.
Q. Was the officer a Malayan police officer?
A. There was a Chinese liaison officer and others, but I can't remember.
Q. What happened to the bodies?
A. They were left there because the police had to photograph them.
Q. Was there any truth in the suggestion that his briefing was to wipe out the village?
A. No, not at all.

Douglas also denied the guardsmen were called together in the village and told that the Chinese were to be shot and that anybody who did not like the idea should say so. At the same time he did not think it remarkable all the males had been killed and that there were no wounded. 'We were good shots,' added the RSM flatly. However, he was unable to remember whether he was the one who gave the order to fire that day.

———∽∿∽———

The final 'Horror in a nameless village' interview that Sunday was with the man who had been in overall command of G Company, 2nd Battalion, at the time of the Batang Kali raid – Captain George Patrick Maule Ramsay. In the intervening years the onetime company commander had enjoyed regular promotion and had attained the rank of colonel prior to retiring from military life and entering London's merchant banking world. *The People* traced Ramsay to his comfortable home in Chelsea where the interview took place.

'I am appalled, if this is true . . . .' Ramsay was quoted as telling the paper's reporter who had obviously provided certain details of the ongoing investigation.

'I remember that weekend well. We were a reserve unit and the civilian police had information of two separate bandit movements, both extremely vague.

'I took charge of what looked to be the most important patrol and the sergeants went with the other patrol. I remember they were Hughes and Douglas.'

Ramsay went on to admit that great surprise had later been expressed over the numbers of Chinese killed in the action. 'We were horrified at the suggestion that our men might have acted improperly,' he added. Following 'misgivings' expressed in Malayan newspapers at the time and complaints from the owner of the plantation on which the killings had taken place, two separate inquiries had been launched – one by the military and another by the civilian authorities. These had exonerated the regiment, claimed Ramsay.

In a further reflection Ramsay added: 'As a matter of fact, we had often been criticised before the incident because of our inability to hit moving targets. Up to that day our bag of terrorists had been very poor indeed.'

Ramsey's choice of the hunting term 'bag' would carry considerable meaning as readers with Far East colonial experience digested the former company commander's thoughts and expressions.

In summarising its overall investigation *The People* carried a closing observation:

'Had there been any survivors among the Chinese villagers who were mown down there might have been a different end to the inquiries held on the spot after the affair. But there were none. Every single man was killed outright, an unusual percentage of fatalities.'

It was an observation that, for all the exposé's journalistic excellence, would soon demand urgent review.

May 9, 1948. War Secretary Emanuel Shinwell pays a special visit to Ocean Dock, Southampton, to farewell 1,500 officers and men of the 2nd Guards Brigade. The guardsmen are Malaya-bound aboard the 'Empire Trooper'.

Chapter 6

'A bona-fide mistake'

A firestorm of British press, radio and television reaction to *The People's* exposé and its editor's straight-from-the-shoulder comments exploded only hours after the paper reached the news stands. By Sunday evening, BBC radio's *World This Weekend* programme had unearthed Victor Remedios whose recollections of Batang Kali had formed such a key aspect of the paper's exhaustive investigation.

Speaking to an interviewer, Remedios reinforced everything he had outlined in his sworn statement and, pointedly, took the story substantially further.

Prior to their Batang Kali mission, he recounted, the patrol had been briefed by an officer who said the villagers concerned were either helping the terrorists or were terrorists themselves. 'We were told we were to wipe out the village,' he added.

Remedios explained that the sergeant in charge informed the patrol what was going to happen. Those who were not prepared to participate should say so. On hearing that, Remedios and another soldier had opted to guard the women and children on the truck rather than participate in the shooting.

At this point the interviewer asked: 'So the sergeant told you that men who had been separated from women were going to be shot, there and then, and if you did not want to take part you need not?'

Remedios replied: 'That's it.'

When it was suggested to him that stark differences existed between evidence apparently given to the 1948 inquiries in Malaya and claims now being made in *The People,* Remedios responded: 'We were told by the sergeant after the incident that if anyone said anything we could get 14 or 15 years in prison. We were more or less threatened by the sergeant.'

'So you got together and conspired to fabricate a story?'

Remedios: 'Yes, more or less.'

'All the platoon?'

Remedios: 'More or less, yes.'

Also interviewed on the same BBC programme was veteran Labour member of parliament, Emanuel Shinwell. He had been Britain's War Minister in the post-war Attlee Government at the time of the Batang Kali killings and, as a cabinet minister, had been jointly responsible for dispatching national servicemen to Malaya.

Asked whether he was surprised by *The People's* revelations, Shinwell replied: 'I

THE Sun

INSIDE YOUR 28-PAGE SUN TODAY

THE FORTUNE TELLERS
Part One of a startling new series PAGES 12 AND 13

WIN A PEDIGREE PUPPY
Day One of a fascinating new competition PAGE 19

FORWARD WITH THE PEOPLE. 6d. Monday, February 2, 1970

ARMY 'MASSACRE' —MPs DEMAND INQUIRY

RSM DOUGLAS
Named in allegation

DEFENCE MINISTER Denis Healey wi be pressed by MPs today to set up a inquiry into an alleged massacre b British troops in Malaya 21 years ago.

Four former members of the 2nd Battalio the Scots Guards are reported to have sai that 25 suspected terrorists were shot whi women and children, herded together in truck shouted and

British daily tabloids join the 1970 Batang Kali press coverage fervour. (Top) The Sun's front page lead story, February 2. (Right) The Sketch story on the same day. (Below) Twenty-four hours later and The Sketch editorial suggests a more comfortable fence-sitting position by the paper which, on the same page, carries a major news story headed "No Massacre Said A General." It quotes remarks made by General Boucher on January 3, 1949.

ARMY 'MASSACRE' PROBE OPENS

SYDNEY BRENNAN

ARMY chiefs begin a top-level inquiry today into allegations that British troops hushed up a

"Pinkville-type" massacre in Malaya 21 years ago.

The allegations, made by four ex-Scots Guardsmen, assert that a patrol of the 2nd Battalion Scots Guards shot 25

suspected terrorists in cold blood.

One of the Guardsmen, Mr. Victor Remedios, now a Liverpool taxidriver, was one of the patrol attached to "G" company of the battalion when the murders were alleged to have taken place.

He claimed yesterday that he took no part in shootings but said he was advised to lie to a military inquiry into the incident.

Mr. Emanuel Shinwell, Labour MP for Easington, Co. Durham, and Secretary of State for War at the time, declared: " I know nothing about this. Neither do I know anything about a military or civil inquiry.

"I assume that, if there had been one, the War Office would have a record of it."

SUSPECTS

The allegations, in a Sunday newspaper, claim that 25 men and youths ages ranging from 16 to 60 were arrested as Communist terrorist suspects in a nameless village in the Malayan jungle.

Women and children were separated from the village men, then, it is alleged, after a night of captivity, the youths and men were gunned down by the Scots Guards patrol.

Officially, the men were shot trying to escape, but according to testimonies

made by four Guardsmen a sergeant ordered the men to shoot down the prisoners, who were Chinese plantation workers.

The four ex-Guardsmen who started the controversy are Mr. William Cootes, aged 40, of Stretford, Manchester, Mr. Remedios, Mr. George Kydd, a farm worker of Arbroath, Scotland, and Mr. Robert Brownrigg, aged 40, of Manchester.

Mr. Remedios said the sergeant told the patrol the village men were either terrorists or had helped terrorists and that they were to be shot.

Mr. Remedios said he got out of the shootings by guarding the women and children

The sergeant has denied the allegations, and said

that the men were shot when trying to escape.

The officer commanding 'G Company at the time, Captain George P. M. Ramsay, later a colonel and now a merchant banker living in Chelsea, was reported as saying: " I am appalled if this is true."

'IMPROPER'

Last night Col Ramsay would only add: "The matter is in the hands of the Ministry of Defence. It would be highly improper to say anything except that the incident is being thoroughly investigated."

The 2nd Battalion Scots Guards (motto: Unita Fortior—Unite and Be Stronger) are now in Germany.

JUNGLE FEVER

THERE is a good deal of hysteria about an alleged massacre by British soldiers in the jungles of Malaya 21 years ago.

The facts are not at all clear.

Did it happen? Did it not happen? The country wants to know.

The Government should dig back in the records and turn up the official files and publish them. They must exist somewhere.

Until then, there is a case for keeping cool.

am not only surprised. I am shocked. I never heard a word about it.' He went on to challenge anyone to find any reference to the events in *Hansard*, the official record of parliamentary proceedings. He also questioned the motives of *The People* and guardsmen who told their stories in its columns. Why had the paper failed to ask the War Office to produce documents relating to the incident?

Shinwell's remarks were significant from several perspectives. Firstly, he had launched an ill-prepared attack on a newspaper. While Fleet Street publications were highly competitive, a closing of ranks was predictable if government authorities unfairly singled out one of their number for attack – particularly on such controversial grounds.

Research of the January 26, 1948, *Hansard* record would, of course, confirm communist MP Philip Piratin's request to Colonial Secretary Creech Jones for a full statement on Batang Kali. It would also carry the Colonial Secretary's response. There could be no question that Creech Jones' remarks that day were geared specifically to removing the killing controversy from public scrutiny.

Shinwell should have considered that such a challenge as he had made would send interested parties, particularly the press, heading for *Hansard*. And once it was established he was in error, wider suspicions would be aroused.

By nightfall that Sunday, Whitehall had decided on a holding action. A spokesman for the Ministry of Defence was being quoted as saying Ministry officials were studying the Sunday newspaper's report. However it was doubtful, the spokesman added, whether any formal comment would be forthcoming in time for the following day's papers.

A behind-scenes application of the gag was regarded as fundamental to the holding action. First to demonstrate its effect was retired Scots Guards colonel turned merchant banker, George Ramsay, who had spoken so openly to *The People*. That evening, when the tabloid *Daily Sketch* contacted the man who had been commander of G Company, 2nd Battalion, Scots Guards, at the time of Batang Kali, his response was curt.

'The matter is in the hands of the Ministry of Defence,' Ramsay told the reporter. 'It would be highly improper to say anything except that the incident is being thoroughly investigated.' There was a familiar ring to the one-time company commander's words. They echoed the formal comments of colonial government and military leaders in Kuala Lumpur 21 years earlier.

The following day, February 2, the *Daily Sketch* reported in a major news story that Army Chiefs would be initiating a 'top-level inquiry' into allegations that British troops had hushed up a 'Pinkville-type massacre' in Malaya. It claimed the Army's investigation would begin that day. The story summarised highlights of *The People's* exclusive account but preferred to leave that paper unnamed. Angled, as it was, on the prospect of an upcoming Army inquiry, the *Daily Sketch* story was way-off base.

Far more accurate was *The Sun*'s approach. Its headline, splashed across the front page, declared: ARMY 'MASSACRE' – MPs DEMAND INQUIRY. The accompanying story informed that the day's parliamentary proceedings would see Defence Minister Denis Healey pressed to set up a formal inquiry. This report openly credited *The People*'s investigation. What was more, *The Sun* had taken up Shinwell's challenge to check *Hansard*. They discovered the ageing politician's unfortunate error and reported the lapse accordingly.

The tabloid's coverage provided further evidence of Whitehall's widening application of the gag. Noting that *The People* had named Charles Douglas, now a regimental sergeant-major, as the patrol leader in the 1948 incident, the paper's final paragraph quoted the soldier as saying he had been ordered by the Defence Ministry not to comment. The military gag was in place.

Predictably, the communist *Morning Star* devoted much of its front page to the Batang Kali story that Monday. It went as far as re-printing the January 4, 1949, headline of its predecessor publication, the defunct *Daily Worker*. The *Morning Star* ran a picture of Shinwell captioned: 'Emanuel Shinwell – Former War Minister who 'never heard a word' about massacre'. Below this was a photograph of MP Piratin. This was captioned: 'Former Communist MP whose Commons' question on the shooting was answered on January 26, 1949.' In the body of the story, which largely harked back to the *Daily Worker* file airmailed from Kuala Lumpur, the *Morning Star* characteristically referred to the colonial government's handling of Batang Kali as 'that hoariest of hoary cover-up stories'.

By this time the Ministry of Defence, after high-level brain-storming consultations, felt confident enough in releasing its first reaction to *The People*'s claims. The Ministry's statement read:

'The allegations reported in The People relate to events in the Far East more than 20 years ago which were investigated at the time. We have called for all the available information and documents, although it is believed that some may be in the Far East, and may therefore have to be traced.

'It is perhaps unfortunate that we were not given the opportunity in advance by the newspaper in question of collating this information.

'The allegations would appear to contradict the evidence originally given, and since they could, in law, amount to allegations of murder, we are taking these very seriously indeed. All the implications will need to be fully and carefully examined. In the meantime it would be premature and possibly prejudicial to discuss the matter further at this stage.

'With the sole exception of RSM Douglas, all the soldiers named in the article have left the Service. At present, RSM Douglas is on leave pending a fresh posting. We will make a further statement as soon as we are able.'

While this was being released, a group of Labour MPs were attempting to raise the Batang Kali issue in parliament through Private Notice Questions – just as *The Sun* had reported earlier in the day. However, the MPs' efforts would ultimately be blocked by the Speaker, Dr Horace King, who chose to disallow their submissions. Not to be deterred, Michael Foot, Labour member for Ebbw Vale, in Wales, tabled a separate demand for an independent inquiry.

Still, the biggest surprise of the day would come from the man who supposedly carried out the colonial government's much heralded official investigation of the mass shooting – none other than the former Attorney General of Malaya himself, Stafford Foster-Sutton. In a broadcast interview he would make a stunning admission. He would categorically deny any formal inquiry had ever taken place.

By then 71 years old and knighted, Sir Stafford had enjoyed a most illustrious colonial career. At the end of 1950, following his stint as Attorney General, he briefly became Officer Administering the Government of Malaya. Immediately thereafter he was appointed Chief Justice of the Malayan Federation, a position he held from 1950 to 1951. Following service in Africa, where he was Chief Justice in Nigeria, Foster-Sutton returned to Britain and had been functioning as President of the Pensions Appeal Tribunal for England and Wales since 1958.

It was the BBC's *World At One* programme that succeeded in locating and speaking to the former Malaya Attorney General. The interviewer sought to clarify exactly what role the ex-colonial had played in the aftermath to Batang Kali. Foster-Sutton explained that immediately he learned of the incident he had called for statements and arranged to meet a sergeant of the patrol, another NCO – he thought a corporal – and Special Branch Chinese and Malays.

'I cross-examined the sergeant and the other men with him and discussed it with the Special Branch men who were with him and I was absolutely satisfied a bona-fide mistake had been made,' he added.

The sergeant had told him that after six or seven days in the jungle his patrol had reached a rubber plantation clearing where a number of suspected bandits had been discovered.

'They arrested them, so to speak,' said Foster-Sutton.

He continued: 'They put them in one hut under guard. The following morning they let them out with the idea, I believe, of taking them to interrogate them to find out what they really were. They must have made, I think, a plan to make a break for it, because they suddenly dashed through the clearing toward a jungle.

And it was then that these men opened fire.'

'What evidence was there for that,' probed the interviewer.

The reply: 'Well, these men, rubber tappers at that time, quite a number of them, were rubber tappers during the day and bandits at night.' Furthermore, the position of the wounds on the victims, he said, had reinforced accounts that they had been shot while running away.

In answer to another question, Foster-Sutton responded: 'There was no formal inquiry at all. Having satisfied myself the statements were true, I made a statement to the press and the matter came to an end. I think we made a statement to the Secretary of State but we made no report to the War Office.'

In the same interview, he claimed any suggestion of a whitewash was nothing but a figment of the imagination. 'I think that anyone who knew anything about it at the time entirely agreed that it was a bona-fide mistake,' he reiterated.

The government's gagging measures had obviously fallen woefully short of objectives. How could the former senior official on whom had rested Britain's entire claim of a comprehensive inquiry into Batang Kali have been overlooked in the latest scramble to control information? After all, his supposedly meticulous investigation of the circumstances had, from the outset, been the one factor justifying repeated official denials of a massacre perpetrated by the Scots Guards.

Now, if the much vaunted inquiry hadn't taken place – and Foster-Sutton was the unassailable authority on this subject – what did his latest revelations do to the perceived validity of the official denials? Nor did it rest there. What impact did Foster-Sutton's curious assertion of a 'bona-fide mistake' have on the historical record? Nothing of this nature had ever before been offered by the authorities as an explanation for the killings.

Fleet Street's reaction was instantaneous. Every London-based daily newspaper organisation assigned reporters to hunt down and question Foster-Sutton. Phones rang constantly at his Pensions Appeal Tribunal offices. When such convenient means of contact failed to achieve results, newspapermen began door-stopping the office premises. As the hours passed it became clear Whitehall had rushed to shore up the oversight.

Foster-Sutton had gone incommunicado. Eventually, late that afternoon, his office was forced to release a decidedly feeble press statement. The Tribunal's president, it said, had been 'debarred from making any comment' on Batang Kali. The statement continued: 'He cannot be helpful as he has ascertained that he is precluded from giving any interviews to press and radio because he holds judicial office.'

Labour MP for Ebbw Vale in Wales, Michael Foot, has an established journalistic background that gives him a decided edge over his parliamentary colleagues when it comes to interpreting Fleet Street reactions.

London Editor, Harry Miller, files his follow-up to The People's initial disclosures and his story makes front page headlines in The Straits Times' February 2, 1970, edition. Editors back home supply some background historical notes from their publication's December 13-14, 1948, coverage – all taken from Miller's original Batang Kali files.

Journalist Harry Miller, whose 1948 Kuala Kubu Bahru interview with patrol leader Douglas had been so heavily relied upon by Foster-Sutton and other colonial authorities – all committed to restricting the release of information on the slaughter – was now living in Britain. He had been appointed London editor of *The Straits Times*. In the dash for interview prospects following *The People's* exposé, Independent Television (ITV) sought out Miller. He appeared on their Monday night's news programme. Miller came across firmly convinced that the Scots Guards action in killing 24 unarmed plantation workers was a lawful military operation and not a massacre. In the interview that followed, he regurgitated details he had reported in December, 1948. But he also added information not included in his originally published story.

The sergeant had told him that he and two members of his patrol had opened the doors and let the Chinese out after their night of incarceration.

'When the Chinese came out of the hut and apparently saw just three soldiers standing around and nobody else, one Chinese shouted and everybody began to run. They split into three groups and took paths leading to the jungle. Patrol members had been placed along these paths at ambush points and their instructions were that if anybody attempted to escape and went along those routes they were to let them pass and then call upon them to halt. If they did not halt, chase them; and if they did not stop, shoot them,' said Miller.

The reason for not shooting toward the escapees as they came out was because patrol members would then be shooting into the village itself, he explained. These expanded details, critical as they were to the story, had been absent from his account published by *The Straits Times in 1948*.

The ITV interviewer then asked Miller if the sergeant concerned had given any order to fire.

Miller: 'No, he did not give any order to fire; it was just one of these automatic instructions down in the manual that they fired when they felt that they had to fire.'

Had he been able to check the story as a reporter?

Miller: 'No, I did not check this story because it seemed to fit in with the tactical conditions at the time and when I was speaking to him he showed me on a map just where he had placed his sentries and it all seemed to fit in.'

Miller's reliance, at this point, on the environment and traditions of the system that had reared him came strongly to the support of Douglas, Boucher, Newboult, Foster-Sutton, Beverley, indeed, the entire Malaya colonial administration in 1948,

A ruthless enemy in an expensive war

By Harry Miller, of The Straits Times, who was in Malaya throughout the emergency.

The incident at Batang Kali in north Selangor, occurred 21 years ago—six months after the emergency had been declared.

"Emergency" was a polite euphemism. It became the smallest and most expensive war of its kind that British troops had been called on to fight. Their battle ended after 12 years. Does anybody in Britain still remember that war, in which British and Commonwealth and Malayan land, sea, and air forces were involved so grimly against a relentless and cruel enemy?

The end came early in 1960, and by that time 500 or 600 armed guerrillas of the Malayan Communist Party had sought refuge in the jungles of south Thailand, from where they have recently been emerging to harry and kill Malaysian and Thai forces arrayed against them.

The "faceless" guerrilla fought from the jungle. His strong support organization outside brought him food, medical supplies, and equipment, including arms and ammunition.

The communist supply organization was gigantic. At its peak it must have numbered about 500,000 people, the great majority of whom in their villages and big towns were unwilling helpers. But as time went on and as the security forces, growing in number and gaining experience, achieved the initiative and then the upper hand and were able to provide for the supply lines were cut, the terrorists went hungry, and eventually they were forced out either to fight to death or surrender. In the last two or three years of the war they did so in hundreds.

It is worth remembering that in the 12 years 1,965 police, soldiers, airmen and home guards lost their lives. So did nearly 2,500 civilians, most of them Chinese.

On the communist side about 6,700 men and women were killed; another 2,675 surrendered. An unknown number died in the jungle from natural causes or from wounds.

Twenty-four hours after the Batang Kali incident Sergeant Charles Douglas, leader of the patrol, told me how they surrounded a small group of huts in a clearing (obviously one of the working areas of a rubber estate) and began interrogating the men after separating the women and putting them into their own huts. That evening one Chinese tried to escape and was shot dead.

One Chinese also said that a lorry load of food was expected the next morning. The patrol intercepted it. The headman on it was taken into custody for questioning about the origin and destination of the food.

The lorry was sent off with the women and children and other men against whom there was no suspicion. The remaining men were brought out of their huts so that they could be sent to base for further questioning.

Suddenly one of them shouted and every man started running. "We called out to them to stop but they continued", Sgt. Douglas said. "My men had been placed around the village in defensive positions with orders that if anyone tried to escape they were to allow them to pass through the positions first and then to shoot at them, otherwise they would be firing into the village. When the men started running they went into the direction of the sentries. There was a terrific ...

Only on ... He was ser ... process of ... able dete ... prove that ... with the c ...

That was one incident. There was another in an adjacent area on the night of December 13. Terrorists murdered Mr. A. M. Blake, an American-born naturalized Briton who was superintendent of a boys' home in Seredah. They shot him down in his study and burnt his bungalow with him in it.

They had no reason to kill him. Mike Blake was working for the Save the Children Fund and he had devoted his life to the interests of orphans of any race.

Malaya terrorists were 'shot in escape attempt'

By HARRY MILLER

London editor of the Straits Times, who reported Malayan emergency, which lasted for 12 years, from 1948 to 1960

TWENTY-ONE years ago in December, 19... Sgt Charles Douglas of the 2nd Ba Sc Guards was 22 years of age, and fresh fac The Scots Guards had been in the country s... October that year.

They had come with the rest of the tall men of the 2nd Guards Brigade — the Grenadier Guards and the Coldstream Guards — to Malaya to fight against the Communist guerrillas against whom the forces of the country—for what they were at the time—had been mustered since June that year.

The despatch of the Guards Brigade to Malaya had created military history, for not even during World War II had any Guards battalion been sent to the Far East to fight.

The men of the Brigade made a reputation. They took to the jungle "as easily"—as I wrote once—"as marching down the Mall" and an American correspondent put it a little more picturesquely when he wrote: "Well, Britain's pride of the palaces are just the same bunch of boys in the bush hats out ...

Take away the fog, sleet and summer sunshine of London and substitute for it the tense heat, rain and thousands of square miles of jungle in Malaya.

The Guardsmen substituted their bearskin hats for floppy green cloth hats. They had a lot to learn. One thing they had to learn was that the enemy in this war was faceless. He was all around them.

Jungle attacks

The terrorists lived and attacked and defended from the jungle. They battened on isolated villages and their people and forced them to provide them with food, medical supplies and any equipment they wanted.

The villagers—they were all Chinese because the Communist terrorists were Chinese and used their own race for their own ends—co-operated out of fear. They took—had to take—more notice of the man who pointed the revolver at them than the British or Malay soldier or policeman who was some miles away.

So, the rubber tapper, the tin miner, the village shopkeeper, produced the required commodities. There were, of course, the voluntary workers, the people who believed in the cause for which the guerrillas were fighting.

But it was not possible to identify the one from the other, nor the terrorists who operated as harmless looking tappers, or miners, or villagers by day and went on the prowl and the kill by night.

Now, the area in which the Scots Guards operated—the whole of North Selangor, in central Malaya—was riddled with terrorists. They had an extremely good support organization outside the jungle. That is why it was only way of finding out whether a man intercepted in the area was innocent was to interrogate him.

On Dec. 12, 1948, there came the news that the Scots Guards had "shot dead 25 out of 26 bandits in North Selangor. If correct it was the biggest success yet achieved in one operation in Malaya since the Emergency had begun. This first report had been flashed to radio from the patrol to the tactical headquarters for the operation.

More than a battalion of troops from the Scots and Grenadier ...

inhabitants. The women separated from the men and into one large hut. The men began their interrogation of the men.

That evening, one Chinese tried to escape and was dead. A search of the hut yielded 15 rounds of 8mm ammunition to the feet of a bandit said Douglas.

Arrangements were made to bring the 25 suspects and 9 men back to base after the next day.

Orders to shoot

According to Douglas he brought the men out of the and the headman from his hut. He came late, the joke to have him identified. As he did so, one Chinese shouted and every man started running.

Douglas told me: "We called to them to stop but continued running."

The guardsmen were in festive positions around the village with orders to shoot anyone tried to escape, any would-be escapee was to be allowed to pass first by shooting into the village.

When the men started running they went to the direction of the sentries.

"There was a terrific amount of firing."

Only one man came out and he was sent back to headquarters for questioning.

The patrol radioed the back of its unit and in for operations that day arrived the Chinese who was identified the caretaker of a hut used terrorists.

The company commander me that the local bag for weekend of operations was killed and 12 captured.

On Monday evening, Malay police headquarters in a red said that the patrol had searching for bandits before burning down two small huts stations and for an attack another area in which as fresh inspector had wounded.

It added that one of the Chinese had, while under interrogation, volunteered the information that they were born and that food would be brought to them the next day.

It also said that the Chinese upon emerging from the and seeing the smallness of guards-police patrol, had broken away and attempted to escape.

Unease developed

Of course, unease developed as the incident because of the nature and mystery of an ordinary incident. The serious concern among the communities, particularly Chinese.

There were two issues: the communities in which the men were shot and the wider question, the instructions issued with troops and police operated.

Had our British Government had radioed its own bandit inquiry promptly, Air Vic-Marshal Sir Foster Sutton, then Attorney General, said in a B.B.C. World One yesterday, he went to see ... wrote, he wrote to the surgeon, and a corporal, he disclosed.

"Whole evidence with Specific Branch officers, and they named a statement which ... named persons tried to escape? was to be chased and recaptured but ... under an diverse statutes to be allowed ..."

In almost unprecedented commissioning arrangements, the highly competitive Fleet Street rivals, The Times (above) and The Daily Telegraph (right), on the same day – February 2 – run similar accounts by Miller. Both stories hold firmly to the 1948-49 colonial government explanations and reject the possibility of a massacre ever having occurred at Batang Kali.

Unbeknown to commissioning British editors, Harry Miller has long enjoyed close relations with the police station at the very heart of Batang Kali investigations. Indeed, shortly before departing for his London posting, Miller is guest of honour at the Kuala Kubu Bahru Police College where, for several years, he has served as a visiting lecturer. The 1959 photograph (above) shows the Commandant of the college presenting a farewell souvenir to Miller. The presentation is on behalf of the Commissioner of Police, Federation of Malaya, and the officers of the college.

not to mention the British government of that day and the present one, as well. It was unnecessary to check the story because the system was saying it was so. There was no need to visit the scene of the killings. There was no need to speak to the families of the victims and other eyewitnesses. The Scots Guards side of the story *was* the story. Miller's was very much the same message as had been relayed earlier in the day by Foster-Sutton on BBC radio.

Monday, February 2, had proved an extraordinarily busy day for Harry Miller. Apart from appearing on the ITV news programme, he had also been required to cover London developments of the story for his newspaper back in Singapore. Additionally he agreed to write separate substantial features for the rival London-based broadsheets, *The Times* and *The Daily Telegraph*. Copy for each had to be submitted by late afternoon. This most unusual commissioning arrangement resulted in Miller by-lined articles appearing in both rival papers the next morning.

In *The Daily Telegraph*, Miller conceded that 'unease' had developed in Malaya over Batang Kali. His piece, headlined *Malaya terrorists were 'shot in escape attempt'*, argued that the unease had resulted from the episode's 'very nature and result; it was not an ordinary incident'.

Miller's article in *The Times*, on the other hand, was headlined: *A ruthless enemy in an expensive war*. Like his feature in *The Daily Telegraph*, Miller went ahead to justify the Scots Guards action in Batang Kali and suggested that whatever had occurred was certainly not a massacre.

Unbeknown to either *The Times* or *The Daily Telegraph* was an interesting sidelight to Miller's professional life in the Far East. Prior to his departure for London, he had been fêted at a formal dinner and presented with a souvenir acknowledging his services to the Malayan Police Force. The presentation, on behalf of Malaya's Commissioner of Police, was made by the Commandant of the Kuala Kubu Bahru Police College. Miller, it was pointed out at the time, had been a visiting lecturer at this college for several years. He had lectured there regularly on a subject he titled 'The Press and the Police.'

As Miller worked on his two features in London, half a world away *The Straits Times* had sent a two-man reporting team to the Batang Kali area to unearth whatever background might be available to story developments taking place in Britain. The team comprised local journalist, Siew Ching Cherd, and New Zealand expatriate, Hugh Mabbett. What the duo would uncover in the next 48 hours would demolish all arguments made 21 years earlier in order to sustain the colonial cover-up.

The team's first dramatic discovery came in the form of 57 year-old Inche Jaffar bin Taib, a former special constable with the Malayan police force. Now working as a rubber tapper, he was one of the three police officers who assisted the Scots Guards patrol on the weekend of December 11-12, 1948. He had guided the British soldiers to Sungei Remok Estate. Inche Jaffar's recollections of events leading to the shooting were substantially the same as had been previously reported. But what he told Siew about the morning of December 12 would have a devastating impact.

He spoke of the arrival of the supply lorry at the plantation clearing and how it was promptly surrounded by members of the patrol. Several men and women were questioned. Food was removed from the lorry and one man from the newly arrived workforce was detained. Then Inche Jaffar recalled the shooting.

'It was about 10 am when the Scots Guards sergeant – he was a young man – told me not to look at the male detainees. I turned my back towards them and suddenly there was a terrific burst of gunfire. Women and children screamed. I turned around. There were dead bodies everywhere. The sergeant warned me that if I breathed a word to anyone about the shooting I would land myself in jail. I counted 25 bodies.'

Inche Jaffar told Siew how the patrol had departed the estate soon after the shooting, leaving the dead where they had fallen. It was several days before the corpses were removed from the clearing and buried at Ulu Yam Bahru, he said.

Siew's report led *The Straits Times'* front page on Tuesday, February 3, under the headline: BATANG KALI: BODIES HORROR. Above it ran the lead-line: *I was ordered to keep mum, says guide.*

A pointer on the paper's front page directed readers to another Batang Kali story on page 8. This account was written by Allington Kennard, one of the old-school British journalists who, like Harry Miller, had enjoyed a privileged career in Singapore and Malaya. Kennard had been a propaganda expert on Admiral Mountbatten's SEAC staff and soon after the Japanese surrender had switched to an executive position on *The Straits Times*. By 1951 he had been appointed an associate editor of the paper. In 1970 he was in retirement but maintaining links to the same publication as an editorial adviser. His rambling feature on Batang Kali essentially echoed the colonial line. It confirmed the cosy relationship existing between trusted expatriate journalists and top echelon colonial civil servants.

Kennard recalled how he had been invited by Britain's High Commissioner to Malaya, Sir Henry Gurney, to explain privately why *The Straits Times* was 'so

New Zealand-born reporter for *The Straits Times*, Hugh Mabbett, accompanied by a local journalist, first tracks down a member of the three-man police party that accompanied the Scots Guards patrol that day on Sungei Remok Estate. Mabbett follows this scoop 24 hours later with the revelation of the mass killing's lone survivor.

AVERAGE DAILY CERTIFIED SALE EXCEEDS 200,000

The Straits Times

The National Newspaper

Estd. 1845   TUESDAY, FEBRUARY 3, 1970   ★   15 CENTS K.D.N. 4517 : M.C. (P) No. 1301

I was ordered to keep mum, says guide
SO REMOTE FROM THE FACTS: PAGE 8

Batang Kali: Bodies horror

By SIEW CHING CHERD: KUALA

Allington Kennard, a retired colonial-era journalist, steadfastly maintains the old government line on Batang Kali in an inside page feature for *The Straits Times*. But the front page headline in the same edition declares: 'Batang Kali: Bodies horror'. Next day, The Straits Times front page banner reads: 'Survivor: It *was* a massacre'.

hostile' towards the authorities on the subject of Batang Kali and why the paper refused to let the matter rest. Kennard quoted his response to Britain's top official in the country: 'Because we know more than has been admitted.' This was far from an acknowledgement that his paper believed a massacre had taken place. Indeed, the remainder of the Kennard article was devoted specifically to reinforcing the view that it hadn't.

The Scots Guards, he said, 'acted completely in accordance with instructions from tactical headquarters'. They were not to let any prisoners escape and would shoot to kill if they had to. Kennard went on to argue that if there was an excuse for Batang Kali it was 'to be found in the almost critical situation that ruled at the time'.

His feature concluded with the observation: 'And whatever else can be said about Batang Kali, the allegation in this London newspaper of 'secret massacre', hushed up at the time, is as wildly remote from the truth as journalistic invention has ever gone.'

Kennard's recapitulation of the 1948 events clashed embarrassingly with the paper's front page lead story.

Embarrassment was not restricted to *The Straits Times*. Back in London *The Times* and *The Daily Telegraph* both gave prominence in their February 3 editions to Harry Miller's unabashed justifications of the official account. Tucked away in both publications, however, were truncated files from staff correspondents in South East Asia reporting the existence of former special constable Inche Jaffar together with his startling disclosures.

The Guardian, on the other hand, treated the day's vastly conflicting news reports by stating, at the outset of its coverage, that three differing versions of the Batang Kali incident had emerged. Two had come from local journalists who accepted that the Scots Guards patrol 'was in a difficult situation' and that the soldiers had shot men who were trying to escape. Their separate reports, it was noted, differed in detail. The third version, reported *The Guardian*, had come from a Malay former special constable, present at the scene, who said the plantation workers had been lined-up and shot. Thrown in for good measure in the paper's coverage was Foster-Sutton's declaration that there had been no formal inquiry at all.

If Fleet Street's serious-minded broadsheets were having problems presenting conflicting news and opinions even-handedly and objectively, the *Morning Star* found itself facing no such restrictions. In a two-column front-page editorial, the communist newspaper proclaimed:

'OPERATION WHITEWASH is in full swing after the revelations about the Malayan massacre 21 years ago.'

The paper took a swipe at former Attorney General Foster-Sutton's remarks to the BBC that the only evidence he had sought was from soldiers involved in the killing. 'Suppose,' said the editorial, 'this eminent lawyer was informed that at the trial of, say, the Kray brothers, the only evidence to be heard was from the accused. Would he regard that as fair? Would he object to a claim that the outcome would be whitewash?' The Kray brothers, at that time, were widely recognised as the most notorious gangsters from London's underworld.

The *Morning Star*'s commentary continued its attack on Foster-Sutton: 'He speaks now of a 'bona-fide mistake', but Colonial Secretary Creech Jones at the time told Piratin not that a 'mistake' had been made, but that the Attorney General 'was satisfied that, had the Security Forces not opened fire, the suspect Chinese would have made good an attempt at escape which had been obviously pre-arranged.'

The editorial referred to the sworn statements made by some former guardsmen and published in *The People*:

'After the revelations by American soldiers about the Son My massacre, these British soldiers have now decided to tell the truth. There is now overwhelming evidence that the original *Daily Worker* story was correct. But the Government and the Establishment will make every effort to avoid admitting this. For it calls into question not only their conduct in this particular case, but the whole character of the Malayan war.'

Thirty-six hours after *The People* broke the Batang Kali story the British Government faced a serious credibility factor. Although yet to be publicly disclosed, there were clear indications it would be adopting the position that a re-opening of the Batang Kali case was unwarranted.

But in order to do this, the basic premise of the Government's argument had to be that the matter had been correctly and properly addressed at the time of the incident, 21 years earlier.

Any delving by investigative reporters would readily reveal that the claimed police and military inquiries had been aborted even before they got underway.

Foster-Sutton's BBC interview had eliminated any possibility that either military or civil authorities could fall back on the findings of an Attorney General's formal inquiry. This hadn't taken place, either. Nor had the Attorney General concerned bothered to seek information from any Batang Kali source other than those involved on the government side.

Furthermore, there were Foster-Sutton's seriously conflicting pronouncements. Twenty-one years earlier he found justification for the shooting on the grounds that a mass escape would otherwise have materialised. Now he was proclaiming something entirely different – a 'bona fide mistake'.

Assertions by former War Minister Shinwell that he had never heard of the matter, together with Foster-Sutton's admission he had held back his opinions from the War Office, placed a large question mark over the reporting procedures adopted in Kuala Lumpur back in January, 1949.

Additionally, sworn statements by four ex-guardsmen, the promise from a fifth that he would testify at an official inquiry along with the overall impact of *The People's* disclosures had presented a dramatically different story to the one maintained by authorities. And, as if this was not enough, there were now the pronouncements of Inche Jaffar to consider. These were critical recollections from an eyewitness. He had accompanied the Scots Guards patrol to the plantation and had been on the scene when the shooting took place.

On the other side of the world he was telling a story in another language, but it was eerily similar to that being claimed in the columns of the British Sunday newspaper.

The next 24 hours were to prove even more alarming for British authorities.

Chapter 7

The lone survivor

As Britain's news media delved deeper, the calculated manipulations undertaken by the 1948 colonial authorities in Malaya became increasingly apparent. There was now little doubt that a cover-up had indeed been instituted 21 years earlier to protect the Scots Guards elite forces' image. Equally important, it was designed to ensure Batang Kali never became a propaganda *cause célèbre* for the communist adversary.

The Wilson Labour Government which, in February, 1970, was looking at general elections by mid-year, had a simple choice as far as addressing the controversy was concerned. It could launch credible investigations or, alternatively, engage in a drawn-out campaign of fudging and misinformation that would likely drag on until the polls. It was taking time for the issue to crystallise for the Cabinet, but further startling discoveries in Malaysia would soon hasten the decision-making process.

The Straits Times' two-man reporting team had been combing the Malay kampongs and Chinese villages in the immediate vicinity of the killing scene. This approach had yielded Inche Jaffar within the first few hours. The next day, while tracing more leads in Ulu Yam Bahru, the reporters heard of the existence of a very 'lucky' man – Chong Fong. They were told the former tapper was a tin-mine worker these days. He lived some six miles away, was married and had nine children. His wife had been the fiancée of his younger brother, Chong Sip, one of the 24 shot dead on the plantation. He had a story to tell, the villagers said, if they could only get him to relate it.

By late morning, reporter Hugh Mabbett had located the now 45 year-old Chong Fong, the lone survivor, together with his wife, Tham Yong, and two other women, Foo Moi and Chai Kiew. All three women had been among the female family members and children who spent the night of December 11, 1948, locked in the dark *kongsi* room on Sungei Remok Estate.

Chong Fong told Mabbett he had not been back to the plantation since the day of the shooting and had no wish to return to the place where so many had died. However, he was willing to recall what happened that terrible weekend. Following this interview, Mabbett drove with two of the women – Foo Moi and Tham Yong – to Sungei Remok, up to the very site of the killings. All that remained of the *kongsi*

AVERAGE DAILY CERTIFIED SALE EXCEEDS 200,000

The Straits Times

The National Newspaper

Estd. 1845   WEDNESDAY, FEBRUARY 4, 1970   ★   15 CENTS   K.D.N. 4517 : M.C. (P) No. 1507

'No attempt to escape'

MORE PICTURES AND EYEWITNESS ACCOUNTS: PAGES 6 AND 7

CPIB has no powers of arrest: Judge

SINGAPORE, Tues. — The arrest of a freelance advertising canvasser by a Corrupt Practices Investigation Bureau agent was "a serious encroachment on the liberty of a citizen," a district judge said today.

The Judge, Mr. K.T. Alexander, then cleared Mr. Pang Yeok Sang, 46, of charges of escaping from the custody of a CPIB investigator and assaulting him.

Mr. Alexander said: "The CPIB has powers to investigate into complaints of malpractices, but does not have powers of arrest.

Legality

The accused was therefore not under lawful arrest at a previous hearing, the court heard arguments on the legality of Mr. Pang's arrest by CPIB in investigator Mr. Lee Than Chee.

He was arrested by Cuthrie three last Aug. 14 when he was suspected of having collected money for a booking contracts possession but on the way to the CPIB

Survivor: It <u>was</u> a massacre

By HUGH MABBETT: KUALA LUMPUR, Tuesday

A SURVIVOR of the Batang Kali "massacre" in 1948 said today that as far as he knew no one was trying to escape when the shooting began.

He added that he escaped because he turned from fright. When he returned perhaps half an hour later, dead bodies lay all around and the soldiers had gone.

The survivor, Mr Chong Hong, is a tin mine worker on The Sungei Remok estate claimed on a Lenkoh newspaper report that

Thais and Indons ordered to play cup tie in Tokyo

LONDON, Tues. — Indonesia and Thailand have been ordered by the International Badminton Federation to resume their controversial Thomas Cup tie in Tokyo on Feb. 21 or 22.

The international championship committee of the IBF took this decision at a special meeting here last night to consider Indonesia's protest against Thailand being declared winners when the tie was played in Bangkok last month.

The committee, numbering 14 world officials, decided that the match should be resumed in Tokyo with the score standing at 3-all.

Same players

The same players must take part, and neutral officials will be in charge. The IBF will appoint the referee.

In the original match —the final of the Asian section of the Thomas Cup—the Indonesian captain Muljadi walked off court in protest against calls by the Thai umpire. Other Indonesian players joined Muljadi in the walkout.

The Thai referee of the match, Phlensak Sonethaikul, declared Thailand winners after the Indonesian walkout.

Decision

Announcing the committee's decision today,

Ninth child for Maria Hertogh

BERGEN-OP-ZOOM, Tues. — Maria Hertogh, the jungle girl whose annulled marriage to the Malaysian teacher Mansur Abadi provoked riots in Singapore in 1951, gave birth to her ninth child—a boy at the weekend.

Six boys and three girls have been born to Maria, now 33, since she married bus owner Jo Wolken Yelt in 1957.

The 1951 ruling awarded Maria to her mother against the pleas of her wartime Malaysian fostermother, Che Aminah.—AP.

The headline for reporter Mabbett's story, together with the story itself, tells a very different account of the Scots Guards actions on Sungei Remok Estate from that being provided by the paper's old-guard journalists.

complex and its adjacent sheds were foundation blocks, now surrounded by new rubber trees. Mabbett walked the length and breadth of the one-time killing zone with the two women who readily shared their recollections with him. He and a staff photographer took pictures.

Mabbett's gripping narrative, when submitted that evening, confronted his editors with major decisions on how it should be presented in the following morning's paper. It blew apart everything Allington Kennard was saying in his prominently displayed feature running in the current day's edition. Additionally, it completely undermined the thrust of the file coming from Harry Miller in London. Already the interview with the Malay former police constable, claiming he had been threatened with gaol should he say anything about the shooting, stood in stark contrast to the stories so far provided by the two old-guard journalists.

In view of such clear contradictions, how were the lone survivor's claims, along with the women's eyewitness accounts, to be portrayed in *The Straits Times* next day? To their considerable credit, the editors chose the bold course. Hugh Mabbett's story led the paper under the headline: SURVIVOR: IT <u>WAS</u> A MASSACRE. A lead-line above this proclaimed: '*No attempt to escape.*' More pictures and eyewitness accounts appeared on pages 6 and 7.

Reporter Siew Ching Cherd wrote the inside page coverage. His account wrapped up other angles on the story. This included statements from the wife of the coffin maker who had sold the cheap wooden planked boxes in which Batang Kali victims were buried. The Mabbett and Siew chronicles now made Miller's and Kennard's positions sound one-sided, remote, and particularly colonial.

Mabbett's text confirmed several critical aspects of the Batang Kali story, all of them in stark contradiction to the official version beside which military and civilian authorities, since 1948, had stood firm in both Kuala Lumpur and London.

Chong Fong was asserting there was no jungle area close to the plantation clearing to which workers could have run. So much for the allegation of three paths leading to the jungle along which Scots Guards sentries had been placed with orders to shoot only after escapees had run past them. The lone survivor was adamant that none of the victims had attempted to escape before the shooting started. Furthermore, he reported that the detained plantation workers had been divided into groups of 'five or six' with a small number of soldiers guarding each group. The bodies had been found, he declared, in tightly formed clusters.

Chong Fong's reference to his incarceration by police for a period of three days after his identification as the 'lone survivor' was of considerable interest. Military claims, immediately after the killings, that one man had been taken away from the clearing for further questioning were in no way linked to Chong Fong. The military had then been referring to Chan Loi, the collapsed tapper, who had been terrorised during interrogation.

It is therefore valid to speculate about the quandary that had confronted officialdom in the closing days of 1948 once it was recognised there had been a genuine 'lone survivor'. How was Chong Fong to be dealt with?

If the cover story was to be maintained that all those killed were bandits trying to escape, then Chong Fong would have to be identified as a bandit and brought to trial under the Emergency regulations. If, on the other hand, he was to be held for lengthy questioning or convenient isolation, those in Ulu Yam Bahru who knew the man and his astonishing experience might well start making awkward approaches.

The final decision on Chong Fong was an expedient compromise. As he told Mabbett, he never knew why he was arrested. In fact, he was held, never questioned, then quietly released. No reference was ever made by the colonial authorities to the one survivor who had miraculously extracted himself from the killing zone after the shooting.

Latest eyewitness accounts from Malaysia made the February 4, 1970, newspapers in London and by that afternoon the Government could no longer dodge Batang Kali questions in the House of Commons. Oxford educated lawyer Marcus Lipton, Labour MP for Brixton, flatly asked whether Defence Secretary Denis Healey would institute proceedings against those responsible for the massacre of civilians in Malaya towards the end of 1948. An irate Defence Secretary still held to the position that two separate investigations of the incident had been conducted at the time – one by the military and another by the civil authorities in Malaya.

'So far as is known,' added Healey, 'no report was received by the War Office from either source of any criminal conduct on the part of the British troops who took part in this incident.' However, he continued, he was treating the matter with 'concern and urgency' and had called for such documents relating to the original investigations 'as might still be available'. Depending on what these revealed, he would decide whether or not to place the matter in the hands of the Director of Public Prosecutions (DPP) for investigation.

More questions from Lipton further irritated Healey. By suggesting in a statement 'a couple of days ago' that published reports could amount to allegations of murder, could not the Ministry of Defence be deterring potential witnesses? Was it not giving the appearance of prejudging the issue? Was such a statement likely to assist the successful outcome of the investigation?

A now vexed Healey shot back: 'We may all have our opinion as to what publications by whom in the last few days will have assisted the course of justice, but there is no doubt that these allegations, if true, are very serious indeed. I think

Three leading figures in the Labour Party of the day – Healey (left) Wilson (centre) and Foot (right) are all troubled by what might have transpired at Batang Kali.

Letters to the Editor

REPORTING THE SHOOTING IN MALAYA

From the Editor of The People

Sir,—Mr. Denis Healey, the Minister for Defence, told Mr. Michael Foot in the House of Commons yesterday that the only approach we made to the Ministry of Defence during our inquiries into the Malayan massacre was for permission to interview the R.S.M. concerned.

This is not so. On any instructions, our chief reporter, Mr. Ken Gardner, asked a press officer at the Ministry of Defence to let us see the findings of the official inquiries into the incident that were made at the time.

The press officer promised to do his best. Later he said that the documents were not available, and explained that in cases where troops were exonerated after an inquiry it was the practice to destroy the papers after three years.

It is also relevant that when Mr. Gardner interviewed the R.S.M., as authorized by the Ministry of Defence, he did so in the presence of an Army P.R.O. with the rank of major.

Mr. Gardner also interviewed Colonel Ramsay, who was the company commander at the time, who informed the headquarters of the Scots Guards of the discussion.

It seems that there is something wrong with the lines of communication at the Ministry of Defence, and that we are owed an apology.

Yours sincerely,
ROBERT EDWARDS,
2-12 Endell Street, W.C.2, Feb 5

(Left) Editor Robert Edwards' letter to The Times, published on February 6, 1970. The following Sunday, Edwards' 'Voice of the People' column (below) leads the paper and asks a basic question.

SHOULD WE HAVE KEPT OUR WORD?

VOICE OF The People
by Robert Edwards, Editor

AN EXTRAORDINARY complaint is made against this newspaper in high places. It is said that we should not have published our report last week of the massacre in Malaya in 1948, when a patrol of the Scots Guards killed 25 prisoners.

This attitude was summed up in Parliament last week by Mr. James Ramsden, a defence spokesman for the opposition, when he said that "raking over the past in the context of this incident, which was twice investigated over 20 years ago, can be of no conceivable value or help to anybody, unless it be to fill newspaper columns..."

Now, then, is a responsible politician, reading critically for Britain's alternative government, who says that having discovered what we believe to be the appalling truth, we should have suppressed it.

A set of emotive adjectives have been used about us last Sunday. "Scandal" was the cry of John Labour about the killing of John Labour far away what happened near Kuala...

WE THINK MR. RAMSDEN'S ATTITUDE IS SCANDALOUS.

Consider: as stated last week, the circumstances which led to our report. Defending, we published an attack off Mr. George Brown in our issue of November 30 for saying of the Pinkville massacre...

the first place, is the argument now that it was wrong for us to keep our word?

Was the American newspaper the Cleveland Plain Dealer wrong to have drawn the attention of the American public and the world to the Pinkville massacre?

If a German editor had had the nerve to risk, not silly talk of criminal libel, but sudden death at the hands of a firing-squad for exposing the gipsing-out of Lidice, would he have deserved such a censure as Mr. Ramsden has administered to us?

The massacre in Malaya will not rank in the annals of infamy with that at Pinkville or, even worse, at Lidice. We said that last week. We say it again now.

Too long ago?

Nonetheless, according to the sworn statement that we had not consulted the Ministry of Defence...

period of time should decide a newspaper against publication.

Is it proper to tell the shocking truth as in the case of Pinkville? Of five years? Or what? Of Pinkville? Or five years? Simply to put the argument shows how utterly unsustainable it is.

If 25 English farm workers had been killed in this fashion during the war, would Mr. Ramsden, or any other living soul in this land, have objected if those responsible were called to account for their actions 22 years later?

It is a sad commentary on present-day attitudes and the growing acceptance of violence that instead of calling on the Army to explain why this affair has been hidden for so long (except it now comes out in the Daily Worker in 1948) so many people in high places have confined their concern to criticising The People's action...

The amazing April Ashley

'I'M SURE THE JUDGE WAS WRONG' says Lord Maugham

LAST WEEK a judge decided that a person who feels like a woman, looks like a woman and wants to live as a woman is, in the eyes of the law, a man.

That woman, now legally a man, is April Ashley, who underwent a sex-change operation which she believed confirmed her female sex.

On Page 11 today famous author Robin Maugham gives his view. It is challenging and controversial.

Mrs. McKay: Two men help detectives

---

it is the duty not only of myself as Secretary of State for Defence but of every Member of this House to recognise that there is a direct conflict of evidence on what may or may not have happened, and I must say that I found the form of the honorable member's question very prejudicial to any inquiry.'

At this point exchanges in the House disintegrated into a slanging match with several members seizing the moment to hurl brickbats at *The People*. James Ramsden, a spokesman on defence for the Conservative opposition, led with his chin when he expressed the view that most people felt 'raking over the past in the context of this incident' was of no conceivable value or help to anybody. It was merely being used, he insisted, 'to fill newspaper column inches' and the general wish was that any new investigation 'be concluded and the incident dismissed'. Measured against all the lame thinking and ill-considered responses made in connection with Batang Kali, Ramsden's remarks on this occasion had to be close to top of the pile. It would not be long before he was dumped on heavily.

Emanuel Shinwell, who had blundered rather badly over his *Hansard* challenge the previous Sunday evening, wanted to know whether *The People's* editor, or any person representing the paper, had approached the Ministry of Defence, or any appropriate government department, 'before publishing these allegations'. Healey replied that, as far as he was aware, no approach was made to any government department.

The wily socialist, Michael Foot, who could boast a substantial journalistic background having himself once been a Fleet Street editor, knew more than Healey did about the manner in which *The People* had conducted its investigation.

He asked: 'Will the Secretary of State examine afresh and very carefully the statement he has just made to the House that no approach was made to the Ministry of Defence by *The People*, the newspaper which originally published these allegations?' And if that was not blunt enough for Healey, Foot added: 'Will he examine this matter in the utmost detail, since I believe there is a direct conflict of evidence on the subject, and, if he finds that he is mistaken in that statement, will he come to the House and make that quite clear?'

Responding to the gravity of the question, Healey modified his earlier remarks. 'I will certainly investigate further, but, as I understand it, the only approach of any nature which was made during the period when this article was being prepared was a request from *The People* to interview the regimental sergeant major who is mentioned in the articles; but no explanation was given of the reason why the newspaper wished to question the regimental sergeant major or of the nature of the articles which it was proposed to publish.'

Liberal Party leader Jeremy Thorpe, had *The People's* editor, Bob Edwards, firmly in his sights. Would the Director of Public Prosecutions, he asked, consider the possibility of prosecuting for criminal libel those who make such allegations?

Healey's reply was a curious one. 'The House will recognise that that is not a question for me. However, I think I express the view of the whole House when I say that it is highly undesirable that articles should be published in newspapers and that persons should be encouraged to make statements in newspapers without any warning being given to them as to the consequences which might follow.'

If the politicians were seeking to deflect public attention away from the realities of Batang Kali by personally attacking a newspaper editor and, as a secondary issue, pouring scorn on his publication, they perhaps should have considered the personality of their prime target more carefully.

Fleet Street demanded toughness in its editors. Robert Edwards was one of the toughest, particularly when he thought a provocation ill-deserved. Unlike the majority of his editing colleagues, Edwards had only one paper a week with which to strike back. So he turned to *The Times* when he decided a quick response to Healey was required. His rejoinder led *The Times*' 'Letters to the Editor' column on February 6 under the heading REPORTING THE SHOOTING IN MALAYA. Dated February 5, it read:

From the editor of *The People*

Sir.– Mr Denis Healey, the Minister for Defence, told Mr Michael Foot in the House of Commons yesterday that the only approach we made to the Ministry of Defence during our inquiries into the Malayan massacre was for permission to interview the RSM concerned.

This is not so. On my instructions, our chief reporter, Mr Ken Gardner, asked a press officer at the Ministry of Defence to let us see the findings of the official inquiries into the incident that were made at the time.

The press officer promised to do his best. Later he said that the documents were not available, and explained that in cases where troops were exonerated after an inquiry it was the practice to destroy the papers after three years.

It is also relevant that when Mr Gardner interviewed the RSM, as authorised by the Ministry of Defence, he did so in the presence of an Army PRO with the rank of major.

Mr Gardner also interviewed Colonel Ramsay, who was the company commander at the time, who informed the headquarters of the Scots Guards of the discussion.

It seems that there is something wrong with the lines of communication at the Ministry of Defence, and that we are owed an apology.

Yours sincerely,
Robert Edwards

The apology was not forthcoming.

This was no deterrent to Edwards who had prepared his next Sunday column well in advance. It led the paper with the headlined question – SHOULD WE HAVE KEPT OUR WORD?

His column began: 'An extraordinary complaint is made against this newspaper in high places' and immediately thereafter the editor began demolishing the position adopted by Defence spokesman Ramsden in the House of Commons.

'Here, then, is a responsible politician speaking officially for Britain's alternative government, who says that having discovered what we believe to be the appalling truth, we should have suppressed it. A lot of emotive adjectives have been hurled about since last Sunday. 'Scandalous' was the cry of some Labour MPs – not over what happened near Batang Kali in 1948, but over a false statement that we had not consulted the Ministry of Defence.'

Then in the paper's inimitable style came the capitalised paragraph: WE THINK MR RAMSDEN'S ATTITUDE IS SCANDALOUS.

In recapitulating the series of events leading to *The People* publishing its February 1 exposé, Edwards recalled George Brown's *spectres in our cupboard* remark and the pledge that, if any such evidence were produced, the paper would search out the truth relentlessly. 'Does (or did) Mr Ramsden think we were wrong to have given that pledge? Does Mr Jeremy Thorpe, the Liberal leader? His chief contribution to the discussion was to suggest that the authorities should consider prosecuting the editor of this newspaper for criminal libel. If it was right to give the pledge in the first place, is the argument now that it was wrong for us to keep our word?'

Edwards zeroed in on what was, in effect, the nub of Ramsden's argument. As the killing had occurred a long time ago the incident should be pushed aside and forgotten. Perhaps the politician would indicate what period of time should decide a newspaper against publication, suggested the editor. 'Is it proper to tell the shocking truth if it happened within, say, two years as in the case of Pinkville? Or five years? Or what? Simply to put the argument shows how utterly untenable it is.'

Edwards went on to elaborate on the points he made in his letter to *The Times*. He branded as untrue hints that the paper's Batang Kali exposé the previous week had resulted from a 'collusion' between the ex-guardsmen involved.

'Our reporters searched the country for them. One after the other they told the same story. One after the other, they then agreed to swear their testimony in the form of legal affidavits.

'In each case they were told by the solicitor who took their oaths that they would be liable to perjury if they lied. Again it is hinted that in the interest of

Two riverside positions are later positively identified by authorities as killing locations on Sungei Remok Estate. The above photograph depicts one of them and is probably that visited by British reporter, Bill Dorran, accompanied by the lone survivor and two widows.

sensational journalism the men were paid to tell their stories and that therefore their evidence is suspect.

'The ex-soldier who originally came forward has spent eight weeks working with our reporters. He has been paid. But no payment has been made to any of the others. They simply wanted to get the truth off their chests.

The People's editor closed his column with the observation: 'Those who say we should not have printed the truth have a misconception of the duty of a free press. If crimes can be committed in dark places and not called to account, they will occur again.'

Reporter Bill Dorran, whom *The People* had flown to Malaysia early in the week, took the exceptional 'lone survivor' aspect a step further. On the following Saturday he succeeded in persuading Chong Fong to make his first visit to Sungei Remok Estate in more than 21 years. They travelled in an open truck, reminiscent of the vehicles used to service the rubber plantations during the '40s and '50s. In addition to an interpreter, Dorran also took along two surviving widows – Foo Moi and Chai Kiew. Both had previously been interviewed by *The Straits Times*.

Dorran watched as the women lit joss-sticks and prayed at the place where they identified their husbands had been shot. Chong Fong took Dorran to the spot where he had fainted from fright and thus escaped the Scots Guards bullets. He allowed the reporter to photograph him there.

Dorran's file from Malaysia accompanied Bob Edwards' hard-hitting column. There was nothing particularly new in Dorran's report that hadn't already been covered by *The Straits Times* scoop four days earlier. What made it significant for the British reader was the lone survivor's return to the scene. That *The People* was sustaining such strong coverage a week after the initial revelations had to be considered by Westminster as a worrying indication that the paper had no intention of backing down.

Even more telling for British authorities was the implicit message contained in Edwards' letter to *The Times*. Chief reporter Gardner had been informed by a Defence Ministry spokesman that documents on whatever inquiries had been held into the Batang Kali incident were no longer available. As explained by the spokesman, all documents, in cases where troops were exonerated by inquiries, were destroyed after three years. If this was to be believed, the documents Gardner sought had not been available since 1952. Healey himself should have been well aware of such conditions and procedures for document destruction.

Ex-Guard: Massacre charge isn't worth Tuppens

A FORMER Scots Guardsman who was serving in Malaya at the time of the alleged massacre at Batang Kali in 1948 today described the allegations · as "ridiculous" and said he was prepared to return to England to give evidence at any inquiry.

He is 43-year-old Cliff Wright, of Devonport in Northern Tasmania, who migrated to Australia 14 years ago after serving with the Scots Guards for 12 years in Italy and Malaya.

Testimony

"I was involved in the operation and it is ridiculous to describe it as a massacre," he said.

HOBART, Friday

"I am prepared to return to England and give evidence at any inquiry into the allegations."

Mr. Wright, who was born at Burton-On-Trent, was commenting on a London report by former Guardsman Allen Tuppen who claimed that at the age of 18, while a member of a Scots Guard platoon, he had been ordered to shoot Chinese terrorist suspects.

"After 12 years in the Guards I refuse to believe any Guards officer would issue such an order," Mr. Wright said.

"I think these people have made these allegations because of the recent publicity over the My Lai affair in Vietnam. Otherwise why wait 20 years to say these things"

Mr. Wright said he was a member of one of five Guard companies based in Batu Arang, in Selangor, in December 1948.

"I knew Tuppen slightly but he was with another company," he said.

The companies' task was to round up about 250 communist terrorists in the area.

Tipped off

"Repeatedly our ambushes failed because the terrorists had been warned. Even in our own base we uncovered cases of arms, ammunition and supplies.

"A village about 40 miles north of Batu Arang was used as supply base and recruiting area by the terrorists but we had never succeeded in surprising them until this operation when our Dyak scouts reported a big gathering at the village.

"I was a member of the right flank company and we heard shooting when the lead patrol surprised about 30 people who were being addressed by one of the most wanted terrorists.

"They scattered on sighting our patrol and did not stop when called them to do so. Most were shot by troops surrounding the village.

Arms, ammo

"We found communist literature, arms and ammunition on many of the bodies and the day's operation was one of the biggest kills during the whole of the emergency.

"I don't say there weren't any in the group who were neither terrorists nor sympathisers but there was a ban on public assemblies and the fact that one of the terrorists was lecturing them was too much to be a coincidence.

"In a situation where a 10-year-old child can be an intelligence agent and your own mates are being killed from ambush it's impossible to just stand up and say "everyone who is not terrorist leave the area"," Mr Wright said.—Reuter.

The sort of knee-jerk reaction from former Scots Guardsmen that has done the unit little credit over the years.

122

Chapter 8

Enter Scotland Yard

It would not have been difficult for Defence Secretary Denis Healey in the second week of February, 1970, to reach a quick decision on the best means of tackling the Batang Kali controversy. Any possibility of arguing that the matter had been fairly addressed in early 1949 was now out of the question.

Statements made by RSM Douglas, Sir Stafford Foster-Sutton and retired Colonel George Ramsay to *The People*, the BBC and other news outlets before the gag was applied had destroyed this option. In addition, no politician could dismiss the power of the affidavits that had formed the very foundations of *The People*'s coverage. Furthermore, there were the latest startling eyewitness reports from Malaysia – from the Malay former special constable, the lone survivor and the widows – that had all made front-page news in Britain.

But the dynamics of politics demanded a decent interval be observed between the Fleet Street frenzy and the formal announcement of what measures the government proposed to take. Moreover, there was ever-growing talk of mid-year general elections and consideration had to be given to the impact a Batang Kali decision might have on these.

The ensuing interim provided an additional forum for unsolicited opinions, particularly those from sources with Scots Guards connections.

Former Scots Guardsman, Cliff Wright, who was serving in Malaya at the time of the mass killing, provided the predictable ex-serviceman's reaction. He pronounced as 'ridiculous' allegations that guardsmen had been involved in a massacre. Speaking from his new home in Tasmania, Australia, the then 43 year-old Wright said: 'After 12 years in the Guards I refuse to believe any Guards officer would issue such an order.' He claimed his unit had been part of the same broad operation launched across Ulu Selangor in December, 1948, to flush out 250 communist terrorists.

'Repeatedly, our ambushes failed because the terrorists had been warned. Even in our own base we uncovered cases of arms, ammunition and supplies. A village about 40 miles north of Batu Arang was used as a supply base and recruiting area by the terrorists but we had never succeeded in surprising them until this operation when our Dyak Scouts reported a big gathering at the village. I was a member of the right flank company and we heard shooting when the lead patrol surprised about 30 people who were being addressed by one of the most wanted terrorists. They scattered on sighting our patrol and did not stop when called upon to do so. Most were shot by troops surrounding the village.'

Wright went on to claim that communist literature, arms and ammunition were discovered on many of the bodies and the day's operation was 'one of the biggest kills' during the whole of the Emergency – another observation with a familiar ring.

'I don't say there weren't any in the group who were neither terrorists nor sympathisers, but there was a ban on public assemblies and the fact that one of the terrorists was lecturing them was too much to be a coincidence. In a situation where a 10-year-old child can be an intelligence agent and your own mates are being killed from ambush, it's impossible to just stand up and say 'everyone who is not a terrorist leave the area',' Wright added.

His comments were first carried in Tasmanian newspapers and eventually published in *The Straits Times* on Saturday, February 7, 1970. They provide an interesting perspective on the unwritten military code that requires loyalty to one's unit irrespective of circumstances. Wright's claim of involvement in the same general operation that resulted in the deaths on Sungei Remok Estate was extremely tenuous. The action he went on to relate occurred several miles away and lacked any direct link to what was taking place on Menzies' plantation. But Wright's boast that the raid in which he had been a participant had resulted in an even bigger enemy death toll is significant. That there may well have been innocent, unarmed people slaughtered in this second action he justified on the grounds of perceived danger and, by inference, this justification was being offered for the Batang Kali action as well.

Two days after Wright's observations were published in Malaysia and Singapore, a letter from Scots Guards historian, David Erskine, was carried in *The Times*. It offered what appeared to be the authorised version of events. Erskine's letter and historical notations were marked by self-serving logic, very similar to that displayed by former front-line soldier Wright.

Erskine pointed out that his book, *The Scots Guards 1919-1955*, had, from the time of its initial publication in 1956, included an account of the Batang Kali incident. He then argued that in the 14 years since, nobody had ever challenged its accuracy. The historian referred to a section in his book detailing the 2nd Battalion's initial successes against communist forces in Malaya during the month of November, 1948. His book then conceded: 'It must be admitted that an incident in December which resulted in the death of 24 Chinese could not properly be claimed in the same category.'

Still quoting from his book, Erskine argued total justification of the Scots Guards action.

'A patrol from G Company under the command of a sergeant was guarding the men of a *kongsi* near the village of Batang Kali who were under strong suspicion of having supplied the bandits with food. Thinking their guard was easily to be evaded, the suspects made a dash for the jungle. Needless to say the guardsmen were on the alert and 24 of the men were shot down as they ran.

'The local press commented in strong and unfavourable terms on this incident for the expression 'shot while attempting to escape' has come to be looked upon with a certain cynicism.

'But in this case the expression was applicable and the action of the guardsmen legitimate. By their own folly, the suspected bandit helpers paid a far heavier price than they would have done had they been found guilty of the crime. The incident illustrates the sudden emergencies which can confront the most junior leader in this type of operation, and the weighty decisions he must take at the shortest notice.'

Erskine drew a further conclusion, again quoting from his book. 'It was many months before there was any further trouble around Batang Kali.'

The historian's volume is today listed on the Scots Guards website as a recommended historical reference book.

What makes his letter to *The Times* so extraordinary is that at the time of writing, virtually every aspect of the official military line on the massacre – a line strictly adhered to by Erskine's rendition of events – had been roundly and publicly shown to be false.

Erskine's tasteless dismissal of what he chose to term the victims' 'folly' is particularly disturbing. The suggestion that the dead had paid a far heavier price than they would have had they been found guilty of the crime becomes justification, on the presumption of guilt. But what if – as is now quite clear – the victims were not guilty of any crime at all and there has never been any evidence to suggest that they were? Indeed, there was and is irrefutable evidence to prove they were not.

His interpretation of history goes on to assert that the Scots Guards had so rattled communist resolve by their killing spree that many months passed before there was any further trouble around Batang Kali. This seeks justification on an assumption. The inference is that, as there was a positive result, the action was justified. Again, the argument – distasteful as it is – lacks any merit. Communist activity across the Ulu Selangor region remained strong throughout 1949. It fell off in other sectors of the country from April to September that year as rebel leaders, emboldened by Mao Tse Tung's victories over the Nationalists in China, prepared a stepped-up anti-colonial campaign. This was launched in October and, as declassified British military documents of the time reveal, in the months that followed, communist-inspired incidents rose sharply to reach over 500 a month Malaya-wide.

The pro-Scots Guards lobby also gained unexpected support from the intensely pro-British and anti-communist Malaysian Prime Minister of the time, Tunku Abdul Rahman. As Healey wrestled with the politics of the Batang Kali issue in early February that year, the Tunku called a press conference in Kuala Lumpur and complained: 'It is unfortunate that people are making such a big thing about something that happened 22 years ago.' Asked whether Malaysia should conduct its own inquiry into the killings, he replied: 'I do not think we should. I cannot see any reason why this incident was ever brought up.

'I do not see any connection between Batang Kali and what happened in Vietnam where occupants of an entire village are alleged to have been killed. During the days of the last Emergency people were rather excited in dealing with the communists or communist suspects,' the Malaysian Prime Minister added.

But when the subject of compensation was raised, the Tunku adjusted his position accordingly. 'It has got nothing to do with this government. But if the British government is considering compensation, I would be happy to lend a helping hand,' he said.

'Mind you,' he went on, 'the Japanese committed a lot of atrocities. They gave us $25 million and we decided to forget everything.'

The Tunku's statement would ultimately prove strongly detrimental to the interests of the surviving widows and familes of the Batang Kali victims. Theirs had been a pitiable struggle against poverty in the years following the mass killing. Newspaper accounts, dramatic as they were, had only scratched the surface of two decades of suffering. In the months ahead the Tunku's word would be interpreted as reassurance for London that, whatever transpired, at least the Malaysian authorities could be relied upon to cause no problems. But this would only become evident later.

As far as Healey was concerned, the Tunku's remarks fell on deaf ears. The Defence Secretary had been demonstrating to the House of Commons that no amount of pressure would deter his resolve to handle the Batang Kali issue expeditiously. Healey had a background that would, ultimately, compel him to examine Batang Kali from a fair, humanitarian standpoint. It was also a training that would enable him to withstand the immense pressures from military quarters all urging the matter be returned quietly to the dustbin of history.

As a schoolboy at Bradford Grammar, Healey was attracted to pacifism. So strongly did his youthful beliefs develop that in 1935 he withdrew from his school's Officer's Training Corps. A year later, at Balliol College, Oxford, he

Malaysian Prime Minister of the day, Tunku Abdul Rahman (above), signals that the events at Batang Kali, 21 years earlier, are of little concern to his government in early 1970. The Straits Times duly reports his views (right).

LE EXCEEDS 200,000

Na New

s Times

70 ★ 15 CENTS K.D.N. 4517 : M.C. (P)

'Forget Batang Kali' plea by Tengku

KUALA LUMPUR, Wednesday.

TENGKU Abdul Rahman said today it was "rather unfair" for anyone to dig up facts about the Batang Kali "massacre" in 1948.

"Let's face it," he told a press conference, "war is war. What about all the atrocities committed by the Japanese during the occupation?"

Asked about a suggestion by Dr. Tan Chee Khoon, secretary-general of the Gerakan Ra'ayat Malaysia, that the NOC should conduct an inquiry into the "massacre," the Tengku replied:

"I do not think we should. I cannot see any reason why this incident was ever brought up

"I do not see any connection between Batang Kali and what happened in Vietnam where occupants of an entire village are alleged to have been killed.

"During the days of the last Emergency people were rather excited in dealing with the communists or communist suspects."

'I CAN'T BELIEVE

Relatives

became involved in politics, dropped pacifism as an ideological approach to life, and enrolled as a member of the Communist Party. When World War 11 erupted, Healey joined the Royal Engineers, saw action in Africa, Sicily and Italy – and opted for yet another political direction. Rejecting communism, he joined the Labour Party and was initially defeated as its candidate for Pudsey and Otley in the 1945 General Elections. Seven years later he entered the House of Commons and by 1959 had become a Shadow Cabinet appointee in the Labour Opposition led by Hugh Gaitskell.

A passage from a speech made by Healey to the May, 1945, Labour Party Conference, provides an interesting insight into the basic motivations of a man who would develop into one of the most feisty, argumentative, arrogant yet acclaimed politicians of his day. 'The upper classes in every country,' Healey told his party colleagues, 'are selfish, depraved, dissolute and decadent. The struggle for socialism in Europe . . . has been hard, cruel, merciless and bloody. The penalty for participation in the liberation movement has been death for oneself, if caught, and, if not caught oneself, the burning of one's home and the death by torture of one's family . . . Remember that one of the prices paid for our survival during the last five years has been the death by bombardment of countless thousands of innocent European men and women.'

It is difficult to imagine how any man, prepared to stand by such sentiments in a renowned public forum at the outset of his political career, could ever brush aside allegations of the Batang Kali massacre that were daily being added to a file in his office. The massacre, it was claimed, had been perpetrated by troops from an elite British regiment against innocent, unarmed subsistence-level plantation workers. The victims' homes had been wilfully destroyed by fire and their destitute families abandoned. And it had all occurred in the name of a colonial war fought primarily to protect a debt-laden UK's most valuable source of foreign funds. The relationship between Healey's 1945 remarks and the decision facing him in February, 1970, was uncanny.

In the event, the Defence Secretary, now ensconced in Labour's right wing, functioned as quickly as he could within dictates of the required 'decent interval'. By late February he had submitted his file to Britain's DPP. It was, inevitably, a somewhat one-sided presentation. It came lacking anything substantive in support of the Army's 22 year-old stand on the matter. It contained no reference material on 1948-49 official inquiries – military or otherwise – because there had been none. Nor did it contain any paperwork on whatever manipulations had been undertaken by the colonial authorities at the time. The three-year document destruction provisions had guaranteed that. The War Office archives could produce nothing as the matter had never been formally referred to that ministry. Colonial Office records, on the other hand, could offer little more than *Hansard* reports to substantiate that this department had, indeed, been informed of – but had taken no action on – a controversial shooting of Chinese civilians at an unnamed plantation in Malaya on the morning of December 12, 1948.

With nothing in Healey's file even hinting at a counter to allegations appearing daily in the press, on radio and on television, the DPP had no option but to call in Scotland Yard and order a formal police investigation. Appointed to head this was Detective Chief Superintendent Frank Williams from the Flying Squad who, a few years earlier, had made his mark as one of the key investigators of Britain's August 8, 1963, Great Train Robbery. He had also figured in several other sensational gangland inquiries both before and after this landmark case. Williams was generally regarded by his peers as being among the country's top sleuths.

Brought in to assist him was Senior Detective Ron Dowling, whose choice on this occasion was highly significant. Prior to his police career he had himself been a guardsman. It was felt he could provide valuable background knowledge and guidance, as the probe got underway, on subjects like troop motivation, interpretation of orders and lines of command as these applied within elite units.

The initial task facing Williams and Dowling was one of locating as many former members of G Company, 2nd Battalion, Scots Guards (circa 1948-49) as possible with particular emphasis on those who had served in the company's 7 platoon. It was an arduous exercise as young de-mobbing national servicemen had, more often than not, moved to where civilian jobs became available. Many left no forwarding addresses. In addition, countries like Australia and Canada in those days had beckoned as migration havens.

The five 7 platoon guardsmen who had spoken to *The People* were quickly located, questioned and requested to sign further statements – this time formal police documents. All five complied. One by one other members of the platoon were tracked down along with several former guardsmen who had not been directly involved on the Sungei Remok plantation but had functioned with the follow-up unit that visited the estate on the morning after the killings.

As investigations gained momentum and locations of those wanted for questioning mounted, Williams and Dowling sent messages, via the police communications network, seeking the involvement of a number of county stations across the UK. Instructions were that those required for the inquiry should, if possible, make themselves available at Scotland Yard. In circumstances where this was impractical, the two investigators found themselves venturing out of London on lengthy forays.

Leader of Scotland Yard's Batang Kali investigation, Detective Chief Superintendent Frank Williams, a highly respected member of London's Flying Squad, whose credentials include prominent involvement in the 1963 Great Train Robbery inquiries.

For some ex-Scots Guards, instructions to attend questioning sessions sowed deep concerns and more than one turned up at an interview room accompanied by a lawyer. Eric Lazenby, formerly of Sheffield, who had nothing whatever to do with the shooting, still received his summons to attend Scotland Yard with understandable apprehension. He could never forget Batang Kali. He had been a member of the follow-up patrol that carried out reconnaissance duties on the plantation after the incident. On entering Scotland Yard he sought the sergeant whose name he had been given to contact. The sergeant signed Lazenby in and, noting his uneasiness, assured the visitor he had nothing to worry about. In the ensuing conversation, Lazenby learned that the sergeant himself had been in the Coldstream Guards.

As the weeks went by the question and answer sessions conducted by Williams and Dowling became longer and more intensive. When dealing with those they had firmly identified as participants in the shooting, both police officers began their interviews with virtually identical preliminary statements. 'As you know,' they would tell the interviewee, 'I have been appointed to investigate the alleged massacre at Batang Kali, Malaya, in December, 1948, where it is alleged that a patrol of the Scots Guards shot down 25 Chinese in cold blood. You, I understand, were a member of that patrol and I would like to ask you some questions about the incident. But before I start I must caution you.'

At this point Williams and Dowling would deliver a formal police caution. From then on it would be up to either officer to decide how best to initiate the probing. More often than not they would begin: 'Do you remember a briefing before the patrol went out?' This question was intended to establish whether or not orders given at the Scots Guards Kuala Kubu Bahru base headquarters, prior to the operation, had involved clear instructions to 'wipe out' all villagers on the targeted estate. The police were well aware that allegations to this effect had been made by one former guardsman on BBC's *World At One* programme and thereafter reported extensively by various national newspapers. What had made this allegation particularly disturbing was the suggestion that the 'wipe out' order had come from an officer.

As the two Scotland Yard men amassed documentation of their interviews, it became patently obvious that they were dealing with substantial corroboration of *The People's* original exposé. All five men who had spoken to the Sunday paper were standing firmly by their accounts. Other interviewees had information that only added more detail to revelations of an appalling episode.

In one sworn statement the following exchange appeared:

Question: Who gave the orders to fire next day when the Chinese were shot?

Answer: One of the sergeants gave the order. I shot into the ground. I remember this because someone said 'What are you trying to do – shoot me instead of them?'
Question: Were they running away?
Answer: 'No, they weren't running away.

Another sworn statement contained this admission by a former guardsman:

'I was in No 7 Platoon of G Company. Just before Christmas, 1948, No 7 Platoon set out on another mission into the jungle. We arrived at the village of Batang Kali. One of the sergeants said words to the effect 'They are going to be shot – you can fall in or fall out. Nobody fell out. I heard shots from the village and lots of shouting. Instinctively, we opened fire. I fired my .303 rifle at the people in the river and on the bank. There were about three or five of them and they all fell dead. Some in the water, some on the banks. One man was hit several times and the top of his head was virtually blown off. After that the huts were burned. The village was empty, quiet. I have often thought of this incident with regrets. As I got older I realised how unnecessary it all was. How wrong it all was. If I was to find myself in these circumstances today I would have fallen out when given the option by the sergeant. The villagers were unarmed. I shot these people while acting under orders. So did my mates.'

———

Two months into the investigation it was clear to both Williams and Dowling that a trip to Malaysia was essential to the final outcome of their work. Interviews had to be conducted with local eyewitnesses and surviving kin. Exhumations and forensic testing on the victims' remains were imperative. At least one Malayan Special Branch officer had accompanied 7 platoon onto the estate and had become intricately involved in activities undertaken there. The Chinese detective was known to be still working with the revamped Malaysian Special Branch. Nothing had been heard from him. He needed to be questioned.

Plans were finalised for both Williams and Dowling to fly to Kuala Lumpur and from there to make their way north to the Batang Kali area. It was just a matter of first wrapping up their work in Britain. This would take another month or two, at most. By their reckoning, they could be in place in Malaysia by late June or early July. The two detectives had, at this point, come to an important decision on *modus operandi*. Not before and not until the Batang Kali end of their investigations was completed would they be ready to interview the leaders of the 7 platoon patrol. This decision said much about the effect evidence gathered thus far was having on the professional approach the two investigators were adopting.

Meanwhile, *The People's* disclosures of the massacre were proving acutely embarrassing to Prime Minister Harold Wilson and his government. Left wing radicalism abhorred imperialism and anything associated with the perceived injustices of the now dissolved British Empire. It could never be erased or forgotten that the Malayan Emergency had erupted, in the first place, during the stewardship of post-war Labour leader Clement Attlee. The slaughter at Batang Kali had occurred within the tenure of his socialist government. Such historical facts were the last matters the Wilson government of 1970 wanted raised with the British public as political parties prepared their General Election campaigns for national polls that would be decided on June 18.

In the final stages of the campaigning, Dowling, a quietly-spoken, reflective policeman, began harbouring serious doubts over what impact a possible change in Britain's government might have on the critical final stage of Scotland Yard's Batang Kali investigation. Dowling was personally convinced at this point that, given the facts already gathered, he and Williams could arrive at rock-solid conclusions once their mission to Malaysia was completed. There was not the slightest doubt in his mind about this and years later he would say so publicly.

With polling only days away, Dowling's concerns intensified. He became all but convinced that a win by the Conservative Party would bring down the shutters on the now three-and-a-half-month-old police inquiry. Outwardly, Williams did not share his partner's pessimism, perhaps confident of Labour retaining power. But this was not to be.

The eventual Conservative victory came on an unusually low voter turn-out.

The next morning, Dowling entered his Scotland Yard office early to await the arrival of his colleague. At the first opportunity he approached Williams and quietly asked: 'Frank, did you see the election result?'

Dowling would later recall that Williams replied: 'Yes. It makes no difference to us. We're going.' But as Dowling would also later recount – they didn't.

A week or two on, Williams received a call from the DPP's office. He was asked to submit a full report on the investigation's findings thus far. The telephone conversation settled any uncertainties. That would be the end of Scotland Yard's involvement. Case closed.

Both investigators were deeply disappointed men. Later in life, Dowling would remember this episode as a 'rude awakening, really'. It had come as a jolting reminder of the frequently unsavoury realities of politics.

On July 9, exactly three weeks after the elections, Marcus Lipton took the opportunity of question time in the House of Commons to raise the Batang Kali issue again. He asked why the newly installed Conservative Attorney General, Sir Peter Rawlinson, had decided against further investigations of the alleged 1948 massacre.

In replying, Rawlinson said: 'After considering the result of the police inquiries in this country, the Director of Public Prosecutions is satisfied that there is no reasonable likelihood of obtaining sufficient evidence to warrant criminal proceedings. He therefore decided not to ask police to continue the inquiry. I agree with his decision.'

Far from satisfied with this response, Lipton rose to his feet and again addressed the Attorney General. 'Does the Attorney General nevertheless agree,' he asked, 'that, in view of sworn statements by four ex-guardsmen claiming to be present at the scene, which were published in *The People*, it is necessary to have the inquiry even though after all these years it is generally accepted that it is impossible to collect sufficient evidence for a prosecution?'

Lipton had introduced a most relevant observation and one that had been overlooked entirely since the time of the killings. What parameters did officialdom assign to determine the validity and basis of inquiries into alleged atrocities? These considerations are, of course, as relevant today as they were when Lipton suggested them in his parliamentary question.

Rawlinson, as it happened, had no wish to pursue the matter and made that plain to the House. 'All I would like to repeat to the House, and to the honourable Gentleman, is my agreement with the Director of Public Prosecutions.'

Sensing that the Labour opposition might be manoeuvring for a showdown on the issue, a Conservative parliamentarian asked: 'Is the right honourable Gentleman aware that the previous Administration strongly took the view that once allegations of this sort had been made it was right and proper that a full investigation should be conducted into them by the Director of Public Prosecutions?'

His question then dovetailed into an equally structured pronouncement: 'That investigation having been conducted and the Director having come to the conclusion which he reached, I trust that the House and the country will accept that a full investigation has been made.'

Rawlinson responded appreciatively: 'I understand the point of view expressed by the honourable Gentleman and I am sure that he is correct in the last point he makes.'

The 'last point' was that both the House and country should accept that a 'full investigation' had been made this time in Britain. This, of course, was not

Britain's June, 1970, national elections. Conservative Party leader, Edward Heath, is an early voter at a polling station in Great Windmill Street, Westminster, London.

Prominent in Prime Minister Heath's Conservative Cabinet is the 50 year-old Attorney General, Sir Peter Rawlinson.

only misleading; it was total deception. The Scotland Yard investigation had been aborted before completion; hardly a full investigation and the Yard had made that very clear. The Attorney General certainly knew this.

The son of a military family, Rawlinson was a former guardsman himself, having joined the Irish Guards in 1940 at the age of 21. He demobilised from that unit in 1946 with the rank of major. Shortly before leaving the Army he was called to the bar at Inner Temple and by 1959 had become a Queen's Counsel. After failing to win the Labour stronghold of Hackney South in 1951, he secured the safe Tory seat of Epsom four years later with a majority of 22,000. He was Solicitor General from 1962-65 and by the time he was appointed Attorney General in 1970 had become regarded as the 'golden boy' of Conservative politics. There was even behind-scenes talk in Westminster that Rawlinson might one day become Britain's first Catholic Tory prime minister. It was not to be as strained relations with Margaret Thatcher would eventually determine.

Rawlinson had woefully misled the House on the Batang Kali issue. He had done so in much the same way as Colonial Secretary Creech Jones had undertaken on January 26, 1949. Major General Boucher and Chief Secretary Newboult had similarly misled and deceived public opinion during their various Kuala Lumpur press pronouncements in the immediate aftermath of the killings.

In an effort to establish the precise means by which Rawlinson and the DPP had agreed to handle the Batang Kali issue, the co-authors of this book made applications under the UK's Freedom of Information Act (FOIA). The first of these was dispatched on July 2, 2007, and was answered by an officer of the Information Commissioner's Office 17 days later.

'I can confirm that advice was given by the DPP to the Attorney General on this matter,' explained the FOIA officer. 'However, this information is exempt from disclosure as it falls under the exemption detailed in the attached Section 17 notice'.

The Section 17 attachment read:

'Section 27 – International Relations – The exemption under Section 27 exists to protect the United Kingdom's international relations, its interests abroad and the UK's ability to promote and protect those interests. Whilst we acknowledge that there is legitimate public interest in disclosure, the information held by the CPS remains sensitive. Disclosure is likely to have a detrimental effect on the UK's international relations with Malaysia and China, prejudicing the UK's ability to conduct business with those states, and further, could potentially damage the UK's ability to defend its interests abroad. I therefore consider that the public interest in protecting the relationship with Malaysia and China, together with the clear public interest in protecting UK interests in these states, outweighs the public interest in disclosing the information into the public domain.'

This decision was immediately appealed under the provisions for such action. Notification dispatched to the Freedom of Information Unit (Appeals) was dated July 20, 2007. It argued strongly for a re-assessment of our original application. Pointing out that the FOIA response had flatly referred to the December 12, 1948 incident on Sungei Remok Estate as 'the Batang Kali massacre', we maintained that far more was at stake than mere 'public interest'.

'At the same time the argument that by refusing to release such information, your office is protecting the United Kingdom's international relations, in particular those with Malaysia and China, is spurious in the extreme.' Our appeal letter continued: 'It would, in fact, be infinitely more prejudicial to British international interests if it could be shown that failure to disclose 'sensitive' material, in this case, was actively assisting in the cover-up of a monumental miscarriage of justice and thereby preventing those directly affected from receiving fair, reasonable and just compensation from the British authorities.'

On August 3, 2007, we received notification from the Deputy Director and Senior Legal Adviser at the Information Commissioner's Office, Wilmslow, Cheshire, indicating he had, in view of our appeal, re-considered whether the information we sought should be released. He had decided it should. This information provided telling insights into the Westminister machinations undertaken in June/July, 1970, to ensure continuing concealment of the Batang Kali truth.

With such intense public interest having been aroused by the issue, it had generally been assumed that the DPP had submitted a formal written advisory of his Batang Kali findings to Attorney General Rawlinson. This was certainly not the case, as the FOIA release revealed.

The DPP's decision referred to in Parliament by the Attorney General came about as a result of a mere verbal exchange between the two men. This had taken place on June 25 – two weeks prior to Rawlinson's announcement in the House that the Scotland Yard investigation had been abandoned. The official file contains no record of the meeting beyond stating that it took place and that no further action was agreed.

The FOIA response clarified one very important point. 'The Director did not send a written submission to the Attorney-General prior to that meeting advising that there was insufficient evidence and that the inquiry should not be continued, though the file does record that that was the course agreed,' said the FOIA reply. It added: 'Subsequent to the meeting the Director did write to the Ministry of Defence giving an explanation of his decision.'

In this letter to the Ministry, the Director indicated that police inquiries in respect of the witnesses in the UK had been completed.

'He expressed the opinion that there was a substantial conflict among the soldiers who were present in Batang Kali; some confirmed the allegations and others denied that anything of the sort had occurred.'

The FOIA Deputy Director further paraphrased the DPP's communication with the Ministry of Defence. 'He went on to point out that the statements of those who supported the allegations had to be viewed with reserve as those men had made statements to the civil inquiry held in Malaya in 1948, and, without exception, they had maintained that the villagers had been shot while trying to escape.

'An alleged survivor, who now claimed to have been an eye-witness to the shooting, had also made a contradictory statement in 1948 in which he had said he had not seen what occurred. Further, neither of the two police officers who had accompanied the patrol had witnessed the shootings.

'The Director concluded that, taking those matters into consideration together with the fact that the incidents took place over twenty-one years ago, the institution of criminal proceedings would not be justified on the evidence obtained. He continued that he considered the prospects of any sufficient additional evidence being obtained through further investigation in Malaysia were so remote that it would not be warranted and therefore he did not propose to ask the police to pursue the inquiry.'

Examination of the DPP's communication with the Ministry of Defence, in this instance, reveals very clearly how the Batang Kali cover-up was maintained at this stage.

It was, for instance, well recognised in senior Scotland Yard circles that the two men in charge of investigations – Williams and Dowling – were of the firm opinion that additional inquiries on their part in Malaysia were essential to the completion of their work. They had written as much in reports to their superiors and arrangements were in an advanced stage for their intended flight to Kuala Lumpur. Any approach to Scotland Yard by the DPP, no matter how perfunctory, would have instantly revealed this quite critical police appraisal of investigations thus far and the requirements going forward.

The DPP and Rawlinson unquestionably knew this. If they didn't, they had simply made no approaches whatever to Williams, Dowling or Scotland Yard's heirarchy. Instead, they schemed to base their decision for halting investigations on the argument that, as there had been a conflict of opinion among the soldiers involved, there was little chance of achieving criminal proceedings from events that had occurred so many years earlier. This was, of course, an unsustainable position.

The two Scotland Yard investigators were well aware of the reasons for the conflict of opinions. If a massacre had indeed taken place, it would be most unlikely, given the possible repercussions, that 14 men involved would all be prepared to incriminate themselves. It was this very conflict of evidence that, from the police viewpoint, made investigations on the spot in Malaysia so necessary.

The DPP/Rawlinson position that the soldiers had all told a 1948 civil inquiry the victims had been shot while trying to escape was nothing short of unsustainable. It had been well explained by Fleet Street, radio and television how all patrol members, immediately after the killings, had been schooled what to say.

Furthermore, former Malaya Attorney General Foster-Sutton had – before being gagged – publicly proclaimed he had never held the much vaunted formal inquiry anyway. He had asked a few questions, quickly made up his mind and even felt it unnecessary to inform the War Office of his conclusions. To make matters worse, Foster-Sutton had initially justified the Scots Guards action as legitimate in the face of a mass escape attempt. Now, he was drastically changing that assessment and maintaining the killings had, in fact, been a 'bona-fide mistake' – legally a most damning switch of opinions. To place any reliance on Foster-Sutton's role was, as far as Rawlinson and the DPP were concerned, devoid of any merit.

So, too, was the added suggestion that as sole survivor, Chong Fong, had made a contradictory statement in 1948, his testimony was unacceptable. Chong Fong had not made a contradictory statement in 1948, although it would take another set of investigations 23 years later, to establish this fact.

On July 10, 1970 – exactly two weeks after the DPP/Rawlinson meeting and a day after the Attorney General's statement in the House – Detective Chief Superintendent Frank Williams signed a substantial police submission on his Batang Kali investigations. Headed 'Statement of Frank Williams', it was type written on Central Office, New Scotland Yard report stationery. It began:

'This statement, consisting of 27 pages, each signed by me, is true to the best of my knowledge and belief and I make it knowing that if it is tendered in evidence I shall be liable to prosecution if I have wilfully stated in it anything which I know to be false or do not believe to be true.'

There was little likelihood that Frank Williams' file would ever be tendered anywhere and the senior police officer knew it. Almost certainly, neither the DPP nor Rawlinson saw any reason to browse through its contents.

Our applications to view this file under the FOIA provisions have been resolutely refused.

The second man in Scotland Yard's 1970 Batang Kali investigations is Senior Detective Ron Dowling, a former guardsman.

Chapter 9

A television commentary

In 1992, a number of the Batang Kali victims' kin had another opportunity to be heard, this time through a television documentary produced by the BBC. The programme, aired as part of an ongoing BBC series called '*Inside Story*', was appropriately entitled '*In Cold Blood*'. This would be 22 years after a general election and new political appointments in Britain aborted the 1970 New Scotland Yard investigations.

It is understandable that the relatives would be buoyed, albeit briefly, by the BBC film. This was television, a medium that had gained inroads in the homes of even the unlettered. They were being interviewed in their language by one of their own. The presence of three former Scots Guards who asked them questions through an interpreter somehow contributed additional substance to the whole proceedings. The assurance of accompanying subtitles made the villagers believe people in Britain might start paying attention to their decades-old plight.

The years had not made the townsfolk of Ulu Yam Bahru any more worldly-wise and sophisticated than their predecessors had been. They were as simple and naïve, a people who, by and large, only wanted to be left alone so they may have more time to eke out a living. They took the visit of the three former soldiers as an indication that, perhaps, Britain would be moved to acknowledge a 'blood debt' and amends would be made.

'I am bitter that's why I sound very angry,' the widow of the man whose head was nearly severed in the shooting would tell the three visiting former guardsmen. 'Everything burnt,' she continued in a hurt, scolding tone, 'nothing to eat, nothing to wear, nowhere to live.'

Retired Senior Detective Ron Dowling who had assisted Chief Superintendent Frank Williams more than 20 years earlier, cooperated with the BBC effort. He talked about his personal interest in the case and his eventual disappointment. Dowling pointed out that, as a former guardsman, it was only natural that he should be drawn to the examination of the episode and the analyses of the facts gathered. He felt it was just right to look into the matter of men being 'accused of something, perhaps, they didn't do'.

Further, Dowling expressed his frustration when the investigations were dropped. He had looked forward to the Malaysia trip but, unlike Williams, had nursed reservations about the matter being pursued and concluded if Harold Wilson lost and Edward Heath won.

Dowling's presentiments were justified. A new Attorney General, Sir Peter Rawlinson, would dash all the carefully plotted moves that might have resulted in the Batang Kali case being satisfactorily closed. Ruefully, Dowling would tell the BBC: 'We could have got at the truth'.

The BBC statement was stunningly clear: 'The charge was of wanton murder'.

In Cold Blood was aired in London on September 9, 1992. It would be addressing two generations of viewers – the old who needed reminding and the young who had to be told. It would make both sit up and ask questions.

⌘

The format of *In Cold Blood* was simple but it generated complex ramifications. Three former Scots Guards who had been members of G Company, 2nd Battalion at the time, but were not raid participants, were flown to Malaysia. There, they were introduced to the kin of the men their colleagues were accused of having shot in cold blood. Interpreters were employed and open, frank discussions were encouraged.

Harry Fuller, Don Houlston and Eric Lazenby were bound by tradition forged by remembrances of the pomp and rituals staged 'for King and country'. Prior to their departure from the UK, they were filmed getting reunited in a pub and toasting each other's health. The documentary included clips of a TV broadcast featuring Scots Guards in full ceremonial uniform. These were accompanied by rousing martial music and a voice-over, heaping the usual praises – 'embodiment of regimental soul', 'symbol of past glories' and 'reminder of fine tradition'. Fuller, Houlston and Lazenby sat on a sofa in London, ostensibly watching and listening to all that.

Understandably, the three felt strongly about their old regiment's integrity. They were aware that the upcoming trip to Malaysia was not a simple excursion to an exotic, tropical country. They had been in its 'thickest, deadliest' jungles once, fighting for a cause that had never been clearly defined for them. They were going back, unsure of the demons the journey would raise. After four decades, a section of their old regiment still stood accused of the mindless killing of 24 unarmed plantation workers. Somehow, having been Scots Guards once, the three felt part of the unresolved case and therefore felt uncomfortable by association.

Fuller was a professional soldier when he was dispatched to Malaya in 1948.

He had volunteered with the Guards at 17 and, at 19, was one of the youngest sergeants in the unit. He stayed in the service for six years. This stint would leave a distinct mark on his view of conflicts and history, especially of the time he served in Malaya. Filmed packing for the trip to Batang Kali, he recalled 7 platoon being split into two sections, the one dispatched to Batang Kali led by a sergeant and a lance sergeant. He remembered meeting this group after the incident: 'They were very happy'. Thus, he got the impression of success and elation. Fuller appeared pretty determined to retain the unsullied view he had of his peers' conduct during the Malayan Emergency campaign.

Houlston and Lazenby, on the other hand, were 18 year-old conscripts when they left their meagre but comfortable working class lives in post-war England. All Houlston knew – 'our impression' – was that he was being sent to this far-flung outpost to help stamp out the 'big bad world of communism'. He would add: 'That took a bit of stamping, that's for sure.' All these years, Houlston had accepted the official line on the Batang Kali episode – it was a successful operation, a feather in the British cap. But he was less adamant than Fuller. He declared not really knowing what had truly transpired on the rubber estate. He had taken at face value what the rest of them were told.

Even less assertive of the righteousness of their regiment's raid was Eric Lazenby. He was a youthful greengrocer in Sheffield when he was conscripted to help safeguard the interests of Britain in the east. Lazenby would tell his interviewers that they had been a 'very naïve 18'. He thought they had been 'much too young' … Like Houlston, he believed what he was told – the platoon 'had done a good job'.

―――

To bolster the fact of the trio's tender age and inexperience at the time, early photographs were shown. This is where nostalgia was used in a bid to balance the gory episode and the reputation of the regiment responsible for the torment. Fresh-faced youths were featured going through their drills and being told about the requirement for following orders without question. These boys would later be seen in train stations or leaving on boats, their mothers waving good-bye. It is difficult to withhold degrees of sympathy and trepidation for these young men who were being packed off to fight a jungle war whose primary objective was to safeguard the flow of British wealth out of its richest colony.

They should have had more training, Lazenby would lament in the telecast; they should have been told what they were doing. As it was, he pondered, they 'just blundered on'.

The film portrayed effectively the dichotomy in the attitudes of the three ex-Scots Guardsmen. Pursuing his obvious and understandable bias towards the honour of his regiment, Fuller, sharing a meal with Houlston and Lazenby, did not hold back. Of the people at Batang Kali, he stated flatly: 'They were our enemies, weren't they? It amounted to that. Ninety five per cent of the terrorists were Chinese. I've always felt that. Nothing has changed my mind ever since.'

His somewhat aggressive approach was in stark contrast to the quiet, tentative demeanour of his travelling companions. Houlston and Lazenby avoided his eyes and turned their attention to the prawns they were eating with their hands.

There was a cogent reason behind Houlston's and Lazenby's ambivalent views towards Batang Kali. The two former 'virgin soldiers' had been members of the reconnaissance party dispatched to the killing scene after the incident. What they saw would haunt them forever. On screen, both men appeared to check back a well of emotions when asked to describe what had confronted them in the village. Their descriptions were to the point, succinctly telling.

Houlston described it as 'appalling', a scene he would never forget. The picture, he claimed, would stay with him 'till the end of my days, anyway'.

Lazenby summed it up by declaring, 'Weren't pretty.'

—*·∾·*—

The meal scene featured called to mind what Fuller had told an interviewer (out of camera range) earlier in the piece. The former Scots Guardsman was staunch in his belief that the villagers were assisting the communists, providing them with food. He based this on the premise that, after all, 'there were no food shops for miles around'. What if they didn't, he was pressed. Fuller's reply: 'Then the terrorists would terrorise them, as simple as that.' On another occasion, Fuller declared that 'these people were communists, one way or the other'. He was not requested to elaborate on this outlandish pronouncement.

Houlston went to Malaysia with his uneasy memories of Batang Kali. Setting out, he said: 'It would surprise me if they were all just lined up and shot in cold blood . . . ah . . . running away, yes, but I cannot see them just being lined up and shot down in cold blood myself.'

Eric Lazenby was more direct: 'What happened there I don't know yet.' He added, "I would want to know."

The relatives of the Batang Kali dead would oblige.

—*·∾·*—

Five interviewees told on camera what they went through on the weekend of December 11-12, 1948. Young TV viewers in Britain heard, for the first time, the unresolved story of how a section of 7 Platoon, 2nd Battalion, Scots Guards, had gone searching for 'enemy bandits'. Their outing left 24 men dead and a village gutted. One day, the women were going about their mundane tasks; the next, they were widows. One day, the children were playing; the next they were homeless orphans.

In her direct, unabashed manner, 74 year-old Foo Moi summed up how the dark, horrific weekend began: 'I was cooking a pot of rice and then suddenly there were soldiers surrounding me.'

These men would likewise gather around her eldest child Wong Mook Sang. One of them would point a gun to his chest while asking him questions about the communists. The then 10 year old boy would reply he did not know.

'I did not know what communists were,' Mook Sang, now in his fifties, told the BBC. In a later scene, he repeated this memory while he stood by the bank of the stream where his father had been felled by Scots Guards bullets.

Fuller would then inquire whether Mook Sang could remember which soldier intimidated him. Mother and son would be incredulous at this question. Mook Sang stepped back, frustratingly amused. How could he remember exactly who it was? He was a small boy! His mother agreed.

But Foo Moi's memories were vivid. She would sound consistently adamant about her recollections. She would mimic the sound of gunfire. For the benefit of the three ex-Scots Guards, she would raise her trouser legs and wade across the shallow watercourse and point out where the bodies had fallen. She told them the exact spot where she found her husband's body.

The grotesque scene at Sungei Remok Estate that confronted them as 18-year-old national servicemen must have returned more sharply to Houlston and Lazenby. Unlike Fuller who appeared willing to interrogate the villagers, the other two gave the impression they wanted to know *from the villagers themselves* more about what had transpired. Houlston and Lazenby were there to learn more – after all, they had heard *their* side and lived with it for more than 40 years!

So they listened to 61 year-old Tham Yong who had lost her fiancé in the raid. She would end up marrying his brother, the incident's lone survivor. The trauma of that December weekend still reduced her to tears. She recalled the repeated questions of the interrogators and her helplessness in the face of it all. She spoke of how she cried and how she was ordered to stop crying. But what could she do, Tham Yong had pleaded with her tormentor. So many times she had insisted she was unable to give them the information they were expecting. But they kept hounding her. To the BBC, Tham Yong claimed to have told the soldiers that even if they killed her, she couldn't satisfy their demand – she simply had nothing to tell. She also recounted how the soldiers had isolated a young man from the group, called him a 'bad man', ordered him to walk some distance until 'there by the woodpile' he was told to stand straight. The man did as he was commanded and 'then he was shot'.

⤙∿∿⤚

Batang Kali's earliest fatality was Loh Kit Lin, Wong Yen's brother-in-law. The BBC tracked Wong Yen down in Kuantan, East Malaysia. She was 79 by this time, and blind. She supplied startling images recalling the afternoon preceding the mass killing. She spoke of another man the Scots Guards had taken aside and interrogated. The plantation worker had been isolated for questioning and was obviously terrorised. The rest of the villagers heard gunshots and surmised he had been killed.

'His ancestors must have saved him,' Wong Yen conjectured. For the man was carried back to his wailing wife and children. He appeared drained and crippled by the trauma. Wong Yen said 'his eyes turned white'.

That was just the beginning. Wong Yen then recalled how the platoon had zeroed in on her brother-in-law. Kit Lin had been looking after her and her children since her husband abandoned his family for a younger woman and moved out of Sungei Remok.

A Cantonese man who had arrived with the Scots Guards – research would confirm he was a Special Branch detective – demanded Kit Lin identify himself. Given the answer, he barked back, 'You're dead!'

The threat was carried out. Wong Yen spoke of how the body lay where it had fallen, a dog pulling at its leg.

The interview with this old blind woman would add another significant dimension to *In Cold Blood*. Wong Yen talked about the inevitable things that happen when war is waged – 'wounding and killing'. She maintained how both sides could be cruel. She asserted that the one who suffers most in wartime is 'the ordinary working man'. She expressed the hope that nobody would declare war again.

But of Batang Kali, she was definite. 'In my opinion,' she stated, 'it was an

Seventy-nine year old Wong Yen, sister-in-law of Loh Kit Lin, the first plantation worker, to be killed by the Scots Guards patrol.

Loh Kit Lin's gravestone in the Ulu Yam Bahru cemetery.

atrocity. No questions asked, no investigations. It was a cruel slaughter.'

She asked her BBC interviewers: 'Do my words offend you?' Her parting shot: 'You can think about it.'

The doubting Harry Fuller would meet his match in Lee Wah Sang, now 56, who had been among the listless, terrified children locked with their mothers in the plantation *kongsi*. Unlike the rest, Lee would speak beyond the subject of the appalling predicament inflicted on the village. He pursued the subject of justice.

He was scared then, he would tell Fuller, Houlston and Lazenby through the interpreter. But now he was very angry.

What was upsetting him?

His answer: He was very angry because the people 'died in a pitiful way'. Because what the Scots Guards did was 'not justified'.

Rather condescendingly, Fuller took pains to talk about the Emergency and how different laws applied at the time.

Lee was unrelenting. If the men were not running, was the shooting illegal?

There was a bit of to-ing and fro-ing at this point. The ex-Scots Guards talked about why something like Batang Kali could not have happened in England and how the Malayan Emergency was such a different case where specific laws applied.

Lee was adamant. Of course, everyone knew that if people ran, they could be shot. That was accepted. That would be legal. But, could they tell him, if the men were not running, would the incident then be illegal?

Lazenby put in his quiet contribution. It would have been illegal, he conceded, but he couldn't understand why they were shot if they were not running away.

Lee kept up the attack. If they were not running away, is it illegal?

Yes.

He delivered the *coup de grace*. 'If they were not running and they were shot, it is illegal. Therefore it was a massacre.'

The declaration earned its desired visceral effect.

The 24 men were not running away. This fact had long been corroborated by testimonies that made newspaper headlines both in Britain and Malaysia in 1970. The BBC film used these materials. The Malay guide who had accompanied the troops to the estate was now dead. An actor read Inche Jaffar's account of how the patrol leader had ordered him to look away moments before the shooting began and how he would be thrown in gaol if he ever talked about the incident.

For the BBC film, lone survivor Chong Fong, by now 67, repeated what he had told *The Straits Times* in 1970. It *was* a massacre. At gunpoint, he and his fellow workers were ordered to walk towards the stream. Then there were gunshots. No, no, nobody was running away.

'The spirits must have pushed me,' he told the BBC. He did not know what happened; he just fell. When he came to, everything was quiet. There were dead bodies about. He gave the scene one quick glance and that was when he ran, 'scared'.

<hr />

Ron Dowling pointed to 'a rude awakening' when the New Scotland Yard's investigations into the Batang Kali incident were halted unceremoniously. He expressed misgivings: 'We could have got at the truth'.

Part of the truth was already contained in the material he and Frank Williams had meticulously gathered. They had listened to former Scots Guards who had featured in the raid. *Inside Story* included these statements in the programme. These segments were read by actors.

The men were not trying to escape. They were not running. They were shot 'in cold blood'.

A former Scots Guardsman spoke of having regrets as he grew older – he had shot men in circumstances he was finding difficult to reconcile. He was filled with remorse at the memory of having killed unarmed men – 'it was unnecessary; how wrong it all was'.

He remembered the gruesome scene of men falling, 'some on the bank, some in the water'; of 'a man shot several times his head was nearly blown off'. His statement spoke of a village being torched and then left 'empty, quiet'.

The ex-soldier was now convinced that if his life could be repeated, he would alter his behaviour at Batang Kali. Members of 7 Platoon G Company had been told by the sergeant that the villagers were to be shot. Patrol members could 'fall in' or 'fall out' as they wished. He should have 'fallen out'.

Reacting to this, Lazenby said he felt sorry for the soldiers who had 'to live with it'. His empathy was based on the thought that 'it could have been me'. He went further and argued the men had been conscripted: 'If we were told to shoot, we shoot.'

The man who allegedly ordered the youthful patrolmen to shoot was 22 year-old Sgt. Charles Douglas. At the time of the BBC production, he was living in retirement in Edinburgh. Obviously, the horror of Batang Kali had not dented his military career. He would not speak of the incident and referred all questions posed to him to the Ministry of Defence who, in turn, refused comment.

Fuller, Houlston and Lazenby shook hands with Foo Moi. Earlier they had watched her burn joss sticks, a tribute to the husband she lost at the same spot by the stream. She talked of hopes that the British Government would acknowledge the plight they had endured for so many years.

It was an awkward moment for the ex-Scots Guards. They stood waiting as the widow gave vent to the anger that had festered over the years spent struggling with children left with nothing. When his turn came to say farewell, Eric Lazenby muttered a few words of personal apology.

This all took place in 1992. By then, Sungei Remok was no longer a rubber plantation. Oil palms had taken over what used to be Tom Menzies' landholding. It had been 44 years since the 7 Platoon raid.

British bureaucracy had thus far succeeded in avoiding responsibility for nearly half a century.

Chapter 10

The Malaysian end

Like the stench of death with which it was so closely linked, the Batang Kali issue, much to the annoyance of those who wanted it obliterated, refused to go away. The televising of the BBC's *In Cold Blood* documentary in the UK in September, 1992 and the programme's subsequent presentation in Malaysia, revived all the old suspicions that Britain was continuing to hide an appalling massacre.

In the wake of reignited Malaysian public interest, a group of Chinese political operatives in Kuala Lumpur now saw the 44 year-old mass killing by the Scots Guards as a golden opportunity for party machinations. Its members were clearly oblivious of the issue's historical complexities. What was more, those behind the politicising failed to consider fully the extent to which the Malay-dominated administration in Malaysia would ultimately view the idea of re-addressing such a sensitive, Chinese-focused event.

Still, by end 1992, the Malaysian Chinese Association (MCA), a component party of the ruling National Front coalition government, led by the United Malays National Organisation (UMNO), had staked its reputation behind a drive to gain formal recognition of the killing as a massacre and an accepted fact of history. MCA leaders coordinated a campaign to secure long overdue compensation for surviving family members of victims. Vocal support from opposition parties soon followed.

Unexpected advice from the then serving Malaysian Inspector General of Police (IGP) Haniff Omar only added to the momentum of the MCA agenda. The police chief went on record as saying that in matters 'pertaining to murder' there was no time-frame for lodging police reports. He further gave assurances that should such reports be submitted on the Batang Kali affair, his force would undertake full and thorough investigations.

On the morning of July 14, 1993, Chong Fong, together with two female eyewitnesses, his wife Tham Yong and Foo Moi, who had both featured with the massacre's lone survivor in the *In Cold Blood* TV programme, arrived at the Batang Kali police station. They were accompanied by a phalanx of local reporters and photographers. The occasion had been carefully orchestrated by MCA officials for maximum publicity. One by one the trio submitted formal affidavits of their experiences. The preparation of all three documents had been closely supervised by the political party's legal advisers. Chong Fong signed his submission in halting

Former Malaysian Inspector General of Police, Haniff Omar.

Chinese characters. The two women were only able to affix thumb-prints to their respective testimonies.

Duty police officers allotted report no 1149/93 to Chong Fong's signed statement, 1150/93 to Foo Moi's and 1151/93 to the submission from Tham Yong.

Two days later, a 12-man police Task Force headed by Superintendent Khew Ching Hoi, then chief of the nation's serious crimes investigations department, was established to examine claims being made by the three former residents of Sungei Remok. Wasting no time, Task Force members later that same day drove Chong Fong to the scene of the massacre and took him, step by step, through the various episodes that had culminated in such a tragic climax. With the assistance of the lone survivor, one of the investigators drew a sketch plan of the estate's former *kongsi* compound and the structures that had once stood there. All that remained of these were concrete and brick foundation points together with remnants of a few scattered wooden stumps.

Despite the passage of years, Chong Fong's memory proved surprisingly vivid. As the sketching progressed, he was able to supply graphic details of the three *kongsi* houses and the positions they had occupied within the clearing. In the company of a police photographer, he once more trudged the plantation pathway still leading to the banks of the stream and the spot where the shooting had begun. With each flash of recall he would summon the photographer, or another escorting officer, to elaborate on a mound of earth, a tree-line, a mid-stream boulder or a position on the far bank of the fast flowing water. He pointed out a lone smokehouse standing on what had been the old clearing perimeter. This, he insisted, had definitely not been there in his day. Chong Fong looked somewhat disparagingly at the rows of oil palms that now covered the estate and had all but eliminated the old compound area. To a former rubber tapper the switch to oil palm cultivation that had taken place in the intervening years seemed a regrettable step.

With light fading, the police party drove the lone survivor home and arranged to meet him the following day at Ulu Yam Bahru Police Station. They then intended to launch into an intensive examination of the police report Chong Fong had lodged two days earlier.

Investigators were calculating that their assessment of the man's value as a witness, together with the supervision and recording of a new statement, could be accomplished in a single day's interview session. The miscalculation was a measure of the team's lack of preparation for the assignment ahead. It would take three days to complete this interview and for much of that time the two-man police team involved would be at a loss to comprehend much of the now 67 year-old's claims and his many and sudden mood swings.

He became particularly irritated when it was suggested to him that, all those years ago, he might well have been a communist himself or at least a communist sympathiser. Nor did he like it when it was put to him that armed communists could easily have used the *kongsi* houses on Sungei Remok Estate as a contact point for food and other supplies.

Why hadn't he reported to the police immediately after he survived the shooting? Why had he gone into hiding instead of lodging a complaint?

Surely, his only purpose in lodging a report and complaint at this time was to secure financial compensation? The first interview session began at 8.30 am. By midday the police realised it was pointless proceeding with Chong Fong in such an uncooperative frame of mind.

It wasn't until the final moments of the second interrogation session that those questioning him began to get an inkling of what Chong Fong's life had been like since the day of the shooting. The interrogator and interpreter had been trying to clear up what they thought were contradictions relating to where the former tapper had gone immediately after fleeing the gruesome scene.

'I deny making these contradictions,' claimed a visibly annoyed Chong Fong, his voice rising. 'There is a mistake. Inspector Yip, the interpreter, made the mistake. When I escaped from the incident I went to see my father at the coffee shop at about 10.30 am at Ulu Yam Bahru and related the whole episode to him. He merely acknowledged what I told him. He did not ask any questions or verify the truth of what I was saying. He did not even ask me as to what happened to my brother. I told him that I do not know what has happened to my brother, Chong Sip. My father told me that he will make a decision regarding the brother. He told me not to talk too much and that he knows what to do.'

The police interrogator followed up with a seemingly naïve question aimed at clarifying why Chong Fong had chosen to hide in his father's shop rather than seek the assistance of the authorities.

By this point the interviewee was shouting. 'I dared not go out of the coffee shop. I helped my father in the coffee shop. I did not tell anybody except my father because I was scared that the white men will get me.'

Given the circumstances, his fear he might become a ready target for follow-up activity by the 'white men' was entirely reasonable and the interrogator quickly realised it. In an effort to calm Chong Fong down the officer decided on a different tack. He switched the subject to a reference the lone survivor had made two days earlier about the MCA's approaches to him.

At this, Chong Fong jumped to his feet and strode from the room angrily cursing MCA officials whose insistence, he maintained, was the only reason he

The Batang Kali Police Station today.

Lone survivor Chong Fong (left).

Tham Yong (above), a witness to the killings, who later marries lone survivor Chong Fong.

Foo Moi (left), who watched her husband being marched off to a riverside killing location, later provides Malaysian investigators with graphic details of events on Sungei Remok Estate.

had made the police report. They had forced him into making it. What was more, they had coached him what to say. Once again the police examination of the lone survivor's story had to be adjourned early. It was 12.15 pm and the recording officer made a note on file that he felt it unwise to continue with the interviewee in his current frame of mind. They would try again the next day at 9.30 am.

Chong Fong's third session under police questioning went ahead as scheduled on July 20 at the same police station. It took place in much the same atmosphere experienced on the two previous occasions. He bitterly resented any form of police insinuation that he might not be telling the truth. He became particularly hostile when police kept pressing their disbelief of explanations he was providing for his actions in the immediate period following the mass killing.

When the recording of Chong Fong's statement concluded the police were barely three days into their investigation and were well short of even a basic appreciation of the incident itself, let alone its overall impact on the man they were interviewing.

They would soon learn that there were very cogent explanations for Chong Fong's bursts of intransigence.

The subject was a semi-literate former plantation worker who had never been able to come to grips with the horror he had experienced. Why had he survived while all his fellow workers, caught in the same catastrophic experience, had perished? He supposed the spirits had deemed it so; but then he couldn't be sure of that either. He had lain low after the mass killing simply because he was terrified for his life. Perhaps his way of dealing with the inexplicable during the years that followed was to withdraw and, when pressed, become antagonistic. It had, at least, provided a semblance of protection. He had married Tham Yong, his younger brother's fiancée. His sibling, Chong Sip, had been killed by the Scots Guards. Might this have explained Chong Fong's marked diffidence towards his brother's fate and his obvious unwillingness to talk about personal aspects of his life?

When police and the military located him shortly after the killings he had been arrested. He had been certain, then, that he would be killed by his captors. But he was unexpectedly released after three days without even being questioned. As he had told reporter Hugh Mabbert in 1970, Chong Fong had no idea why he was detained at that time. An angry Chong Fong explained that, since the 'white journalist' talked to him 23 years earlier, people had endlessly questioned him. It was an incident he simply could not explain. Why did he survive? He had no answer. Endless promises had been made to him in order to gain his co-operation in telling his story. Journalists had done it. Acquaintances had done it. Political operatives had done it. None of the uninvited intrusions into his life had yielded

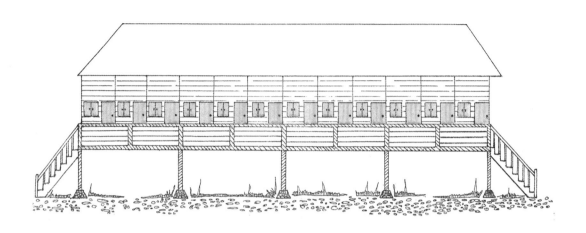

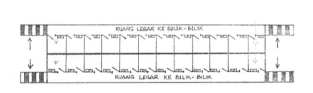

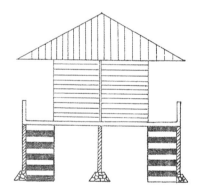

In order to clarify important aspects of their inquiries, Malaysian police assign an artist to provide accurate drawings of Sungei Remok Estate's kongsi houses as they presented in late 1948.

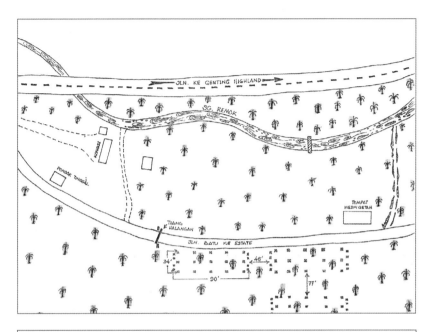

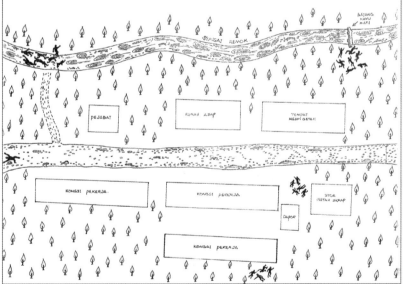

In further pursuit of clarifications, Malaysian investigators work on diagrammatic representations of the plantation's accommodation and work quarters. They need to be certain of the relationship between these positions and the various killing sites. Identified on one diagram are the locations where Scots Guards fire felled unarmed plantation workers. Also identified are the numbers involved in each cluster of corpses.

any positive results. Nothing had alleviated the abject poverty that had dogged him for years.

Now the police were at it again and from his perspective they were *at him.* They harboured doubts. He was being made to justify something that had both victimised and traumatised him since his youth. What made it worse, their questions seemed to be portraying him as an element of the massacre's cause – either a communist at the time or a sympathiser. And he had been neither.

Speaking about life on the plantation during the initial Emergency months, he told his interrogators: 'We could carry out our daily work without any fear or harassment from anybody. There was no curfew and our movements were not restricted except that food was controlled. Each of us was restricted to six tins of rice per month.'

His statement continued: 'Our normal routine work started at 4.00 am. There was no muster then. All of us had a fixed area to tap which was allocated to us by the *mandor* (plantation supervisor).'

When it came to describing the Scots Guards raid, Chong Fong's statement records:

'On the day in question, at about 5.00 pm after I finished my bath at the river and I was dressing up in my room, I heard white men calling out loudly, gesticulating for all of us to come out of the *kongsi*. There were about three white men near my *kongsi* ordering us out. My brother, Chong Sip, did not share my room in the *kongsi*. He was next door.'

On leaving his quarters, said Chong Fong, he noted that there were about 12 soldiers, all dressed in jungle green, within the compound clearing. They were accompanied by a Chinese man. Each of the troops looked about 20 years of age and all of them were armed.

'The white men separated the men from the women as we all came out of the *kongsi*. I can remember seeing Foo Moi, and Wong Ying among the women who were there. The group of men and women separated were about 50 metres apart. The lone Chinese who came with the white men was with the women folk.'

Chong Fong's statement recalled that five soldiers stood guard over the 25 male plantation workers. 'I could see the women folk about 50 metres away, nearer to the river. They were all standing together. There were seven white men with them. The children were there with the women.'

He went on to describe how the group of male plantation workers were locked for the night in a *kongsi* room measuring about 20 feet by 12 feet while the women and children were confined to another room.

'The next day, at about 7.30 am, three white men came to the room and signalled us to come out of the room. We were out assembled at the same place as the previous evening. I saw ten white men who signalled us not to move.' Chong Fong explained that he could not tell whether the soldiers that morning were the same ones present the previous evening. 'I presume they were the same persons. They all looked the same to me. I cannot recognise any one of them nor give a description of them.'

His statement continued: 'We were all standing there until about 9.30 am. The white men were having a discussion about 15 feet away. They were assembled in a circle.

'We were then separated by three white men and formed into five groups at random. There was no selection according to age, height or size. I was in a group of five persons. I cannot remember who were in my group.'

Chong Fong recalled that the groups, thus formed, were kept separated three to four feet from each other. Chong Sip, he said, was not in his group.

'Then two white men pushed my group of five persons with their long rifles and made us walk forward towards the river. I was in front of my group. We walked about 100 yards towards the river. I was wearing a blue shirt and greenish yellow shorts. I do not know what the others were wearing but some were wearing long pants and others were wearing short pants. We were unarmed.

'Suddenly I heard a gun shot. I fell down and fainted immediately on hearing the gun shot. Roughly about half an hour later – I did not possess a watch – I recovered and saw three to four bodies with bloodstains. I did not examine them. I ran for my dear life.'

At this point of his evidence Chong Fong described how he made his escape from the plantation by running along the course of the stream.

Confusion among the police ensued over whether he had gone to his uncle's or his father's coffee shop. This ultimately led to the abandonment of the second interrogation session. By the following day the confusion had been clarified and it was established by the police that the lone survivor had indeed gone to his father's establishment in Ulu Yam Bahru.

The final three pages of the statement Chong Fong made to the investigating team reflect, very accurately, the initial attitude adopted by the Malaysian police towards their overall examination of the massacre claims.

Dealing with the report he made under MCA auspices, Chong Fong stated: 'The MCA people did not explain the contents of the typewritten letter. They told me that I was lodging a police report. They did not say what the report was and whether it was pertaining to the incident that happened 45 years ago. I do not have the slightest idea what the report is all about.

'I can read a bit of Chinese characters. I know that the documents that I signed at the police station and earlier in my house were not typewritten in Chinese characters. I do not know whether it was typewritten in English, Malay or any other language. I do not even know how to read the alphabet A, B, and C. That is all I have to say.

There followed a concluding question and answer segment to the recorded statement. Among the questions posed to Chong Fong by the police were the following, along with the answers he provided:

Q: Sungei Remok Estate was alive with CT (communist terrorist) activity in 1948. How come you say that there were no CTs in the general area?
A: Inside the Sungei Remok Estate there was no CT activity but elsewhere, outside the estate, I do not know.
Q: Are you a CT sympathiser?
A: No. I hate them.
Q: Were your parents CT sympathisers?
A: No.
Q: Were there any shootings/arson prior to this killing incident?
A: No.
Q: Do you know that the CTs were causing a lot of trouble, shooting and killing during this period in other areas?
A: There was a curfew in other areas but not in Sungei Remok Estate.
Q: You did not show any remorse when your brother was killed in cold blood. Why?
A: I do not know why. I do not feel sad for him.
Q: Do you hate your brother?
A: I do not hate him. I seldom talked to him. My relationship was not close with him.
Q: Did he deserve to die the way he did?
A: I don't think so; I do not want to take any action now or then.
Q: Why did your father fail to avenge the death of his son?
A: I do not know.
Q: Are you a CT?
A: I swear I am not one. My brother was also not a CT.
Q: What is your purpose in lodging this report?
A: I lodged a report because the MCA pulled me to lodge a police report. I did not want to lodge a police report because I am old.
Q: Do you expect to be given any compensation by way of cash or kind?
A: No. I do not expect anything. I will accept anything from anybody.

Photographs of stump lines of Sungei Remok Estate's original kongsi houses, associated office and tool storage structures. From these positions investigators are able to make very accurate assessments of evidence as it becomes available. The two pictures above indicate stump positions for two kongsis in relation to the estate road.

A somewhat blurred photograph indicates the position on the estate road where Loh Kit Lin was shot by the Scots Guards patrol leader and later received the coup de grace from the second-in-command.

Further photographic evidence shows the two pathways leading from the estate's living quarters down to the nearby river. It was along these tracks that Scots Guards escorted separate groups of plantation workers to their deaths.

Q: Do you like the attention and publicity that has been given to you for the last few days?
A: I have no interest in what is happening and all the publicity in the newspapers. Nobody else has interviewed me except the police.

In time key members of the police Task Force, assigned to the Batang Kali Massacre investigations, would come to appreciate the significance of these reactions and thereafter were able to evaluate Chong Fong's recorded statement as critical to the work they had undertaken.

Three days after concluding this initial interview, the Task Force received a TV tape of the BBC's *In Cold Blood* programme. It was July 22. At a planning committee meeting that same day Task Force members viewed the documentary. It is very clear from their file that attitudes of key investigators towards their assignment became more thoughtful and reflective from then on.

When they embarked on the case the selected officers possessed very rudimentary historical knowledge of the Malayan Emergency period and certainly of the incident they were re-examining. By the very positions they held in the police force, their perceptions of the era had been coloured by extensive government propaganda to which they had all been subjected. The communists were evil. The security forces – police and military – were at all times blameless.

Remarks by Superintendent Ron Dowling during the TV programme, particularly the importance he placed on the need for the Scotland Yard men to travel to Malaysia for on-the-spot inquiries, had a substantial impact on the Malaysian police audience during that initial viewing. Not lost on the local team was the surreptitious way in which the British Attorney General in 1970 had conveniently derailed the Scotland Yard probe – a key feature of the documentary. When these two factors were considered jointly, it was quite obvious to all concerned that the Malaysian investigators were now being required to provide the very evidence Scotland Yard had always regarded as vital to finalising Britain's Batang Kali review. The problem was, of course, that nearly 45 years had elapsed since the mass killing and 23 years had gone by since the UK's formal inquiry had been sidelined.

Chapter 11

Evidence mounts

The Task Force's July 22, 1993, meeting resulted in a significant realignment of Malaysia's Batang Kali Massacre investigation, just seven days after the probe had begun. Primary trigger for this was the review of the BBC's *In Cold Blood* tape. Initially, the idea had been for an inquiry specifically directed at reinforcing or disproving the police reports submitted by Chong Fong, Tham Yong and Foo Moi. It was thereafter decided that a far broader approach would have to be undertaken if the investigations were to reach firm, meaningful conclusions.

It was agreed that a scene-by-scene analysis of the BBC programme would be invaluable to the task ahead. To this end a complete transcript was compiled of all remarks made throughout the documentary, whether part of the overall commentary, off-camera background pronouncements or those made during the numerous on-camera interviews. Where translations were needed, these were done into English. This became the working language for the exercise.

A list was ordered of all those featured throughout the programme as well as all BBC production staff involved, including the interpreters employed locally and even on-the-spot journalists who had been consulted during the filming process. In each case, contact particulars were recorded. An extensive collection of still photographs was also extracted from the tape. Based on such data, investigators drew up a folio of requirements for interviews and signed statements.

Task Force members were surprised by the relatively scant information provided by a Special Branch report they had received at the outset of their work. It recounted, in very general terms, events that had taken place on Sungei Remok. Much of this information appeared to have been culled from newspaper cuttings. But two specific observations in the text provided interesting avenues for inquiries and substantiation.

When it came to deal with the search of estate *kongsi* houses undertaken by the British troops on the evening of December 11, 1948, the report stated: 'The search lasted about two hours until 1900 hrs. During the search they did not obtain any evidence whatever that would indicate communist sympathies among the locals.' This, of course, contradicted all previous official claims that ammunition rounds had been discovered in a *kongsi* room.

The other aspect of the report that struck a note with the Task Force was

Wounded in a nearby communist ambush just prior to the Scots Guards action on Sungei Remok Estate, Police Inspector Harnum Singh is in retirement by the time the Malaysian investigating team tracks him down. Still, he is able to provide vital information.

its evaluation of security force tactics in late 1948. It claimed that following the failure of operations highlighting the staging of ambushes in November that year, the British had changed tactics. The new military approach late that month and in early December concentrated on house-to-house searches throughout jungle-fringe areas. These, as it happened, also failed to detect any firm evidence of communist activity. Despite this, the new techniques employed by the British troops, including the Scots Guards, had been to order all people from the jungle-fringe houses they were targeting. The dwellings were then torched as a matter of course. 'Many houses belonging to the Chinese in Kampong Sungei Masid, Ulu Yam Bahru and Sungei Genting Manik were destroyed in this manner during this operation,' said the report. The clear inference of these observations was that unnecessarily cruel tactics on the part of the British at this time had achieved nothing.

❦

To accommodate their expanded parameters, Task Force members sought input from sources of expertise able to provide accurate appreciations of the 1948 security environment throughout Malaya, particularly those reflecting conditions in the Ulu Selangor region. Police and Special Branch records offered a means of tracing addresses and contact numbers for officers of that era, but, by then, in retirement.

It very quickly became evident that all key records dealing with Emergency security from 1948 onwards had been removed and taken home by the British upon the granting of independence to Malaya in 1957. There was not a single document or reference to the Scots Guards killing spree on file anywhere in the country and this despite the fact that the British had originally claimed no less than three separate departments had undertaken investigations into the event. The clean-out had been meticulous. To the Task Force, this appeared highly questionable and, of course, made research efforts considerably more difficult.

❦

Early inquiries were able to uncover the role played just prior to the mass killing by Inspector Harnum Singh. The then retired officer had been attached to the Kuala Kubu Bahru police station. He was involved with follow-up investigations of the arson attacks on Sungei Tempayan and Ulu Yam Lama railway stations.

Singh was wounded in a communist ambush not far from Sungei Remok. Records showed he had been admitted for treatment at the Kuala Kubu Bahru Hospital for bullet wounds to the shoulder.

Quickly traced, Singh explained he was in hospital on the day of the Scots Guards action and knew little about its details. However, he had often visited the estate during his duties in the area and was quite familiar with its layout. He was able to confirm that the nearest jungle to the *kongsi* clearing was a substantial distance away on the estate's eastern boundary. This was the first confirmation received by the Malaysian inquiry that the clearing had certainly not been surrounded by jungle but rather by rows of rubber trees.

Singh's information immediately highlighted another important contradiction in original descriptions of events provided by colonial civil and military authorities.

There were 14 men in the Scots Guards patrol that morning. The Guards and government subsequently claimed the platoon leader had posted three groups of sentries to cover the three alleged entrances to the surrounding jungle. The word 'groups' indicated there must have been more than one Scots Guardsman positioned at each entry point. At very least this would have called for the commitment of two to three men at each of the claimed entrance positions – anywhere from six to nine soldiers in total.

Given Singh's evidence, the numbers maintained by the colonial authorities simply didn't add up.

Eyewitness evidence indicated at least eight Scots Guardsmen out of the 14 had been involved in escort work – down to the two positions by the stream and to separate points behind the *kongsis*. Neither the platoon leader nor his second in command, according to claims, had participated in escort or sentry duties. The newly arrived contract workers were being detained that morning in the plantation office. This required two guards. Two other guardsmen had clearly been detailed to supervise the departure of the plantation supply lorry and its occupants including the women and children. All in all, that accounted for the entire 14-man platoon. Where did the additional six or nine guardsmen, supposedly in concealed sentry positions, come from?

There was a further interesting insight Singh was able to provide. It concerned attitudes of Scots Guardsmen immediately following the December 12 incident. The inspector's home billet at Kuala Kubu Bahru had been in quarters directly opposite their military camp. The same unit, he explained, also occupied an adjacent Chinese School. 'Some of their tents were pitched right in front of my house and across the road,' he told the investigators.

His signed statement revealed: 'On one or two occasions the soldiers, on seeing

The police billets, where Inspector Singh resided at the time of the Batang Kali raid remain functional today, situated opposite the grounds that once housed the Scots Guards HQ at Kuala Kubu Bahru.

me with a sling on my shoulder and arm, inquired as to what had happened to me. I related this incident and what had happened and the response of one or two of them was to the effect: 'Those fucking bastards on the estate deserved to die by being shot'.'

Forty-three years after the fact, Malaysian investigators well appreciated such remarks neither proved nor disproved guilt or intention. But they were part of the picture and were certainly worth noting. These sentiments would later link with a quote former national serviceman, Alan Tuppen, had given *The People* in 1970. Tuppen had said he and his comrades in 7 platoon understood the objective of the mission that day. It was to 'wipe out a particular village and everyone in it because . . . they were either terrorists themselves or helping the terrorists in that area.'

By then investigators were wondering whether they might well be probing a case of 'massacre under orders'. But it was also too early to entertain rash judgements and they avoided doing so, preferring to concentrate, for the time being, on gathering information with a wider focus.

———∽∾∿∾∽———

Expertise was then sought from retired Police Superintendent Lim Cheng Leng who, like Singh, had not been directly involved with any aspect of the Sungei Remok case but held impressive anti-insurgency credentials. Lim was traced through police records. He had been the first recipient of British High Commissioner Gerald Templer's Medal and Commendation in the early 1950s. This had been awarded for results he had achieved during the Emergency in action against communist guerrillas.

Lim had closely studied Malaya's counter insurgency history and, he told the investigators, there had never been an operation that yielded numbers anywhere close to those the Scots Guards had claimed at Batang Kali. He told the investigating team that throughout his career the most number of kills he ever personally achieved in a single action was five. The overall record, he continued, was created in 1976, during the second Emergency, when an operation near Bentong, in the state of Pahang, resulted in nine communists killed.

In a statement he made and signed for the Task Force, Lim explained that during the Emergency's initial months there had been no proper guidelines for security forces on how to tackle the insurgency. It was a time, he said, when 'every suspect was somehow arrested and put away'. This sort of approach had failed to benefit the accumulation of worthwhile intelligence and 'ground operatives' eventually came to realise they must take risks in order to 'get to the enemy'.

Lim noted that the controversial Malaysian 'Psy-War Warrior', the late C.C. Too, while serving as assistant to the head of the Emergency Information Service (EIS) sometime after the mass killing, had been ordered to drop the idea of an inquiry he proposed to make into the event. He was warned the authorities involved were powerful men not to be crossed.

The information Lim had been able to supply in his statement to police thus far was important to their overall assessment of the background against which the Batang Kali incident had occurred. But it was what his statement revealed next that became critical.

No formal documentation of the killings, Lim maintained, had been undertaken by the military at the time. Nor had there been any finger printing identification of the victims. Nor had there been any post mortems undertaken on the victims' bodies. Nor had any Sudden Death Reports – known by their acronym SDRs – been submitted. Nor had the basic Order of Battle (ORBAT) document been amended to show that 24 communist suspects had been eliminated on Sungei Remok Estate.

All these steps would have been critical requirements in the normal course of events. Lim's statement indicated there had, at very least, been monumental dereliction of duties on the part of the colonial authorities in the mass killing's aftermath – and strongly suggested a cover-up had, indeed, taken place. Subsequent inquiries along these lines undertaken by the Task Force strongly reinforced Lim's opinions.

—◊◊◊—

Employing the same records that turned up contacts for both Singh and Lim, Task Force officers endeavoured to identify the Chinese police officer attached to 7 platoon, G Company, during the 1948 raid. This proved a more difficult assignment. After 'discreet inquiries' – the term used on the official police file – information was obtained indicating a retired Special Branch detective, one Chia Kam Woh, alias Ah Woh, was the man in question.

Four weeks into their investigation, two Task Force members travelled to the Malaysian police headquarters at Bukit Aman, in the heart of Kuala Lumpur, in order to press the Special Branch into releasing information that might lead them to Chia. They came away with a telephone number and an address, both of which were wrong. It took another month to establish the correct contact details. In mid-

The 1993 photograph (above), taken from inside the Ulu Yam Bahru Police Station grounds, illustrates the compound's close proximity to the town cemetery opposite where all Batang Kali victims are interred.

September two investigators called on the retired Special Branch man.

At first, the conversation between Chia and the policemen was amicable. It was established he could converse 'quite well' in the English language, a skill obviously essential had he been an interpreter with the Scots Guards. After 15 minutes or so of introductory banter, conducted in English, the police indicated they were there to get a statement from the 69 year-old retiree about his supposed role in security operations in the Batang Kali area during December, 1948. Chia immediately became evasive and refused further communication in English, insisting it continue only in his dialect.

He said he had joined the police force in February, 1946, and, after recruit training at the Police Depot in Kuala Lumpur, had been assigned to a Criminal Investigation Department (CID) within the Federal Capital area. Thereafter he was dispatched to Kuala Kubu Bahru on general duties where he had assisted in all types of investigations and had been involved in jungle patrols with the Scots Guards, the only British troops known to be operating in that area.

'On the day in question I was assigned to do duties with a group of about 40 to 50 soldiers on a hill-top at Sungei Remok Estate, in an ambush position,' said Chia in his recorded statement.

He went on: 'Meanwhile, another group of soldiers of about the same number entered Sungei Remok Estate. Detective Gopal and DPC Ali were in the second group. We were at ambush position at about 2.00 to 3.00 am. At about 5.00 to 6.00 am we heard gunfire and subsequently we joined them at Sungei Remok Estate. By the time I reached there I saw a lot of dead bodies. I also witnessed the burning of three *kongsis*. After that we went back to Kuala Kubu Bahru. I do not know what happened subsequently.'

Chia's last posting was with E3 (Special Branch) between 1956 and 1979. He retired with the rank of Sub Inspector in November, 1979.

Police noted that Chia appeared to be very worried and reluctant to cooperate. They decided he had to be further interrogated if the truth was to be established. Soon after this interview, those actively pursuing Task Force inquiries began noticing a drying-up of cooperation from Special Branch. Undeterred, they maintained the momentum of their investigation and went to the extent of amassing a collection of old photographs of police attached to the Kuala Kubu Bahru station during the general 1948-49 time-frame. One of these photographs was of the then 24 year-old Chia.

Two weeks after Chia signed his statement, police located and began interviewing Madam Chong Koon Ying, a sundry stall owner then living and working in the Setapak area of Kuala Lumpur. Evidence thus far gathered suggested she was one of the older children detained on Sungei Remok Estate the night before the killing.

Her father, Chong Mun, had been identified as one of those shot dead. Although unschooled, Madam Chong, who was nine years old at the time, was remarkably articulate and possessed an extraordinary memory for names and details. During two lengthy sessions with her, police were able to amass a wealth of specific information about families who had lived on the estate and, more importantly, where their individual members were currently living and contactable.

There was an amazing correlation between her vast recollections and the data the Task Force had thus far been able to put together from a variety of sources. Those responsible for interviewing her and taking down her statement were impressed, not only by Madam Chong's power of recall, but also the detached and dignified way in which she recounted the harrowing past.

Of the Batang Kali episode's latter stages, her statement noted: 'We were ordered into a lorry which was full of workers. It was the same lorry that arrived earlier. Before the lorry moved, I heard gunshots. I was unable to see anything as I was small and blocked by the others. We were all standing inside the lorry. There were also gunshots as the lorry was moving.

'We were taken to Ulu Yam Bahru. Some of the workers went back to their respective houses. Some did not have a home. We were housed with friends. We lost all our belongings and were left with whatever we were wearing.'

Madam Chong's statement continued: 'After about five days I came to know that my father was one of those killed by the soldiers. My mother was given a chit by the police to collect my father's corpse at the estate. My mother identified the body of my father by the shirt he used to wear as his body was highly decomposed. My father was buried at the Chinese cemetery in front of the police station. The coffin was donated by Lim Chye Chee, the contractor of the estate.'

Investigators were convinced Madam Chong would prove a reliable witness. Once her statement was completed, they produced ten 1948-49 vintage photographs of police officers who had been attached to Kuala Kubu Bahru police station. Included in this photographic line-up was a mug-shot of Chia Kam Woh, aged 24. She was asked whether she could identify anyone of the ten.

Madam Chong scanned each one and picked out Chia's picture without hesitation. She went on to identify Chia as the Chinese man who had accompanied the soldiers onto the estate. She recalled the man was 'good looking'. His features – particularly the eyebrows and the face – appeared to be the same as those in the photograph she had chosen. She admitted she was not 100 per cent sure, but went on to add: 'I cannot forget that face.'

Three months into Malaysia's Batang Kali massacre inquiry, it became clear that the bulk of investigative work was being undertaken by no more than three or four of the originally appointed 12 Task Force members. Some of the initially established force had even been deployed to other duties.

Moreover, the Special Branch remained aloof. It was as though those in the police department's inner sanctum of power were having second thoughts about the wisdom of pursuing what had originally been a politically inspired effort.

Still, the momentum established by the early expansion of the inquiry and associated instructions for a variety of interviews and signed statements had produced a flow of documentation that was difficult to stem. A meeting called at Bukit Aman police headquarters in early October, 1993, involving a Deputy Director of the Malaysian CID and Task Force members, gave further hope that resistance encountered within the police department could be overcome and investigations pursued to a meaningful conclusion.

The gathering reviewed in detail the minutes of an earlier Task Force meeting. It concluded with orders from the Deputy Director that a progress report be submitted with a view to getting cooperation from the Special Branch.

As inquiries proceeded, those in charge began to perceive an amazing continuity of information coming from, in the main, unconnected sources. There were, of course, instances of conflicting evidence.

One of these occurred during an early interview police conducted with Lee Sheng, alias Loh Kar Siah, the smokehouse keeper on Sungei Remok Estate at the time of the raid. Aged 66 and still living in Ulu Yam Bahru, he recounted being a passenger on the lorry bringing supplies to the estate. His description of the scene he encountered within the *kongsi* compound agreed with other accounts.

Luck had been on Lee's side. Although he resided in one of the estate's three *kongsi* houses, the then 21 year-old, who operated the smokehouse with a staff of three, had departed the clearing the previous afternoon to visit his parents in Ulu Yam Bahru.

Alighting from the supply lorry that had been stopped by British soldiers, he noticed the body of a Chinese man in the centre of the estate road, intestines spilling from a stomach wound.

The statement Lee gave police explained there were about 20 passengers on the lorry including a number of women and children. The newly arrived male workers were separated from the women and children and escorted by two British soldiers to a storeroom beside the smokehouse where they were locked-in under guard. Up to this point his statement gelled with other recollections.

What puzzled investigators, however, were his following memories. 'We were guarded by two British soldiers. At about 9 am to 10 am I heard the sound of shooting coming from the *kongsi*. It lasted for about 10 minutes. Later, after about 20 minutes, a male Chinese, believed to be a detective, opened the door and announced that all the persons in the *kongsi* had been killed, the kongsi burnt down, and ordered us to go back to the lorry. When I boarded the lorry, the ladies and children were already there. None of them were harmed. All those who came earlier in the lorry were all there including the lorry driver. We all went back to Ulu Yam Bahru.'

Lee's claim to have been on the estate throughout the shooting and to have left after the *kongsis* had been set alight did not mesh with reports that the departing lorry had begun to move shortly after the killing began.

In an unusual admission, the former smokehouse keeper confessed to having gone back to the estate some days later. There he had collected latex from abandoned rubber trees. He had sold this for a total of $20. The investigators decided to hold Lee's observations in abeyance. They would concentrate on the overwhelming mass of statements providing a cohesive pattern of events. If necessary, they would address Lee's contradictory observations before submission of the final evidence to coronial authorities.

As far as the investigators' intentions at this point were concerned, their efforts would conclude with a final presentation to the coroner. Thereafter, decisions would be in the hands of the authorities.

Meanwhile, from the east Malaysian coastal centre of Kuantan came a very moving signed declaration by Wong Yen, the elderly blind woman whose quietly delivered sentiments had provided such sad, thought-provoking, yet dramatic concluding moments to the *In Cold Blood* programme. The story she related in her statement was entirely consistent with observations and claims she had made in the BBC documentary. She described how her brother-in-law, Loh Kit Lin, was accused by the Chinese detective of supplying durians to the communists. Shortly thereafter, the detective had turned on Loh and declared: 'You're dead.'

The durian incident was becoming one of many focal points for the probe. It made little sense that estate workers might be involved gathering durians for jungle dwelling communists. The prized fruit was heavy, prickly and difficult to carry in bulk on foot for long distances. Durian trees grew in the wild and would have been easily accessible to communist jungle camps. Even those cultivated on local plantations were readily available for the picking. What was more, the fruit, by its very consistency, rich flavour and reputation could never be considered an essential staple of the insurgents. Guerrilla food requirements were well documented to be rice, sugar, salt and, if possible, tinned goods. To accuse a plantation worker of collecting durians for the communist effort had all the hallmarks of desperation on the part of the Chinese detective concerned. It was almost as if, in the absence of any tangible evidence of involvement with the communists, the detective had seized on any excuse to justify a pre-determined plan of action. In this respect, Wong Yen insisted that, as far as she knew, her brother-in-law had never been involved in any durian collection arrangement with anyone.

Police had asked her to clarify one remark she made during the *In Cold Blood* documentary to the effect that her dog had tugged at the leg of her brother-in-law's body in an effort to awaken him. She had claimed her affectionate pet had constantly followed Loh Kit Lin around the estate as he worked. Wong Yen explained in her statement: 'On the second day when I returned to the scene, I saw my brother-in-law's thigh had been bleeding and the pants were torn, as if torn by a dog. That is why I presumed that it was my dog which did it.' It was, perhaps, an unimportant point. But police read it as illustrating the old woman's desire to help the investigation and, at the same time, to be as accurate as possible.

She was also able to confirm the discovery of groups of bodies she and three other women had made when they returned to the estate the day after the shooting. One group was by the hillside at the rear of the *kongsis*, she said. Other bodies were by the stream. In addition she was able to fill in details of attempts estate residents had made to retrieve personal belongings before the Scots Guards burnt down the *kongsi* houses. The agony the women had gone through during the day-long wait in vain for their men at Ulu Yam Bahru on the morning of the shooting was implicit in her statement.

———∽∾∽———

The longest witness statement gathered by the Task Force came from the lone survivor's wife, Tham Yong, who was 62 years of age when she was interviewed. She had figured prominently in the BBC's television programme. Tham Yong had also been widely quoted and photographed by the press following *The People's* exposé in 1970 and the subsequent initial discovery by reporters from *The Straits Times* of her husband's astonishing escape. Her August, 1993, declaration to investigators took five days to complete and ran a total of 19 pages. She was able to provide a remarkably precise run down, not only on those who had perished, but also of victims' family members. Additionally, she helped police identify victims' graves in the Ulu Yam Bahru cemetery.

Investigators recorded a similarly detailed interview with female rubber tapper, Foo Moi, the second woman to lodge a police report at the instigation of MCA political activists. She was able to supply precise information on the Chinese detective's interrogation of estate workers on the day before the shooting and also graphic descriptions of how the 'white soldiers' had escorted the male detainees to the killing zones the following morning.

In her statement, taken down during three interview sessions, Foo Moi noted how her position on the lorry that morning, prior to her departure from the estate, had enabled her to look back towards the *kongsis* and watch as the British troops divided the male plantation workers into separate groupings. 'Each group was escorted by two to three white man soldiers with rifles pointing at them. Two groups walked towards the river and the other walked towards the hill behind the *kongsi*. One of the two groups which walked towards the river passed beside the smokehouse. My husband, Wong Yan, was in that group and was walking in front.'

Her statement went on: 'As soon as they reached the river I saw the three white man soldiers start to fire at them and they collapsed. At the same time, I also heard gun shots coming from further up riverside and also from behind the *kongsi*. The white man soldiers then set fire to the *kongsi* houses, office and smokehouse. The lorry driven by Chong San took us to Ulu Yam Bahru.'

Like the other eyewitness statements made to the Task Force, Foo Moi's recollections contributed to a recognisable and overwhelmingly consistent pattern of events. There were, of course, variations of emphasis here and there. But from the Task Force's viewpoint – or at least the viewpoints of its still-functioning members – these were far too minor to be considered detracting from the overall impression that a massacre had indeed taken place. It was also becoming increasingly clear to them that the act had been wilfully covered up by British authorities at the time, and since. They wondered, in the final analysis, whether their current endeavours at uncovering the truth would be sustained in Malaysia, or whether they would be dismissed, as all similar past efforts had been treated.

Chapter 12

Recording diminished lives

Only when the Task Force began studying the mounting collection of signed statements in detail did the massive narrative of human suffering before them have its full impact. Every meeting with a surviving kin was yielding accounts of uncomprehending loss and continuing filial piety. More used to experiences with petty thieves, thugs and destructive rabble-rousers, the police officers could not ignore the interviewees' resilience and their remarkable will to get on with life. This was an investigation like no other.

The aftermath of the raid – what the women and children had to confront following the deaths of husbands, fathers and brothers – was part of the whole Batang Kali equation. With each passing year, their hardships had multiplied. The legacy of that particular 1948 Scots Guards weekend mission was a collection of marginalised lives, scarred by recollections of mindless butchery.

The investigators were family men themselves, with wives and children. At the same time they also knew they had to remain detached. This made their probe doubly difficult. They had to stay dispassionate in the face of misery.

They had to proceed with open minds.

———

Wong Mook Sang, surviving son of Wong Yan, the plantation clerk, confided: 'My mother and I did not want to bring back all the sad memories by reporting Batang Kali to the authorities . . . Since my mother said there is hope of getting some form of compensation, there is no harm trying.'

Foo Moi, his mother, was 75 years old at the time of the interview. Mook Sang provided a summary of her life dispassionately. An aunt had adopted Foo Moi when she was orphaned at five. She never went to school. Her childhood had been a patch of odd jobs, like cutting grass in rubber estates. When she got married, she just shifted from working with her aunt to working with her husband. If rubber tapping is a higher occupation than grass cutting, then one could say her life was a notch improved. She and her husband had a room in a *kongsi* house in the clearing at Sungei Remok.

The rubber tapping was as back-breaking as the grass cutting. She accepted her lot. And what was her reward? She once thought it was the four children until the day she watched her husband being shot from behind by soldiers. After that, the children became liabilities. She re-married and had more children but her life remained an exercise in making ends meet.

Mook Sang was 11 when his mother was widowed. When he was 17, he left home. 'I was,' he volunteered, 'seeking for greener grass.'

He was 53 years old when he spoke to Task Force representatives in Sabah, East Malaysia, where he worked as a ban-saw operator in a sawmill. He hardly took holidays to save money. Every month, he sent his wife part of his salary. He tried to visit his family each Chinese New Year. After this obligation was met, Mook Sang went, if he could, to see his mother back at Ulu Yam Bahru and give her some 'pocket money'.

'My father's death,' he declared, 'caused us much suffering and misery.'

What did he remember of the Batang Kali episode?

'I can still remember it vividly,' he began. A soldier tempted him with a bunch of rambutans and asked, through a Chinese interpreter, whether he had seen any communists on the estate. If he helped the soldiers, he could have the fruit; otherwise, he would get shot.

His police statement continued: 'I told the soldier and the interpreter that I had no idea what communists were and I told them I have never seen those people. The soldier looked fierce and he pointed a pistol at my chest. Now I can say the pistol looked like a revolver. He told me to tell the truth. I was so scared. I could not even speak.'

He learned of his father's death from his mother. 'I did not actually witness the killings of my father and the other villagers at Sungei Remok Estate. I was small at that time. I only knew I was frightened and cried during the incident and held tightly to my mother.' But he had heard the gunshots and he would never forget the unrelieved wretchedness that followed his father's death.

He quit school. His brother did not get sufficient education either. His sisters were very small. To earn sustenance for the family he helped his mother tap rubber. That was what he did until he left home.

'My life,' Mook Sang said matter-of-factly, 'has been a tough one.'

But it was the way he concluded his statement that left his interviewers with something more to ponder: 'We leave it to the wisdom of the authority but definitely not to blame the Malaysian government. Those days were still British colonial rule.'

Obviously, the Batang Kali killings had left an attitude of wariness towards the workings of the system and the fairness of authority. The fear of undeserved recriminations was learned fast and only too well. It stayed, seared in the minds of those left behind. And it would appear they had passed on this inheritance of fear to their children.

———∿∿∿∿∿———

It was not difficult to cultivate the culture of fear. Women like Chong Koon Ying grew up remembering being told by her mother to stop complaining about being hungry in a dark room because 'there were soldiers outside'.

She spoke of the infant sister her mother tried to breast-feed all night in the mistaken notion that attaching the child to her would keep it quiet and save them from courting further trouble from their irate guards. Taken out of detention the next morning, the then nine-year-old Koon Ying had wanted to go home: 'I wanted to return to my room which was next door but I was not allowed by the soldiers.'

She did not claim to be an eyewitness to the horrific scenes that followed but for the investigating team she recalled 'being small and being blocked by the others'. But, like Mook Sang, she heard the gunshots. She mentioned the *kongsi* room she had known as home being set on fire.

Coaxed to look back, she spoke of the meals she earned as a child assisting an old woman collect latex. Her baby sister was eventually given away. Koon Ying did not know what happened to her sibling. All she had was the girl's name. This, she felt, was of little use. Koon Ying was convinced it would have been changed long ago by her sister's adoptive parents.

———∿∿∿∿∿———

Distrust of authority was the earliest clear lesson another police interviewee, Wooi Kum Thai, absorbed as a little girl. Her parents were both rubber tappers on the Menzies plantation.

Recalling the night before the killings, she told police: 'My mother warned me not to make noise as the soldiers outside would kill us.' As the eldest child, Kum Thai explained, she had been detailed to look after her younger siblings. Petrified at the prospect of being punished by the guards for causing trouble, she decided the best position to take was next to her mother.

Her statement recounted being driven in a lorry away from the clearing with other women and children. Homeless, they ended up in dilapidated accommodation in Ulu Yam Bahru. They had been in this house for three or four days when they were informed of two deaths that directly affected them: her father's and her uncle's.

The years that followed were a chronicle of desperate moves to survive. Still, a space was given each year to respect the dead. 'On Cheng Beng (All Souls' Day), I accompanied my mother to visit my father's grave,' Kum Thai told the police.

But the daily struggle took its toll. They never had sufficient food and nothing to save Kum Thai's youngest sister from malnutrition. The toddler died within two years of the Scots Guards action.

'My mother died when I was 12,' Kum Thai continued. 'She was sick but there was no money to see a doctor.' The widow was 45 years old.

At the time of giving her account to the investigating team, Kum Thai was providing shelter to a younger brother who assisted her 'selling fowls'. For some reason, she had not visited her father's grave at the Ulu Yam Bahru cemetery for at least seven years. Still, she sounded relieved when she said that her brother continued to observe the tradition started by their mother.

—◈—

As their file of statements expanded, investigators grew to appreciate the full extent of the deprivation that had been thrust on widows and families. A case in point was that of Chan Kai, a 55 year-old tapper shot by the guards. Police were able to identify this tapper's grave with the help of a surviving son, Mok Sang. Chan Kai had left behind a 33 year-old widow, two sons and infant twin daughters. Statements revealed how the widow, after burying her husband's remains, had been forced to seek rubber tapping work herself, leaving the care of her two sons and the twins to friends.

She was at work when one of the twins fell sick. She had little time to grieve over the baby's eventual death. She had also been too engrossed earning a living to note her second son's erratic temperament. Exhausted, she would put it down to the lingering unease the boy could be suffering after a night of horrifying uncertainty at Room 4 of the first *kongsi* house.

The boy had whimpered all night and begged and begged for food only to be shushed and commanded to be quiet because the 'white soldiers' were waiting outside and would get him if he did not stop complaining. Then they were unceremoniously bundled onto a lorry. The same boy had latched onto his mother's skirt as she wailed and tried, together with the other women, to get off the moving vehicle. The boy had watched 'white soldiers' push the screaming passengers back.

His mother was among them.

'My brother is mentally deranged,' Mok Sang informed the police investigators. At the time, the man was an inmate at an asylum in Tanjung Rambutan.

The series of adversities that visited Chan Kai's widow affected her so deeply it took years before she could talk about her sorrows. When the *kongsi* houses were gutted by fire, she lost the meagre memorabilia she had of the life she shared with the father of her four children. Not a single photograph of Chan Kai remained. She mourned this fact till the year she died at 70.

'I don't have a photograph of my father,' Mok Sang told the investigators. 'Every year, since I was a little boy, I accompanied my mother to visit my father's grave every Cheng Beng Day.

'But I was already 13 years old when she told me that he was killed by British soldiers.'

As they met more people directly affected by the raid and gathered more accounts, the Malaysian investigators found themselves gathering impressions peripheral to the issues they were aiming to clarify.

It struck them how life had hardly advanced for most of the victims' families. A handful of the grown children had struck out on their own, moving to other towns for better job opportunities. On the whole, however, one could not speak of progress or hints of prosperity, even in relative terms.

The Task Force could readily assess that over the years, there was nothing by way of higher education or promising enterprise the victims' families could celebrate. The children and the children's children had, at one time or another, dropped out of school to earn a living. Advancement in life had been marked by little triumphs: the purchase of a small house where everyone in the family lived until one married. Owning a wristwatch was a milestone. Having a telephone installed and the luxury of new clothes were considered accomplishments.

Lim Kok, nine years old at the time of the Scots Guards mission, fared better than most. It might be argued that circumstances in the aftermath were stacked in his favour. His benefactor was the Sungei Remok contractor, Lim Chye Chee, whose nephew – Kok's father – had been among those killed.

Surviving kin assist in identifying the graves of Batang Kali victims. Here is a selection of photographs taken then at the Ulu Yam Bahru cemetery.

Wong Teck Foong

Chan Kai

Chong Mun

Lam Kow

Chong Sip

Wong Hing

Ng Kong

Wong Yan

185

Lim Tian Sui had been 'kepala' (headman) for his uncle on the estate, tasked to supervise the work of grass cutters who were trucked in daily to the Menzies property.

'I remember my father going to work before sunrise,' Kok recalled in his statement to the police. 'He went in the same lorry with the workers.'

A particular afternoon in his childhood stood out in his memory. 'It was in 1948,' he told the probe team. 'I can't remember the exact date. I saw my mother crying in our house in Ulu Yam Bahru. From her I learned the soldiers in Sungei Remok Estate killed my father. I don't know who came and told my mother about my father's death.'

Lim Kok said that, at the time, he did not give particular attention to what had happened. He just remembered how his mother had gone to collect his father's body and placed his coffin by the side of the house before it was interred at the cemetery in front of the police station.

But the widow wanted her eldest child to know the relevant details of their loss and the extent of the horror done. 'My mother told me that my father's body was headless,' Kok stated.

Kok's future was decided soon after the burial. His granduncle, Chye Chee, took him to live with the contractor's family in Kuala Lumpur. For the first time in his life Kok stayed at a proper house with running water and rooms specifically assigned for receiving guests, eating, sleeping and bathing. He attended the Methodist Boys' School and had at least 10 years of education, passing his Senior Cambridge in 1958.

The work ethic was as strong as ever because Kok was soon earning his wages and paying for his way, like his father before him. Having been fostered out enabled the youth to be pushed a few rungs above grass cutting. He became a clerk for many years and, eventually, a supervisor at a petrol station, which, to all intents and purposes, meant being 'kepala' to workers who pumped fuel into cars. In 1979, he left this job for a higher paying one. He was determined to do better. When the Malaysian police spoke to him, he seemed to be on his way to becoming at least like his granduncle. To Kok's mind he probably was already a step ahead of his benefactor. His enterprise – he was now a freelance lubricants seller – was based in the city and he did not have to round up workers in a lorry before sunrise. He now referred to himself as 'a businessman'.

But he had remained a filial son. He looked after his mother once he was able and he never forgot the father he lost when he was nine years old. Every year, he returned to Ulu Yam Bahru to clean his father's grave for All Souls' Day.

The aftermath of the action at Tom Menzies' rubber plantation had its reverberations in the lives of those who had given succour to the lorry load of dumbstruck women and terrified children.

Ng Foong was 43 years old when his brother, Ng Kong, was killed in the search-and-destroy mission at Batang Kali. He was 88 when the Malaysian Task Force interviewed him in 1993.

What he had to say added yet another dimension to the investigators' thickening file – the plight of early immigrants to Malaya from China and how often the dream of a better life got dashed for them. Once landed, they remained shackled to the chains that had always hampered their efforts to advance in life. They confronted the old issues – ignorance, the expedient needs for food and shelter and the requirement to feed and clothe those they had left behind. The struggle for survival remained essentially the same, only lived in a different setting. Often, life presented the additional burden of loneliness and the challenge of gaining acceptance in an isolated and therefore initially hostile community.

The Malaysian police gleaned these observations after meeting and talking to Ng Foong. In 1927, at the age of 22, he had left his pauperised village in China. He travelled to Malaya where his much older sibling had gone earlier. Foong had only money for his passage and information that his brother, Kong, had settled in a place called Ulu Yam Bahru.

Foong found work as a rubber tapper in a small Malay-owned holding. He did not immediately seek out his brother. A reunion did not appear imperative; survival did.

'After some time, I met my older brother,' Foong told police. 'I found out Kong had been rubber tapping at Sungei Remok Estate.'

Both brothers had led tough lives. Foong thought he had certainly been luckier. At least he found time, at 37, to get married and start a family after ten years in Malaya. Kong, 12 years older, was a bachelor all his life. He lived very quietly in shared accommodation in one of the plantation *kongsi* houses where he was employed as a labourer. Kong had departed China in the early 1920s and had spent a lifetime feeding the mouths he had left in the old village.

Kong had accepted his role as everybody's provider with quiet dignity – rising at dawn, doing his job, cooking his own food. All he wanted was to be left alone to do as he pleased when his tasks were done – to chat or to nap, to watch the children at play or to make the odd trip to Ulu Yam Bahru and get acquainted with his brother's infant son. His brother would have four children.

'I can't remember the date or the day,' Foong informed his interviewers, 'when I learned from a group of women that British soldiers had killed many men at

Sungei Remok Estate. I was later told my brother was also killed.'

Being Kong's next of kin, Foong was summoned to the police station four or five days after the shooting. There he was given a permit allowing him to collect his older brother's body. Together with relatives of the other victims, Foong travelled to the estate in a lorry which also carried coffins for the dead.

At the plantation, Foong was assailed by the stench of highly decomposing bodies and felt helpless. He walked around and peered at every collapsed heap. He was on the verge of giving up when an assigned collector alerted him to a corpse where a card, bearing Ng Kong's name, was found.

Foong's statement recalled how his brother's coffin was made of planks, a donation from the contractor. He had sat beside it all the way back to Ulu Yam Bahru.

Foong told the police quietly: 'All I could do was visit his graveyard to show respect to him.'

The Malaysian investigating team could not help but be overwhelmed by the emerging magnitude of the challenge they had been assigned. They had started off believing they were experienced and hard-nosed professionals familiar with antagonisms, confrontations and bloodshed. But Batang Kali was proving to be an entirely new learning curve.

Chapter 13

A letter to Interpol

Nearly six months into their massacre inquiry, the three or four Malaysian police officers on whom had landed the main burden of responsibility decided it was time to appeal for far greater cooperation from the country's Special Branch. In the hope of harnessing top-echelon influence, they sought another meeting with the deputy CID director who had earlier proved helpful with their research work. The meeting was granted in early January, 1994. Task Force members, after appraising their superior officer of the probe's progress thus far, quickly reverted to the problems they were encountering with a decidedly less than supportive Special Branch.

The officers recounted the interview conducted four months earlier with retired Sub-Inspector Chia Kam Woh. They complained Special Branch had ignored their requests for guidance on what steps might be taken to further interrogate him. They explained their certainty that Chia was the only surviving member of the three-man local police group attached to the Scots Guards at the time of the mass killing. The Task Force thus felt Chia had to be further questioned. Its members did not mince words. They wanted Special Branch to consider whether Chia could be given 'an immunity against prosecution' as an incentive to come clean.

Complaints against Special Branch did not end there. Back in August, barely a month into the inquiries, the investigators had sent two letters to E3 executives. One had sought assistance tracing Special Branch officers who had served in Kuala Kubu Bahru in 1948. The other requested a run-down of communist terrorist activities in the same general region over the same time-frame. Five months later, neither request had elicited any response.

Before the meeting concluded, the deputy director had agreed to write personally to the then head of Special Branch, Dato' Norian Mai, in an effort to gain long overdue assistance. In late March, the Task Force finally received a muted response to the original approaches made months earlier. It came in the form of a six-page typed report headed 'The Batang Kali Incident – Security Situation in Selangor in 1948'. The requests for tracing former officers were ignored completely. Neither was there any response to the advice sought for a continuing interrogation of Special Branch retiree Chia.

The report, however, provided one or two interesting pieces of information.

It confirmed indications that the British had carried out a meticulous clean-up of all secret documents compiled on the Batang Kali incident. Not only had it been impossible to trace even a mention of the killing in department archives but, the highly secretive Special Branch was claiming, 'most of the records on security matters for the period 1948-57 are believed to have been taken back by the British upon the Independence of Malaya'.

Much of the report was devoted to an outline of the CPM's historical development from the mid-1920s onwards. It told how the economic depression of the 1930s had provided the communists with opportunities for exploitation and how these had led to serious strikes in local coal and tin mines. The CPM's cooperation with Britain's clandestine Force 136 during the Japanese occupation years was also listed along with a summary of communist activities in the immediate post-war period. All this amounted to little more than a history lesson for the investigators and made no useful contribution to their inquiries into the massacre.

But, the very last page of the report managed to focus the Task Force's attention. Headed 'Comment', this segment read:

'It would appear from available records that the security situation for the period under study was tense and that the initiative was largely with the CTO (Communist Terrorist Organisation). The Police Force was in the process of being built up to meet the threat, and military reinforcement in many cases comprised very young national servicemen (17 years – 20 years+) from Britain who had never seen combat and who now, for the first time in their lives, were plunged from a cold country into a guerrilla warfare situation in a very hot tropical jungle.

'Further, it has to be noted that in 1948 the CPM/CTO was identified mainly with the Chinese although it had some Malay and Indian membership. To the young British soldiers, it might have been difficult to distinguish between a Chinese Communist and an innocent Chinese. Apart from this, several abortive attempts to flush out the Communists in the jungles at that time were believed to have been caused by tips given to the CTs by the nearby rural folks. This might have compelled the frustrated British soldiers to turn their guns on whoever they suspected to be the culprits.'

The comment concluded with the telling passage: 'In view of the absence of any SB records on the victims of the Batang Kali incident, nothing conclusive can be drawn as to their innocence or otherwise. But whatever the state of security then, unless the victims had breached the Emergency Regulations which warranted the military to resort to the use of lethal weapons, there was certainly no justification for their killing.'

Suggesting that the Scots Guards patrol might have experienced difficulty distinguishing between communist and non-communist Chinese seemed an extraordinarily weak point to make. According to all evidence the Task Force had accumulated in Malaysia, the inescapable conclusion was that the British soldiers had lined up groups of male detainees they had held overnight and had opened fire with the clear intention of killing them all. They had not counted on a lone survivor.

If the Special Branch had found itself unable to draw conclusions as to the victims' innocence or otherwise, Task Force members felt very differently. As far as they were concerned, results of their inquiry had fully settled such matters.

There had not been a scrap of evidence suggesting anyone of the Sungei Remok Estate staff, or resident families, had ever been connected, directly or indirectly, to the communist cause.

Quite to the contrary, there was ample evidence indicating those living on the plantation held strong anti-communist sentiments.

Similarly, there was nothing to indicate the victims had, in any way, breached Emergency regulations. Their food supplies were within the colonial authorities' imposed rationing restrictions. Suggestions that they might have been engaged in providing communist forces in the area with food or other assistance had proved unfounded.

Those killed had been unarmed. They had not tried to escape. They had been shot as they stood on the positions to which they had been escorted. The eyewitness statements were quite conclusive on all these aspects.

That being the case, there could be absolutely no justification for the Scots Guards action.

In the early days of 1994, Task Force members began planning their schedule with a view to bringing inquiries to a close. Among the numerous clarifications requiring their attention was the matter of the petition they knew had been sent to Her Majesty Queen Elizabeth 11 of Great Britain. They understood this document bore the signature of Chong Fong and the fingerprints of Tham Yong and Foo Moi, the same trio whose police reports had initiated their massacre probe. The petition had, on August 8, 1993, been handed personally to the then serving British High Commissioner in Kuala Lumpur, Mr Duncan Slater.

Investigators felt it essential at least to have details of this petition on file. Moreover, they were keen to establish exactly what sentiments had been conveyed

PETITION

TO HER MAJESTY QUEEN ELIZABETH II

Through the British High Commission at Kuala Lumpur

We, FOO MOI (F), and THAM YONG (F), the relatives and dependents of victims of the shooting incidents at a village in Batang Kali in Malaya (as it then was) some time in December 1948 where twenty-four village men were killed in cold blood by a patrol of soldiers of the Scots Guards and CHONG FOONG, the survivor of the said incidents hereby humbly say as follows:-

1) There had previously been two official enquiries over 20 years which had never satisfactorily explained what had happened on the December 11th and 12th in 1948 at Batang Kali.

2) The British Broadcasting Corporation (BBC) in its investigative documentary series "Inside Story" broadcasted a documentary entitled "In Cold Blood" on the said incidents over BBC 1 on 9th September 1992.

3) The BBC produced evidence from the eye-witnesses, survivor, ex-guardsmen involved in the shootings and investigators which contradicted the official version of events and pointed to a cover-up by successive governments of a massacre by British soldiers who shot on orders at innocent civilians who were not armed nor running away.

We, the abovenamed who were eye-witnesses to the said incident therefore most humbly pray YOUR MAJESTY THE QUEEN to order that right be done in this matter and in the name of justice to refer this Petition to the present government to establish the truth and to open up the files and take the necessary action to prosecute the person or persons involved in the cold blooded massacre of the twenty-four innocent menfolk of Batang Kali and due compensation be made to the dependants and relatives of the victims for their loss and suffering.

FOO MOI (F)

THAM YONG (F)

張洪
CHONG FOONG

The petition to Queen Elizabeth 11 sworn by Batang Kali eye-witnesses Foo Moi and Tham Yong and lone survivor Chong Fong.

192

to Her Majesty and what, if any, response had been received from Buckingham Palace. Approaches to the High Commission produced the required document the following January. It bore all the obvious signs of continuing behind-scenes orchestration by the MCA. The wording and presentation were clearly beyond the capacities of the signatories. Further inquiries quickly confirmed police suspicions. It had been prepared at the MCA political headquarters under the direction of senior party officials.

While the High Commissioner's office had received no indication of a formal Palace reaction, the investigators' decision to acquaint themselves with the petition produced a useful result. Even though elements of the police hierarchy were revising their views on the massacre inquiry's advisability, political commitment to the process still looked strong. From the investigating team's viewpoint, the petition's wording, particularly its closing paragraph, appeared to leave no possibility of subsequent wavering from the course of action it was seeking:

'We, the above-named who were eyewitnesses to the said incident therefore most humbly pray YOUR MAJESTY THE QUEEN to order that right be done in this matter and in the name of justice to refer this Petition to the present government to establish the truth and to open up the files and take the necessary action to prosecute the person or persons involved in the cold blooded massacre of the twenty-four innocent menfolk of Batang Kali and due compensation be made to the dependants and relatives of the victims for their loss and suffering.'

By now, Task Force members were buoyed by the results their inquiries had produced. Surely their efforts would not go the way of previous endeavours by their British counterparts?

Around this time the investigating team had also identified a need to establish, once and for all, the exact contents of the diplomatic letter of complaint dispatched to Colonial Chief Secretary Newboult by Chinese Consul Li Chin nine days after the Batang Kali killings. Parts of its text had been made public shortly thereafter.

Published by the local press, these segments contained the initial revelations that all victims had been unarmed and that the killing had been 'out of all proportion' to the claimed threat. Investigators felt the unpublished parts of the diplomat's correspondence might well provide additional critical insights. After all, the Consul's information had come from eyewitnesses who had personally recalled their experiences for him only days after the incident. However, despite extensive searches carried out by and on behalf of the investigating team, no trace of the Consul's letter was ever found. It was then assumed that the original and all copies had been carefully packed away by the departing British in 1957 – or, perhaps, even before that – along with other possibly incriminating pieces of documentation on the incident.

By mid-1994, those leading the Malaysian inquiry had decided that only two main channels for investigations remained to be pursued. A concentrated effort was needed to secure the interrogation of ex-Special Branch man Chia Kam Woh. In addition, it was agreed that no Batang Kali massacre inquiry would be complete without evidence from Scots Guards who had taken part in the killing.

Reticence on the part of Special Branch to become involved in getting Chia to tell the truth appeared to be spreading to other police departments. This widening lack of cooperation presented as the only real stumbling block to a neat closure of the Malaysian end of inquiries. Task Force members were annoyed, but far from defeated. Even without the truth from Chia, they reasoned, evidence they had accumulated locally was more than enough to establish the fact of a massacre to a coronial or any other court.

Still, to miss out on the inclusion of a truthful account from the only surviving local member of the 1948 Scots Guards mission would not only be perceived as unprofessional investigative work but would always hang as a question mark over police force machinations. To say investigators were dismayed at this prospect would be an understatement.

Several meetings of the investigating team had been devoted to the issue of how best to handle the key but delicate area of gathering evidence from the former Scots Guardsmen concerned. One get-together in early June at the Bukit Aman mess had even been joined by the then newly appointed Inspector General of Police Rahim Noor. A tinge of disappointment had been injected into the gathering when the tough-talking IGP expressed the opinion that, perhaps, investigations in Britain might not be needed. Nobody took up the remark for further exploration and the subject of conversation moved on with, investigators hoped, no firm decision having been made.

Suggestions that the Malaysian team should rely on Scotland Yard's long-range assistance, and specifically its archival records, had been widely discussed on earlier occasions and rejected. Whatever had been behind the incoming British Conservative government's move in 1970 to abort and close the Scotland Yard inquiries had introduced a grey area the Task Force felt best avoided. All had viewed the BBC's *In Cold Blood* documentary on numerous occasions. All had heard retired Senior Detective Ron Dowling's wry comments about his meeting with colleague,

Detective Chief Superintendent Frank Williams, on the morning after the 1970 British general elections.

Strong apprehensions among Task Force members about seeking access to Scotland Yard archival material were, in the circumstances, understandable. What if they found nothing! The proposal to gain their London counterparts' cooperation for a series of interviews with former Scots Guards – measures to be conducted by Malaysian officers – seemed much the better approach. Their requirements were clear-cut. Initially, they wanted to speak to all guardsmen featured in *The People's* exposé and those whose statements had been revealed in the BBC documentary. If this first step proved successful, they would then seek to inspect all Scotland Yard files on the case and would, thereafter, make decisions about interrogating the remaining members of the patrol. Finally, they wanted to speak to Dowling and, if possible, Williams.

—◈—

In mid-June, 1994, Task Force leaders also met with the then Director of Malaysia's CID, and an array of senior officers. On this occasion, all gathered at the Bukit Aman headquarters viewed the *In Cold Blood* programme once more. Again, its significance was roundly recognised. During discussions that followed, the CID Director asked for Task Force recommendations going forward. The police were now feeling political pressure on the massacre issue. Questions had recently been asked in the Malaysian parliament as to the progress and likely outcome of the latest Batang Kali moves.

The meeting received a full briefing of the problems still being encountered with Special Branch as far as Chia Kam Woh's evidence was concerned. Also explained was the now urgent final requirements for sending Malaysian investigators to London.

The CID Director informed the gathering he would personally look into the difficulties associated with Chia. Furthermore, he instructed his head of prosecutions to liaise with both the Attorney General's office and Interpol, the international police organisation. The Attorney General would make the final decision on actions to be taken by Malaysia once the inquiry had closed. Interpol was to be the conduit for arranging the vital working visit to Britain by two Task Force investigators.

In a final observation before the meeting adjourned, the CID Director impressed on those present that, as it had been seen fit to petition the Queen, the

```
IP London                           44(0)71 238 8112




(IP)KPN(PR)71/5/105(2664/as)              23/5/1995


"BATANG KALI MASSACRE" — BATANG KALI POLICE REPORT
NO : 1149/93, 1150/93 AND 1151/93
---------------------------------------------------------

Introduction


The Royal Malaysia Police (RMP) is investigating on a case
of alleged massacre carried out by the 7th Platoon of the
'G' Company of the 2nd Battalion Scots Guards, who were
operating in Malaya then.  The alleged massacre took place
during the height of the Emergency of Malaya  in 1948.  In
this incident, a total of 24 chinese, suspected to be
terrorists were killed.  This incident has attracted a lot
of publicity both in our country as well as in Britain.  The
case, although happened in 1948, has not come to a
conclusion yet.


                                              ..2/-
```

On May 23, 1995, almost two years from the outset of Malaysia's Batang Kali investigations, the Kuala Lumpur police HQ dispatches a request for the assistance of Interpol. It seeks the international police organisation's help in facilitating a series of interviews with former Scots Guardsmen active on Sungei Remok Estate on the day of the slaughter.

Task Force had a duty to exhaust all avenues of investigations. The case, he said, had transcended national interests and had become one of international concern. Given the highly dubious nature of officialdom's role throughout the drawn-out saga, the CID chief's exhortations on this occasion might well have been dismissed by the investigators as just more added smoke to the screen.

But the meeting had involved the participation of some of the most powerful figures in the Malaysian Police Force. That special importance had now been placed on the approach made to the British monarch seemed to elevate matters to a level of significance previously unachieved. The Task Force still saw hope in retrieving the truth about Batang Kali from beneath the carpet of concealment where it had languished since the run-up to Christmas in 1948.

***

Some weeks later, two senior diplomats from the British High Commission in Kuala Lumpur drove to the Kuala Lumpur police headquarters for a meeting with high-ranking Malaysian police officials. Proceedings began with a briefing for the diplomats on the then current state of local investigations into the mass killing. Preliminaries over, Police Chief Rahim Noor informed his British visitors it had been decided two Malaysian investigating officers would be sent to Britain to conclude the Task Force's work. It was vital, the IGP emphasised, that neither the British nor Malaysian authorities make any public comment on the Batang Kali affair, or release any press statement, until the officers had returned from London and investigations were finalised.

The diplomats were informed that, in the meantime, Malaysia would go through the exercise of exhuming the victims' remains and carrying out forensic examinations. Once these were undertaken, the Malaysian officers had returned from London and their final investigation file had been submitted, British and Malaysian authorities would be in a position to issue a joint release. With close liaison existing between Britain and Malaysia at this point, the whole matter could be satisfactorily concluded.

The full message was unstated but obvious. Malaysia had no intention of taking the Batang Kali affair even to the coroner's court, let alone measures beyond that. London could rest assured the Malaysian investigations would never result in Britain facing further embarrassment on the matter. Nor would she have to confront the unseemly possibility of having to part with huge, long overdue reparations to family members of victims.

In 1970 'The Batang Kali Massacre' filled 3 pages of "The PEOPLE", a popular British Sunday Newspaper, and was quickly followed up by most other British papers alleging, "could be murder"; "New Version of Malayan Shooting" and "Order and Investigation"; British General and Leading government official had backed the Scots Guards Sergeant at the time of shooting"; "Accused British Soldiers have the right of reply and must use it"; "Government should dig back in its files and turn up the official records and publish them"; "Operation Whitewash is in full swing..... But attempts to hushup the truth today, as in 1948 and 1949 must not be allowed to succeed".

Our local newspapers also gave extensive coverage at the time of incident in 1948 and in 1970, the B.B.C crew did make a documenatry film locally on television.

On 4/2/1970 the Ministry of Defence in London launched an enquiry in the alleged massacre   Sworn testimony of some of the guardsman taken gave an insight into what really happened.   Sufficient evidence had been adduced to prove that, the villagers were killed without reason and that they were not trying to escape as claimed.   In fact, the enquiry revealed that, "A Bona-fide mistake had been made".

None of the evidence taken at the enquiry was ever made public and the report was never sent to the war office in London.   The team of investigators from Britian did not leave for Malaysia to investigate as the Labour Government had lost in the General Election in June 1970.   The new Conservative Government halted the investigation.

In 1992, a new research by "Inside Story", the British Broadcasting Corporation (B.B.C.) Television Investigative – Journalism Programme brought out buried evidence.   The documentary entitled, "In Cold Blood" included "Confessions" of some of members of the 7th Platoon "G" Company, 2nd Battalion Scots Guards and interviews with Scotland Yard officers, investigating the case in 1970.   Besides this, "Inside Story" also managed to get several Defence Ministry files which also contained statements taken from the soldiers, and showed that the victims were neither armed nor trying to escape.   The testimony of the eye-witnesses and even "Confessions" from former Scots Guards in the 45 minutes documentary pointed to a cover-up by the successive governments.

..5/-

The last sentence on page 4 of the Malaysian request to Interpol suggests conclusions being drawn by Malaysian investigators after their 22-month-long extensive inquiry.

Neither of the British diplomats offered objections to the suggestions put forward. They dutifully promised to report all remarks back to London. All in all, it had been a productive discussion; a little one-sided, perhaps, but most satisfactory nonetheless. A real win-win situation. That is, as long as you were not involved in the original Scotland Yard investigation. Or, you did not play a part in the MCA's campaign for justice and due compensation. Or, you were not a member of the Malaysian police inquiry team. More importantly, the neat arrangement regarding simultaneous press releases would have been all quite acceptable as long as you were not a kin of any of the Batang Kali dead.

⌐∿∿⌐

Controversies in the public arena, particularly those exhibiting international connotations, have a tendency to clog civil servant activity arteries wherever governments function. Malaysia has certainly not been immune to such afflictions and by the end of 1994 had begun strongly exhibiting many tell-tale symptoms over the Batang Kali issue. Police deliberations exploring the best means of securing Scotland Yard support and assistance had dragged through weeks into months.

It was not until May, 1995, that Bukit Aman finally settled on a list of requirements in the UK for a chosen two-man investigating team to leave for London. Long-standing liaison channels through Interpol, it was decided, would be the best means of achieving the right sort of facilitation on the part of the British police.

On May 23, 1995, Supt. Koh Hong Sun, Assistant Director NCB/ Interpol, wrote on behalf of the Malaysian IGP to his UK opposite number. The superintendent's five-page typed letter requested Interpol London's assistance in quite specific areas.

Help was needed, wrote the superintendent, in identifying the members of 7 Platoon, G Company, Scots Guards, who had operated in Malaya in December, 1948. Once done, the Malaysian team would then need arrangements for recording the statements of the identified former guardsmen.

The letter went on to ask for 'copies of confessions or statements made by some of the platoon members to Scotland Yard and the BBC'.

'As soon as the members of the platoon have been identified,' wrote Superintendent Koh, 'kindly let us know in advance so that we can send our officers to London and record the statements of the persons involved.'

His letter then provided a run-down of the security situation in Peninsular

199

Malaya in 1948 together with a general briefing on the Batang Kali incident as the Malaysian police investigators now saw it.

Significantly, the superintendent chose to draw Scotland Yard's attention to the fact that soon after the killings – on January 29, 1949, to be precise – Britain's colonial Chief Secretary in Kuala Lumpur had received a letter from the Chinese Consul-General requesting the issue of compensation be addressed. This matter, Koh emphasised, had 'since been left unattended'. Other references in the letter provided interesting pointers as to the mindset of the Malaysian investigating team at this stage of their inquiries.

At one point the letter noted:

'On 4/2/1970 the Ministry of Defence in London launched an enquiry into the alleged massacre. Sworn testimony of some of the guardsmen taken gave an insight into what really happened. Sufficient evidence had been adduced to prove that the villagers were killed without reason and that they were not trying to escape as claimed. In fact, the enquiry revealed that 'a bona-fide mistake had been made'.

Two paragraphs later, Supt. Koh informed Interpol:

'In 1992 a new research by 'Inside Story', the British Broadcasting Corporation (B.B.C) Television Investigative-Journalism Programme brought out buried evidence. The documentary entitled 'In Cold Blood' included 'confessions' of some members of the 7th Platoon 'G" Company, 2nd Battalion, Scots Guards, and interviews with Scotland Yard officers investigating the case in 1970. Besides this, 'Inside Story' also managed to get several Defence Ministry files which also contained statements taken from the soldiers, and showed that the victims were neither armed nor trying to escape. The testimony of the eye-witnesses, and even 'confessions' from former Scots Guards in the 45 minute documentary, pointed to a cover-up by the successive governments.'

—∿∿—

On April Fools' day, 1995, a leading member of the Malaysian investigative Task Force signed off the Batang Kali investigation file. Above his signature ran a three-page commentary on the work that had been undertaken by the Task Force since its formation on July 15, 1993 – almost two years earlier.

The officer noted categorically: 'It is evident from the witnesses that this massacre did take place in COLD BLOOD. However, he pointed out, 'all avenues/resources available have NOT been exhausted, in order to complete investigations so that a decision could be made by the proper authorities.'

The similarity between the British police position in July, 1970, and the Malaysian police position in April, 1995, was singularly eerie.

The Malaysian Task Force commentary continued:

'It is recommended that the following action be completed:

'(a) The statements of the SCOTS GUARDS, including those who made confessions to SCOTLAND YARD officers and BBC be recorded, with the assistance from A/G and Interpol.

'(b) Retired S.I. 182 Chia Kam Woh to be further interrogated in order to ascertain the truth and if required be used as a crown witness.

'(c) The views of the chief pathologist be sought with a view to exhume the graves.

'(d) This IP/SDR be referred to the Coroner for his findings.'

—◈—

Travel arrangements for the Malaysian investigators immediately ran into snags. Bukit Aman assumed responsibility for organising airline bookings. Interpol was further approached to confirm flight time-frames suitable to Scotland Yard. Then on the night before two Malaysian police officers were due to depart Kuala Lumpur's International Airport, on the initial stage of their UK investigations, each received a telephone call. They were informed Interpol was reporting Scotland Yard unprepared to host the proposed visit and associated interviews. These would have to be postponed to another day.

But another day never came. A further plan of action – or rather inaction, in this case – had overtaken the arrangements proposed months earlier by the Malaysian Police at the instigation of the investigating team. Scotland Yard would not be involved.

—◈—

Nine more years would pass from the Task Force's final submission of its investigative report before the Malaysian authorities announced publicly – but decidedly quietly – the official word on the nation's Batang Kali Massacre inquiry.

A-G closes file on Batang Kali massacre due to lack of evidence

THE Attorney-General's Chambers has closed the case on the Batang Kali massacre of 1948, Datuk Seri Abdullah Ahmad Badawi said.

The Prime Minister said the file was closed on Dec 30, 1997, after no evidence was found to charge anyone in the matter.

He told Lim Kit Siang (DAP-Ipoh Timur) in a written reply that based on police reports lodged by a survivor of the massacre, police had investigated the case under Section 302 of the Penal Code.

"The complainant in the case had said that on Dec 11, 1948, a group of more than 10 British soldiers had embarked on a rescue mission and detained Chinese occupants of the Sungai Remuk Kongsi in Batang Kali Estate," said the Internal Security Minister.

He said the detainees had been accused of being communists and sympathisers.

Abdullah said the complainant had alleged that the women and children were taken to Ulu Yam Baru the next day while the men were shot.

The complainant had said that he had escaped being shot as he had fainted.

"Investigation papers were opened on July 14, 1993, after the police report was lodged.

"The results of the investigations were submitted to the Selangor Criminal Investigation Department chief and Bukit Aman CID director," he added.

The investigations were then referred to the A-G's Chambers, which decided to close the case.

Finally, the Malaysian Government makes public its decision on the Batang Kali investigations. This is reported, tucked away in The New Straits Times, on September 16, 2004.

It came in the form of a brief written response to a parliamentary question posed by opposition politician, Lim Kit Siang, representing the country's Democratic Action Party (DAP) seat of Ipoh Timur.

A ten-paragraph story in Malaysia's *The New Straits Times* newspaper on September 16, 2004, revealed that the country's Prime Minister, Datuk Seri Abdullah Ahmad Badawi, in his dual capacity as Internal Security Minister, had gone on record declaring the Batang Kali case closed.

In fact, Malaysia had effectively sealed the file more than six years earlier. According to the Prime Minister's curiously delayed announcement, closure had actually taken place on December 30, 1997. The reason? After police had investigated the case under Section 302 of the Penal Code, no evidence had been found to charge anyone in the matter. The Attorney General's Chambers had therefore closed the case.

As to why it had taken the authorities six years and nine months to reveal this information there was, quite predictably, no explanation.

Given the tight government control of the nation's press and media worlds, Kuala Lumpur authorities could be confident such information entering the public arena in this way would make little impact locally. That is exactly what occurred. As a result, there were no repercussions whatever in the British press or anywhere in Westminster. For some, there is solace in the fact that, given properly manipulated situations, memories and the prospect of justice both fade with the passage of years.

From the time of the Batang Kali Task Force's formation, it had taken the Malaysian authorities more than 11 years to release a statement on the massacre inquiry's results. When the disclosure finally came, it was astonishingly and embarrassingly similar to that presented by British Attorney General, Sir Peter Rawlinson, in the House of Commons more than 34 years earlier.

Both pronouncements were based on conveniently terminated investigations. Both secured the continuing cover-up.

Chapter 15

The Batang Kali massacre and British propaganda

We gave the matter of locating our CPM base headquarters a great deal of thought
for obvious reasons. At first we considered locating somewhere in southern Johore so
that we might be near the population centre of Singapore. However, we eventually
rejected this idea after reviewing the security risks it would involve. We then though
of situating ourselves in the Labis-Segamat area of northern Johore with the ultim
aim of moving into central Pahang which offered such conveniently isolated ju
prospects. In the end, it was the rush of events at the outset of the Emergen
would determine the details of our strategy and the position of the nerve c
our campaign.

The original plan had been for me, after collecting our tin-mining
the Kampar capitalist, to move back to Labis and call a final meeting
Committee. There we had hoped to conclude arrangements and
switch to armed struggle. In fact, some of our key men, in ex
developments, had already moved to a temporary base in Johore

As it turned out, Yeung Kuo, had a similar narrow escape fr
and at around the same time. Although he had moved perma
this stage, he had gone back to Penang in mid-June to visi
daughter. As soon as he heard the State of Emergency
Siput, he felt it best to leave his in-laws' George
nearby. The police raided his in-laws' residence
was subsequently banished to China.

Yeung Kuo decided to make for Selang
safely and headed for the Ampang area of t
the local comrades. As he had spent
Japanese occupation and in the m
recognised figure there, particula
in the confusion, he found h

For all their ea
managed to
revolutio

*Former Secretary General of the
Communist Party of Malaya, Chin Peng,
in his memoirs, My Side of History, first
published in 2003, leaves no doubt about
his understanding of what took place on
Sungei Remok Estate.*

Chapter 14

Lessons of history

Exactly a year before Malaysia revealed she had jettisoned her Batang Kali Massacre probe, the memoirs of former Communist Party of Malaya Secretary General, Chin Peng, reached the bookshops. *My Side of History*, a 527-page tome, was simultaneously released in Malaysia, Singapore, the United Kingdom and Australia. It became an instant best-seller in both Malaysia and Singapore. Reviews in the UK and Australia made the point that Chin Peng was one of a handful of historical figures – including Gandhi, Nehru and Nasser – who, jointly, could claim credit for the 'final dissolution of the British Empire'. Critics observed that the 'winds of change' that eventually blasted through Africa, had first manifested in Malaya.

My Side of History provides, from Chin Peng's perspective, a substantial review of the Malayan Emergency years.

Chapter 15 of the book is headed *The Batang Kali massacre and British propaganda*. This section carries reproductions of UK news stories published at the time by both *The Daily Telegraph* and *The Times*. In a final comment on the mass killing the former guerrilla leader writes:

'*Batang Kali had been a massacre by an enemy whose political leaders on the other side of the world had simultaneously decided it would be more advantageous to their colonial cause to describe us as terrorists. That the December 12, 1948, executions remain a British secret is a measure of the advantage held in warfare by the side that dominates propaganda. The UK Ministry of Defence has remained tight-lipped. All police files on Batang Kali are classified to this day. At the outset of my book I referred to the way victors edit history. This is certainly a case in point.*'

Chin Peng recalls that at the time of the massacre he was at a jungle location in the Cameron Highlands, some distance from the killing scene. But, he notes, he began receiving initial reports on the incident soon after the event. It would, however, be some months before his underground network was able to provide him with more substantial details.

Even then, he writes, it would take decades before he could piece together the truth of what had really occurred at Batang Kali.

From the outset, his underground reports had branded the Scots Guards action a 'calculated massacre'. They had also indicated the victims were unarmed.

Veterans' fury at 'Malay massacre

Rebel leader's new book revives allegation that the Scots Guards executed civilians in campaign of terror

KURT BAYER
AND GRAHAM OGILVY

FROM Waterloo to the Falklands, they fought with undoubted bravery and distinction. But claims of war crimes during a bloody conflict in south-east Asia have resurfaced and threaten to sully the name of the Scots Guards.

The man who led the insurgency against British rule in Malaya has published an account of the war in which he repeats claims that members of the Scots Guards massacred unarmed civilians.

Chin Peng alleges in *My Side of History* that troops from the second battalion killed 26 civilians in cold blood, pretending they were communist bandits shot while trying to escape.

The Ministry of Defence has always denied the claims and last night insisted there was insufficient evidence to bring criminal proceedings against Scots troops over the events in village of Batang Kali on December 11 and 12, 1948.

Veterans of the campaign also condemned the claims, branding them "complete nonsense".

Peng, before leading anti-British rebels in the 12-year-long Malayan Emergency, was given an OBE and decorated by Lord Mountbatten for his key role in the resistance movement against the Japanese during the Second World War.

But his book has once again shone the spotlight on a dark episode in post-war history that the British military establishment must have hoped had been forgotten.

In it he claims that calculated terror was applied by the British

Peng: Had received the OBE

deliberate "cold-blooded massacre" to subdue the population.

Britain's success in winning 'hearts and minds' in the Malayan Emergency was later lauded as a model for defeating communist insurrection.

Peng, 79, now lives quietly in Bangkok, but in the 1950s he was the British Empire's most wanted man with a $250,000 bounty on his head.

Speaking exclusively to Scotland on Sunday, Peng called for an independent investigation into the shooting by the Scots Guards of 26 young villagers at Batang Kali.

At the time, the killings were presented as a victory. A Scots Guard patrol of 14 men was said to have captured 26 communist 'bandits' in a single engagement with no British casualties at all.

According to the official version of events, one prisoner was subsequently shot while trying to escape on the night of December 11 and the remaining 25 were killed in a similar attempt the following day.

In his book, Peng paints a

evidence from female villagers, one male survivor and a former Malayan police officer, he claims that all of those who died were unarmed rubber tappers and tin miners from the Chinese ethnic minority.

He alleges that one prisoner was summarily executed to terrify the others on December 11 and the remaining 25 were divided into three groups and executed the next day.

Peng, who was General Secretary of the powerful Communist Party of Malaya (CPM), is also adamant that there was not a single member of the CPM among those killed.

He told Scotland on Sunday that any official inquiry into the action by the Scots Guards would reveal, "meticulous preplanning at a very senior command level".

Peng also alleges that Scots Guard soldiers used extreme "terror tactics" to subdue and control Malaya's rural population. He said: "There can be no other logical explanation for the killing of so many unarmed civilians in such a calculated, clinical fashion."

Peng also believes that members of the unit involved were told by their sergeant that there would be a mass killing and were offered the opportunity to withdraw. He claims: "That members of the involved unit should have been given the option of withdrawing from the killing, prior to the event, strongly supports the conclusion that it was a calculated act."

Peng's claims are partly based on the testimony of villager Chong Hong, who claims he had a remarkable escape from Scots Guards' bullets. "The sol-

Front line: At the height of the Malayan Emergency, Scots Guards watch areas of jungle they have mined for communist bandits t

Denis Healey, to order an inquiry. A team from Scotland Yard was assembled to travel to

by their troops were unlikely to be exposed to public scrutiny.

"Equally important, Batang

and added: "I was not at the incident, but there was a very strong feeling in the battalion

WAR WITHO
The Malayan Emerge

The weekly newsaper, Scotland on Sunday, is quick to respond to claims of a Batang Kali massacre made by Chin Peng in his memoirs.

What was more, none of the *kongsi* residents on the estate, he relates, had ever been members of the CPM. Sceptics would argue that it would be in the octogenarian's continuing interests to make such claims. On the other hand, if anyone had access to the sort of information that could clarify these aspects once and for all, it would surely be Chin Peng.

Since the release of his book, he has additionally confirmed that subsequent research further substantiates the repeated assurances by former residents of the three *kongsi* houses that nobody on the estate was involved in what security forces classified as *Min Yuen* support activities. In short, the sort of information the former insurgency leader could have provided Malaysian investigators would have concurred with accounts rendered by the apparently anti-communist, surviving family members of Batang Kali victims. Pointedly, Malaysian investigators never considered seeking his opinions.

Chin Peng's book drew virulent reaction in the Scots Guards heartland. On December 4, 2003, the Edinburgh-based *Scotland on Sunday* newspaper published a major feature beneath a banner headline reading: *Veterans' fury at 'Malay massacre' claim.*

Asserting that Scots Guards veterans of the Malaya Campaign were scathing of the claims being made about Batang Kali in *My Side of History*, the newspaper account went on to seek the reaction of a number of prominent former guardsmen.

General Sir Michael Gow, a former General Officer Commanding Scotland, one-time Governor of Edinburgh Castle and Commandant of the Royal College of Defence Studies from 1984-85, was quoted as saying: 'I served with that battalion, although I arrived a few months after the alleged incident. I would say that these allegations are complete nonsense. Our unit was completely professional and nothing of that sort happened. What some people forget is that it was a hell of a slog out there. We lost a lot of men, including some good friends.'

Scotland on Sunday also quoted Major General Sir John Acland, a veteran of the Malaya Campaign, the Cyprus Campaign, Kenya's Mau Mau Uprising, the Zanzibar Revolution and Northern Ireland riots. Also a former commanding officer of 2nd Battalion, Scots Guards, the general pointed out: 'I was not at the incident, but there was a very strong feeling in the battalion that nothing wrong happened.'

Former Tory leader and onetime Scots Guardsman, Iain Duncan Smith, told the same paper: 'I was too young for Malaya. But the Scots Guards are one of the most professional units in the world. The way the British forces conducted themselves contributed to the success. Modern Malaysia owes a great deal to Britain for dealing with the insurgency.'

These reactions differed significantly from viewpoints then being relayed to the

Former Conservative Party leader, Iain Duncan Smith, once a Scots Guardsman, comes to the defence of his old unit in the Scotland on Sunday story.

publishers of *My Side of History* by former UK military personnel with Malayan Emergency backgrounds. Some sought direct communication with Chin Peng himself. Fifty-five years and so much recurring controversy later, it was obvious that a body of ex-service opinion desired far more than the accepted regimental version of events. Bland suggestions to the effect that Scots Guardsmen could never have committed the Batang Kali Massacre as the regiment's noble traditions and renowned professionalism would have made such behaviour impossible were wearing thin. There were reports of how several junior officers in the battalion, in no way connected to the killing but deeply troubled by what had taken place, had, in the months that followed the raid, made private forays back to Sungei Remok. Quite aside from command pronouncements and explanations being provided at the time, they felt exploring the terrain for themselves might help dissolve lingering doubts and unease.

One former Scots Guards officer, in an exchange of letters with Chin Peng, told how he had arrived in Malaya in early 1949. Although four months had elapsed since Batang Kali, he noted, the incident had 'still left ripples in the pond'.

On one occasion he had taken advantage of a lunch break from patrol duties to visit the scene of the killing as it happened to be 'not far away'. He went in the company of Sgt. Douglas, the man who had led the 7 platoon action. The sergeant, he said, 'showed no guilt'.

As the two men walked around the scene, Douglas had explained how he thought the amount of food at Batang Kali had been excessive. He had told the *kongsi* manager very sternly he expected cooperation the following morning. The sergeant claimed he had posted his men at the end of narrow pathways to stop any food going out or anyone coming into the plantation clearing. When the supply lorry came up the approach road it went over loose planks on a wooden bridge. This had resulted in a noise like a burst from a machinegun. The plantation workers screamed and started running. Once one shot was fired, patrol-members reacted accordingly.

The letter writer said Douglas' story had been separately confirmed for him by a senior officer who happened to be in attendance when the platoon leader, shortly after the incident, was interviewed by a representative from the Judge Advocate's Department.

Endeavouring to clarify the Scots Guards side of the story for Chin Peng, the correspondent offered extra background. The company's second-in-command, on the weekend concerned, had assembled an 'ad-hoc force'. This had comprised drivers, cooks, storemen, clerks, orderlies, etc. The 'ad-hoc force' had then been divided in two – the second-in-command taking charge of one section and Sergeant Douglas leading the other.

It was thus not surprising, went the writer's explanation, that troops on this occasion performed 'rather erratically' when faced with a stampede of screaming people 'who outnumbered them by more than three to one, running at them in the half-light of dawn'. Interestingly, the Scots Guards Regiment has never offered a formal public statement on these matters.

Given the programme of concealment undertaken by civilian and military authorities throughout 1949 and since, these details are probably the closest anyone has come to the very private and closely protected Scots Guards regimental rationale for the Menzies plantation slaughter. It is therefore valid to judge the veracity of these latest claims against irrefutable facts, working through them point by point.

It is difficult to see how the sergeant could have judged that there were excessive food stocks on the estate late on the first day of the raid. His patrol's search certainly made no such discovery nor were there ever claims to this effect. Indeed, at the outset of the controversy, emphasis was placed by the colonial military establishment on the supposed seizure of Sten-gun ammunition from a *kongsi* bed – a claim later shown to be without foundation. Twice, during his 1970 interview with *The People,* Douglas made the point that his patrol had not discovered any ammunition.

His exact words then were: 'There was an inquiry by, I think, the Judge Advocate General, and we heard ammunition had been found.' Later in the same interview, when questioned further about the ammunition Douglas said: 'They were found by the Chinese afterwards.' Given the fact that all structures in the plantation clearing were gutted by fire immediately following the shooting, this particular claim seems totally without merit.

The suggestion that Douglas, as the result of the excessive food supplies, had demanded the cooperation of the *kongsi* manager on the evening before the shooting must also be seriously questioned. The *kongsi* manager arrived on the plantation in the lorry the following morning along with the food supplies. These were subsequently shown to be in full conformity with Emergency rationing restrictions.

The insinuation that the sergeant had pre-positioned sentries sometime prior to the shooting is impossible to sustain. The restricted manpower of the patrol indicates he lacked the numbers for such a commitment. The overwhelming body of evidence provided to both *The People* newspaper and Scotland Yard by former guardsmen involved, together with eyewitness accounts from victims' widows and the lone survivor himself, all confirm that no sentries were posted. And if these factors were not enough, the finding of four separate tight groupings of corpses is undisputed. No sentry activity took place.

Lt. Colonel Michael Gow, 2nd Battalion, Scots Guards photographed in December, 1965 (above). General Sir Michael Gow (right) arrives at Edinburgh's Holyrood Park to take the salute at a Beating Retreat ceremony in 2003. Gow chooses to pour scorn on the possibility of a Batang Kali massacre when talking to Scotland on Sunday. Such allegations, he declares, are 'complete nonsense'.

Major General Sir John Acland shows off his KCB after his investiture at Buckingham Palace in 1980. His remarks to Scotland on Sunday are well considered. Pointing out he was not at the incident, he adds: '. . . but there was a very strong feeling in the battalion that nothing wrong happened'.

The excuse that the early morning supply lorry had triggered a panic among the detained labour when it crossed the wooden approach bridge to the plantation is equally unacceptable. The lorry left Ulu Yam Bahru with the food supplies and extra contract workers at 6 am for the less than 15-minute drive to the estate. When it crossed the bridge all detained men, women and children were still locked up. It had been halted, surrounded by guardsmen, emptied of its passengers and its food stocks unloaded well before the women and children were escorted from their detention room. All men who had arrived in the lorry, including the driver, were then taken away for questioning. The lorry remained stationary on the estate road while the interrogations, with guards in place, were underway. By this point it was well past the 'half-light of dawn'.

When the male plantation workers emerged under guard from their confinement, the women and children had already been placed in the lorry. Eyewitness accounts leave no doubt that the shooting erupted before the vehicle began to move off and long before it could have driven back over the wooden bridge. In short, whatever sound the lorry may have made on the bridge during its arrival or departure from the estate that day simply had no influence on the events that transpired there.

Equally implausible is the claim that the male labourers began a stampede from a point immediately outside their overnight detention room. As quoted in Chapter 3, the Attorney General's Supplementary Statement, issued on January 3, 1949, argued that an escape scenario had been carefully hatched by the detainees overnight.

The Attorney General averred that a shout was 'no doubt the pre-arranged signal for putting the plan into effect'. This, of course, all flies in the face of the wooden-bridge-sounding-like-a-machinegun argument. Once again, all evidence collected in both Britain and Malaysia thoroughly demolishes such contentions. It beggars credibility that supposedly terrified, screaming men, fleeing for their lives, would have the presence of mind to converge on four separate points where they were felled – this, irrespective of the Attorney General's preposterous observation that they had, without hesitation, formed into three neatly pre-arranged groups as they departed.

In this context, the other over-riding reality that must be taken into consideration is that those supposedly attempting to escape were all unarmed. And those from whom they were supposedly fleeing were equipped with sophisticated automatic weapons.

When media reaction following *The People's* 'Horror in a nameless village' disclosures smoked-out former Malaya Attorney General, Sir Stafford Foster-

Sutton, the truth of the initial killing cover-up was there for the taking. Foster-Sutton's admission he had never led a 'formal inquiry' into the mass killing and had never reported the matter to the War Office quickly revealed that, in fact, none of the claimed three separate official inquiries had ever taken place.

His one-sided 'findings' in January, 1949, had justified the results of the Scots Guards raid on strict military grounds. Twenty-two years later he was judging it all 'a bona fide mistake' – a drastically revised conclusion. When Foster-Sutton conceded he had never held a formal inquiry, the entire British colonial argument in support of the Scots Guards fell apart. The purported formal inquiry and its avowed conclusions had been the very cornerstone of the British position. Clearly, Foster-Sutton had been a willing party, along with Malaya Commander, Major General Boucher, and Chief Secretary, Sir Alec Newboult, in formulating a calculated deception to justify Batang Kali.

But rather than independently exploring and developing the 'cover-up' angle, press, radio and television journalists in Britain, once Scotland Yard entered the picture, left this to the detectives. This was predictable. There were countless other stories seemingly more relevant and certainly closer to home. By the time the British investigators had dropped away, the issue had faded, just as the politicians had hoped.

The original deception, suitably assisted by a compliant colonial press, resulted in large part from perceived requirements to preserve the saving graces and myths of Empire as its final dissolution appeared unstoppable. Of course, personal self-interests were a factor. But nobody would have admitted these were paramount. Without preservation of saving graces and myths, the historic basis on which colonial masters argued the morality of their past and fading positions would likely have disintegrated entirely.

This was particularly so in the closing stages of the 1940s – a decade dominated by World War 11 and the emergence, immediately thereafter, of re-invigorated nationalist sentiments throughout South East Asia. There were serious concerns in London over how the Malayan Emergency and continuing involvement of British troops could be portrayed and validated before the UK public.

Presentation of communism's international threat coming from behind the Iron Curtain was far easier to explain on the home front than involvement in anti-insurgency activities in jungles on the other side of the world. The possibility of British forces being linked to crimes in an undeclared war in those jungles only exacerbated problems. And underlining all was the acknowledged need for Britain to retain Malaya for as long as she could keep extracting foreign earnings seen as vital to the repayment of her overwhelming war debts.

Two decades later, the perceived requirements, as far as British interests were concerned, were markedly different. The Emergency had been declared over in July, 1960. The decade to follow saw the Vietnam era unfold and a determined reluctance on the part of the UK to become directly involved in yet another South East Asian regional conflict. Britain became committed to an 'east of Suez' military withdrawal and took her troops home.

By 1970 the Empire was being viewed as little more than a quaint notion of history. Now the perception, from the political standpoint, was a need to preserve national prestige in world forums. For the military, it was a requirement to maintain, unblemished, the façade of discipline, dignity and honour.

Thus the Batang Kali Massacre regurgitation came as a decidedly unwelcome distraction. The decision? The cover-up must continue.

Whereas it had been colonial Malaya's Attorney General who was instrumental in setting it in motion in 1949, it fell upon the British Attorney General, Sir Peter Rawlinson, to ensure the deception be kept firmly in place in 1970. When he addressed parliament on July 9 that year he stressed it had been the DPP who had decided to halt the Scotland Yard investigations and call off the detectives' Malaysia trip. These decisions, he said, had followed a 'full investigation'.

Quite clearly, there was nothing 'full' about the Scotland Yard inquiries at that stage. The Attorney General must have known it as Scotland Yard was well aware of it. Police research at the Malaysian end had long been recognised as fundamental to a balanced appreciation of the mass killing. This view had been communicated to the DPP's office by Scotland Yard early in the British probe. Concurrence had been secured and flights booked for the two Scotland Yard men, Williams and Dowling. The DPP had appreciated the argument and it would be incredible had Rawlinson been kept in the dark on such an important issue. What was missing from a 'full' British investigation was the gathering of evidence in Malaysia. Only then could final decisions be made.

Just as baffling was the ultimate reason Rawlinson gave for calling off the inquiries. As noted in Chapter 8, it had been concluded there was 'no reasonable likelihood of obtaining sufficient evidence to warrant criminal proceedings'. Given the circumstances of tidily aborted investigations, this was undoubtedly true.

An almost identical reason was provided by the conveniently supportive Malaysian authorities 34 years later, when they quietly justified the abandonment of their unfinished Batang Kali inquiries. In each case, official explanations, lame as they now seem, passed without question. It was, again, as the politicians had hoped.

Given the piecemeal manner the Batang Kali truth has emerged over the decades and now the never before revealed details of the Malaysian side's abortive investigative effort, significant questions are raised.

In both Britain and Malaysia doubts over the 'likelihood of prosecutions' have been used to justify the abandonment of continuing inquiries. Has this excuse ever really been a fundamental consideration?

Could nothing of value have resulted from continuing inquiries, even if these had lacked the promise of specific prosecutions?

Was it not possible to establish an illegal act had been committed, irrespective of prosecution probabilities?

If substantiation of such an act was forthcoming under these conditions, could this not lead to rightful compensation?

In an age of massively advanced forensic science, is it valid to abandon any exhumation activity or related killing inquiry on the vague notion that a prosecution, or prosecutions, might be unlikely?

Are there not deep moral issues involved here as far as the responsibilities incumbent on nations sending men to war and reviewing campaign aftermaths?

Does the lapse of time ever diminish the requirement for the establishment of truth?

Should following generations be deprived of the lessons that can be derived from history – particularly when lessons stem from the horrifying fact of a mass killing in the time of an undeclared war?

As far as Batang Kali is concerned, it is both incongruous and deeply disturbing that the information needed to complete the British investigations should now be readily available in a Kuala Lumpur police file. At the same time, that required to wrap-up the Malaysian side sits in Scotland Yard files protected by the tightest possible restrictions.

A coordination of the separate investigations, even at this late stage, could produce a formal finding. The elusive 'full investigation' would then have been achieved. The historical record could be set. Official efforts could be undertaken to address long overdue obligations.

Finally, an appreciation of the truth could be established in the hope of ensuring such a lamentable course of events as Batang Kali, does not recur.

Epilogue

THAM YONG

She shuffles cautiously across the spotless sitting room dominated by a Chinese altar. She is 78, bent and shriveled by illness. But there is something about the eyes that suggests the gift of grit. She settles in the wheelchair only after the unexpected guests have identified themselves.

The intrusion into her day is met with surprising equanimity. She apologises for having to strain with her words. She raises her hand and brings it close to her throat. It is the cancer, she informs.

Tham Yong confirms her husband Chong Fong died in April, 2008. At this point, she volunteers to show her identity card that proves she is, indeed, Tham Yong, widow of the only man to survive the 1948 mass killing on Sungei Remok Estate. This gesture on her part is a curious one until one realises that, since 1948, the woman had, on various occasions, been called upon to confirm her identity. People had sought to establish first who she was before asking their questions – the journalists Chiew Cheng Cherd, Hugh Mabbett and Bill Dorran, the BBC TV crew, MCA political operatives and the members of the police investigating team.

What she tells people hardly departs from what she told the police who were endeavouring to get at the truth of Batang Kali in 1992.

Her birth year is 1931. Tham Yong does not know the exact dates. At three, she had been given away to a man who travelled from China and settled in Malaya. In Kuala Kubu Bahru, he gave her away to an impoverished couple who worked in a tin mine. They were very poor and didn't send her to school. She also knew they didn't like her ' because when I was 7 or 8, I became naughty.'

Life became more difficult when the Pacific war broke out. At 12, Tham Yong became a rubber tapper in a small Malay-owned holding. Shortly after, her adoptive mother took her to Sungei Remok Estate where they worked and lived together in one of the kongsi houses. Then, in exchange for $200 in Japanese occupation money, Tham Yong was left with another set of 'parents'.

Tham Yong became part of Chong Choi's family and Wong Kiew was now her 'stepmother'. The couple had three sons – Chong Fong, Chong Sip and Chong Chen. Chong Fong was a rubber tapper at Sungei Remok, Chong Sip and Chong

Chen were studying in Ulu Yam.

The remaining years of the war passed quietly for the workers on Sungei Remok. For the first time Tham Yong felt she had a home. Wong Kiew was pretty determined to sustain this. In early 1948, she called in Chong Fong, Chong Sip and Tham Yong to discuss the future. Wong Kiew wanted Tham Yong to marry into the family and the 17 year-old was asked to choose between the two brothers.

The choice was an easy one for Tham Yong: it was Chong Sip. He was even-tempered, a student and had ambition. He wanted to be a teacher. Chong Sip asked Tham Yong to wait until his studies were completed. She agreed. They had always got on well and kept their pact to themselves. At this point, she started to nurse hopes of an improved life. In three years, Tham Yong thought, she would stop rubber tapping.

In 1948, Chong Choi opened a coffee shop in Ulu Yam Bahru and Tham Yong started serving there. She welcomed this development as she also found time to see more of her fiancée.

His mother tried to rush Chong Sip into marriage and discourage his ambitions. Wong Kiew pointed out that the family could not afford to send him to teachers' training college. Chong Sip was undeterred and explained he would work for the money. In fact, he informed his parents, he was working on the Menzies plantation to earn extra money during the long school holidays from November, 1948, through to January, 1949. Furthermore, he had also struck a durian-collecting arrangement with his close friend Loh Kit Lin from which he hoped to share profits.

To be with him, Wong Kiew and Tham Yong moved back to the *kongsi* and worked on Sungei Remok plantation for the stipulated period.

This obvious display of affection did not escape the spurned Chong Fong and his relationship with Chong Sip was further strained.

Chong Sip's determined efforts for advancement would cost him his life.

At 78, Tham Yong is still visited by the memory of December 12, 1948. She alights from a lorry in Ulu Yam Bahru with the other traumatised women and children. She recalls weeping with Wong Kiew under a tree. It is there that Chong Choi finds them and he takes them back to his coffee shop.

Tham Yong is there when Chong Fong reaches his father's establishment. The 19 year-old is out of breath and deathly pale. There is blood on him. He is disoriented and falls in a heap on the floor. Chong Choi asks his son to get up and sit on a chair. Uncharacteristically, Chong Fong does not protest; he gets up and does what he is told. Chong Choi makes a cup of coffee and sets it on a table, in front of the agitated youth. Then father and son talk softly and quietly. Wong Kiew has stopped crying and advises Chong Fong to rest. He stands up slowly and as he

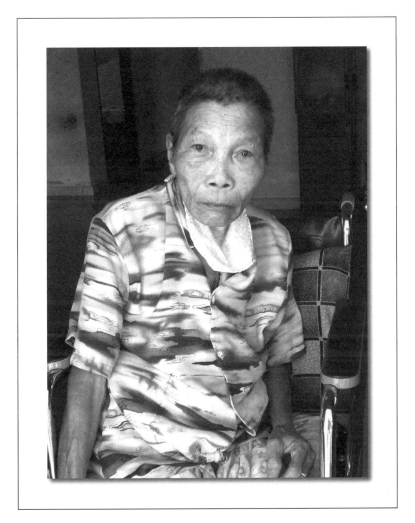

Tham Yong, Ulu Yam Bahru, August, 2008.

turns to leave, his mother asks after Chong Sip. Chong Fong only shakes his head.

Much of the exchange between Chong Choi and Chong Fong escapes Tham Yong who is seated at a distance. The blood on Chong Fong's clothes fills her with foreboding. Quietly she runs through her mind how, being told by the 'white soldiers' they could retrieve some personal belongings, she had rushed through the verandah and called out Chong Sip's name. And he had answered. Tham Yong remembers how he had asked her to take the money he had carefully hidden in his room. She is able to retrieve the savings tucked in a trouser pocket: $70. But soon she is being brusquely told by a soldier to return downstairs. Rattled, she throws the clothes over the verandah rail to the ground below. The 'white soldiers' do not allow her to pick them up.

The next day, Tham Yong goes back to Sungei Remok with a few other women, including Wong Kiew. They trudge in the blazing sun. Who would ever forget the gruesome scene that awaited them? They walk back to Ulu Yam Bahru in silence but the gravity of it all and their exhaustion make them stop at a Malay kampong where the villagers advise them to rest and offer them glasses of water.

It is Tham Yong who identifies the decomposing body of her fiancée a few days later. It takes a long while to retrieve the remains of the 24 Sungei Remok dead. She cannot forget how these were shoved into planked coffins and how the women painstakingly labelled each box.

She rides with Chong Sip's coffin at the back of the same lorry that took them away from the plantation on the morning of the shooting. Tham Yong relates how the weather turned and the skies opened up. She and the other women try to shield the boxes from the lashing rain.

Chong Sip is interred at the Ulu Yam Bahru cemetery. Then life resumes. Chong Choi keeps his coffee shop open and Tham Yong assists him. Where would she go?

The decent interval between death and a new beginning is observed. Then it is decided that nothing much has changed. Wong Kiew still wants Tham Yong to be her daughter-in-law. More importantly, Chong Fong is still interested. He has nothing to do with Chong Sip's death. Now that his brother is gone, it does not seem wrong to make his intentions known.

Tham Yong marries the surviving brother. Life continues to challenge them and new struggles surface. But in the nearly sixty years they are together, Chong Fong and Tham Yong never cease to wonder whether anyone in authority will ever recognise the injustice of December 12, 1948.

Tham Yong survives her husband and finds herself left with the legacy of hope that justice will one day triumph.

Index

Ministry of Defence (UK) 97, 98, 138.

Min Yuen 15, 16, 19, 23, 207.

Morning Star 98, 108, 109.

Moscow 35.

Mountbatten, Admiral Louis 43.

My Lai 77, 78, 79.

My Side of History 204, 205, 207, 209.

N

Nanking 29.

National Liberation Front of Vietnam (NLF) 77.

Newboult, Sir Alec 51, 63, 64, 66, 68, 69, 103, 136, 193, 214.

Ng Foong 187, 188.

Ng Kong 185, 187, 188.

Norian Mai 189.

O

Order of Battle (ORBAT) 171.

Orang Asli 10.

P

Peking 29.

Penang 20, 48.

Pensions Appeal Tribunal 100.

Piratin, Philip MP 73, 97, 109.

Prince Charles 55.

Q

Queen Elizabeth *11* 191, 192, 193, 195.

R

Rahim Noor 194, 197.

Ramsay, George Patrick Maule 92, 93, 97, 118, 123.

Rape of Nanking 55.

Rasa 56.

Ramsden, James 117, 119.

Rawang 16, 19, 21, 22, 31.

Rawang Tin Fields 20.

Rawlinson, Sir Peter 135, 136, 137, 138, 139, 142, 203, 215.

Remedios, Victor 88, 89, 95.

Ridenhour, Ron 77.

S

Scotland on Sunday 206, 207, 208, 210, 212.

Scotland Yard 129, 131, 133, 136, 138, 139, 141, 149, 150, 164, 171, 194, 195, 199, 200, 201, 210, 214, 215, 216.

Photo Credits

p.6, Institute of Southeast Asian Studies (ISEAS); p.12, Media Masters Pte Ltd;
p.18, The New Straits Times; p.21, Media Masters Pte Ltd; p.24, Media Masters
Pte Ltd; p.28, New Straits Times; p.33, The New Straits Times; p.37, PA Photos;
p.41, Media Masters Pte Ltd; p.44, Media Masters Pte Ltd; p.53, The New Straits
Times; p.67, Army P.R. Photo; p.74, PA Photos; pp.80-81, PA Photos; p.94,
PA Photos; p.101, The Daily Telegraph, London; p.104, The New Straits Times;
p.107, The New Straits Times; p.115, The Daily Telegraph, London; p.127, Media
Masters Pte Ltd; p.130, PA Photos; p.135, The Daily Telegraph, London; p.140,
BBC; p.152, Wong Wing On; p.155, Media Masters Pte Ltd; p.169, Media
Masters Pte Ltd; p.208, The Daily Telegraph, London; p.211, The Daily Telegraph,
London; p.212, The Daily Telegraph, London; p.219, Media Masters Pte Ltd.